ISBN 978-0-942702-28-6

Printed in South Korea by Four Colour Print Group.

© Dimensions Educational Research Foundation, 2018

Cover and interior design by Scott Bilstad. Editing by Emily Rose and Tina Reeble.

Typeset in Adobe Caslon Pro.

Photographs and images are protected by copyright law. Images © / Adobe Stock.

This book may not be reproduced in whole or in part by any means without written permission of the publisher.

For more information about other Exchange Press publications and resources for directors and teachers, contact:

Exchange Press
7700 A Street
Lincoln, NE 68510
(800) 221-2864
ExchangePress.com

Oh Boy!

Strategies for Teaching Boys in Early Childhood

Francis Wardle, PhD

Dedication

To my dear wife, Ruth, who partnered with me to raise four wonderful children, and who has valiantly fought ovarian cancer during the almost two years I have been working on this book. As we go to press, she is still fighting the good fight!

Table of Contents

Introduction:
Why We Need to Focus on Young Boys 1

Chapter 1:
The Challenge of Boys 9

Chapter 2:
Causes: How Did We Get Here? 27

Chapter 3:
Young Boys Are Unique 47

Chapter 4:
The Solution: Theoretical Underpinnings 75

Chapter 5:
Policies and Program Practices 107

Chapter 6:
Curricular Approaches 129

Chapter 7:
Aspects of a Classroom 161

Chapter 8:
Play in the Outdoors 195

Chapter 9:
Men in the Lives of Young Children 219

Notes 247

Bibliography 277

Glossary of Key Terms 293

About the Author 303

Acknowledgments 305

INTRODUCTION

Why We Need to Focus on Young Boys

This book focuses on the specific needs of young boys in early childhood programs. For our purposes, early childhood covers children from birth to eight-years-old (second or third grade). As a result, the book includes infant and early childhood programs, including kindergarten and early elementary in a variety of settings—private, public, religious, and home-based. The obvious question, of course, is why focus on boys? Why not simply write a book on the unique needs of all young children? This is a legitimate inquiry, and while many of the ideas, recommendations, and best practices that work well with young boys also work well for girls, much of my research, observations, and personal experiences have led me to the conclusion that young boys, as a group, generally struggle more than girls in early childhood and elementary programs.[1]

My own observations are based on considerable professional and personal experience. I have been a Head Start director, Head Start education manager, elementary school teacher, and an administrator of a national child care company. I have also helped to raise four children—including one boy, and I now have four grandchildren, three of them boys. In examining this issue, I also looked back at my own childhood and early education growing up on a farm in rural England. I was a typical boy who loved exploring the outdoors and enjoyed a variety of physical activities, but struggled extensively with academic tasks and expectations during my early education.[2]

My intent with this book is to suggest that many of the struggles young boys have in our early childhood programs and schools are not simply a result of bad behavior. Rather, boys struggle because of a much more fundamental problem: a mismatch between how most young boys develop, grow, and learn, and the kinds of expectations, outcomes, activities, and discipline approaches used in programs during the early years. I think a radical change is needed in order to fully meet the needs of young boys. A place to start is recognizing that typical boy behaviors like lack of attention, risk taking, poor emotional regulation, full body movement, and messy exploration of the physical world—are the norm—not the exception. This book hopes to aid programs as they begin to acknowledge and celebrate this norm.

Chapter Summaries

This book explores a range of issues that describe and address the challenges faced by many young boys in early childhood programs. The following is a chapter-by-chapter summary of the topics that will be discussed.

Chapter 1:
The Challenge of Boys

Chapter 1 examines the problems many young boys experience in early childhood and elementary programs today, documenting a variety of national statistics on suspensions, expulsions, boys placed in special education, and those held back a year before entering first grade. Chapter 1 also argues that now is the appropriate time for a radical change in how we educate young children, similar to other changes in the history of early education produced by Froebel (Kindergartens), Dewey (progressive education), Bruner (the process of education), and the creation of developmentally appropriate practice.

Chapter 2:
Causes: How Did We Get Here?

Chapter 2 discusses some of the historical, social, and educational causes as to why so many young boys struggle in our programs. The expanded use of organized child care programs, the creation of Head Start, and the contemporary view that the central function of early childhood is to prepare students for a successful school experience are examined. Chapter 2 also explores the increased academic expectations in early childhood and elementary programs, and suggests how these factors impact young boys.

Chapter 3:
Young Boys are Unique

There is an increasing body of evidence that shows boys and girls are biologically different. These differences include basic brain development (both structure and maturation), verbal skills, emotional regulation, and physical development. Not only are boys and girls different, but in many ways, the development of boys is delayed compared to girls the same age. Another large body of evidence suggests that these initial biological differences are compounded by the way the environment responds to boys and girls. For example, as is suggested in Chapter 3, many girls' verbal skills are ahead of those of some boys, yet mothers tend to talk more to their girls than they do to their boys. Conversely, behavioral expectations in many programs appear to frustrate the needs of boys to be messy, spontaneous, and physical. These environmental influences are both physical and social. Additionally, in our early childhood programs, increased academic and behavioral expectations can cause many of the challenges faced by young boys.

Chapter 4:
The Solution: Theoretical Underpinnings

If young boys have a unique set of physical, emotional, social, and intellectual needs, then one way to care for and educate young boys is to find a way to address all of these needs. Theoretically, this is known as the goodness-of-fit theory. In order to achieve this important goodness-of-fit, Chapter 4 highlights a variety of helpful early childhood theories, including Gardner's theory of multiple learning styles, Vygotsky's zone of proximal development and scaffolding, Erikson's psychosocial stages (the first two), and Dewey's learning by doing theory. In describing these theories, this chapter offers real-life suggestions that programs can use to maximize the physical, social, emotional, and cognitive development of young boys.

Chapter 5:
Policies and Program Practices

Chapter 5 explains some of the specific policies, trends, and practices that have had a negative impact on young boys in programs including a push-down of academics, reduction of play and the use of the outdoors, an increase in the number of boys placed into special education, and zero-tolerance behavioral policies. This chapter also examines ways to change these approaches through advocacy.

Chapter 6:
Curricular Approaches

Chapter 6 identifies a variety of curricular approaches that provide the best goodness-of-fit to the diverse needs of young boys. This includes a focus on social competence, increased use of the arts, integrated physical activities, and hands-on learning approaches in early childhood and elementary school settings.

Chapter 7:
Aspects of a Classroom

Chapter 7 explores appropriate academic and behavioral expectations for young boys. It covers ways to make the classroom environment and instruction more "boy-friendly." Many more boys are placed in special education programs than girls. While special education is designed to help struggling children be more successful in school, in many cases, boys are inappropriately placed in these programs for a variety of reasons that will be discussed.

Chapter 8:
Play in the Outdoors

Chapter 8 discusses why outdoor play is so effective for boys and describes ways that programs can provide an array of outdoor learning opportunities. This chapter explores playground design, equipment, safety, complexities of play, and ways to bring the classroom into the playground. It also identifies outdoor opportunities for young children in the community beyond the early childhood program and school, and issues a clarion call to justify quality outdoor play for young children in all of our programs, including those who struggle behaviorally and academically.

Chapter 9:
Men in the Lives of Young Children

Chapter 9 focuses on ways to increase the number of men young boys interact with when attending an early childhood and elementary school program. The chapter discusses some of the barriers that exist that make it difficult to involve men in programs that serve young children. The chapter also provides a variety of suggestions to increase the participation of male family members as volunteers, and how to recruit and retain more male teachers and caregivers.

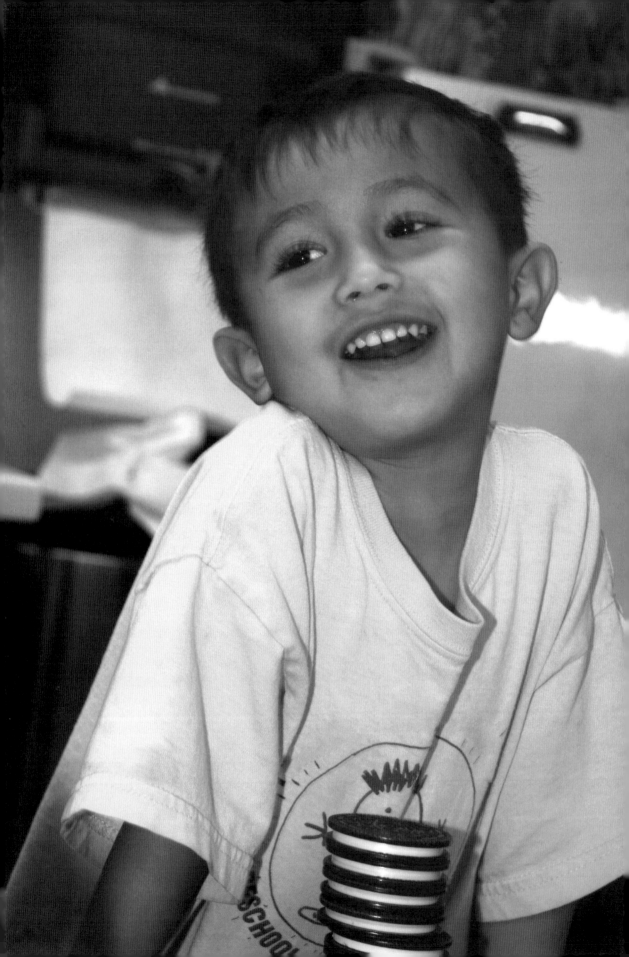

CHAPTER 1

The Challenge of Boys

Today, many of the challenges faced by young boys are a direct result of the United States' perspectives on early childhood education. The historical and political contexts of these perspectives will be explored throughout this chapter. One of these contexts is the continued debate about the exact purpose of K-12 education within American society as a whole; another is the specific role that early childhood education should play in relationship to K-12 education.

One of the main reasons for closely examining any specific problem is to try to find different ways to fix the problem; to find solutions. This, of course, is the ultimate purpose of the book: to present a variety of ideas to help maximize the care and education of young boys. While this chapter focuses on defining the problem—the challenge of boys in our early childhood and elementary school programs—other chapters provide direct and explicit ideas, concepts, activities, policies, and methods to help us address the problem.

What We Know about Boys

Based on a variety of objective indicators, boys can struggle more in early childhood and elementary school programs when compared to girls. Some of these indicators demonstrate that more boys are:

- identified with a variety of special needs including developmental delays, *attention deficit hyperactive disorder* (ADHD), and specific learning disabilities;
- recommended to be assessed for possible special education services;
- expelled from early childhood and elementary programs;
- receiving extra help through recovery programs, Response to Intervention (RTI) programs, and other remedial programs;

- struggling with issues of emotional regulation, which can cause a variety of problems in the program;

- on some form of discipline plan;

- held back from entering first grade because they are deemed not ready for school; and

- reported to simply struggle in programs, be it sitting still during circle time, biting, not following the rules on the playground, or falling behind in academic subjects.[1]

There is very little specific data about discipline issues in preschool programs, because the field is so diverse—public school programs, Head Start, family child care, community non-profit programs, religious, and for-profit programs—it's almost impossible to collect this data in a meaningful way. However, in 2014, the U.S. Department of Education Office of Civil Rights published data on public school early childhood and kindergarten programs for the 2011-2012 school year.[2] Highlights of this data indicate that:

- in preschool, boys received more than three out of every four suspensions. While boys represented 54% of the preschool population, they represented 79% of the children suspended once, and 82% of children suspended multiple times; and

- of the more than 140,000 kindergarten students held back in 2011-2012, while boys represented 54% of all kindergarten students, 61% of those retained were boys. In all ethnic and racial groups, boys were retained more than girls.[3]

Not only do boys tend to struggle in our programs, but many teachers—who are almost all females—can show a preference for working with girls.[4] When I first became a Head Start director, one of the initial problems I had to solve was at the beginning of each school year when the teachers would argue about who they wanted enrolled in their classes, showing a strong preference for girls.[5] This preference was probably due to several factors. Research consistently shows that in many cases young boys are simply more difficult to care for than girls.[6] Therefore, teachers will tend to work with girls if they have a choice.[7] In some cases, women are more comfortable working with girls, just as men may be more comfortable working with boys.[8]

An increasing body of research also suggests that not only do men and women interact differently with young children, but young children seek out men or women based on the kinds of stimulation they want.[9] For example, fathers tend to encourage their young children to explore and take risks, try out new things, and engage in high intensity play, while mothers nurture, care, and comfort. When a child wants stimulation and high intensity play, she turns to her father; when she wants caring, comfort, and nurturing, she turns to her mother.[10]

Minority Boys

Young boys as a group struggle in many of our early childhood and elementary programs, but minority boys do so even more.[11] In one of my college classes, a student reported an experience when observing in a local public elementary school. She overheard a discussion in the teachers' lounge about a difficult first-grade boy. One of the teachers offered to her colleagues that the student in question would not succeed in school "because he is the three Bs." The three Bs meaning *boy, behavior problems,* and *Black.*

There are many reasons minority boys struggle. Some have to do with the lack of match between their needs and the program. Other reasons are a direct result of both institutional and personal biases that may exist in many of our programs. For example, far more minority boys are suspended and expelled from these programs than non-minority boys.[12]

The minority boys who struggle most in our programs are Native Americans, African Americans, Hispanics, and boys of two or more races.[13] It is well known that many programs are more effective working with White, two-parent, middle-class families than minority and non-traditional homes.[14] This is due to a variety of reasons, including the fact that the vast majority of child care and elementary school staff and administrators are White and middle-class themselves.[15] Additionally, the minority and non-traditional parents' experiences when they themselves attended early childhood and school programs were oftentimes negative.[16]

Expectations of Boys

Young boys and girls act, behave, and learn differently in many ways. Young boys tend to be identified with far more special needs than girls. For example, boys are three to four times more likely to be identified as having ADHD when compared to girls.[17] We also know that more boys than girls experience discipline problems in our programs.[18]

However, are these differences because more boys actually have ADHD, or engage in more unacceptable behavior in the program when compared to girls, or is it also because we expect boys to be more active and have discipline problems? In other words, do we expect boys to be hyperactive and impulsive, and to misbehave? Do they, in fact, fulfill our expectations? Are these behaviors self-fulfilling? When boys run around in the classroom full of energy and seem to lack focus, do we automatically assume they have ADHD? When girls do the same thing do we think they are having a bad day or simply acting out of character?

It is also very clear that some boys are developmentally slower than girls in many areas, and that young boys often struggle developmentally with emotional regulation, specific learning disabilities, and ADHD.[19] In other words, there are also real developmental differences between young boys and girls, including brain and language development.[20] Clearly, some of these differences cause many young boys to struggle in our programs.[21] Is this because boys are not meeting developmental milestones, and therefore, need intervention? Or do the program's expectations not match the typical development of young boys?

A central question to the discussion in this book is whether these differences are a function of genetic gender differences, cultural and social gender expectations, or an interaction of both? The three areas of concern regarding boys are:

- *emotional regulation* (the ability to control ones' behaviors, including in learning academic content);

- early language development; and

- certain disabilities (especially specific learning disabilities and ADHD).

Why It Matters

Why does it matter that boys struggle? After all, one of the purposes of early education is to provide early intervention so that barriers to learning can be addressed before students face the academic challenges of K-12 school.[22] The early years can be used to assess the needs of young children and to provide interventions to those who struggle academically and behaviorally, and to prepare them so that they will be successful in school. The current focus on the early assessment of young children also enables us to collect needed data to make informed decisions to help prepare our students for a successful K-12 school experience.

However, this approach causes a variety of problems for young boys. First, too many boys are being suspended and expelled from early childhood programs across the country.[23] This is not only very difficult for parents, but it is also destructive for a young child, who is continually being told he does not belong in a program.[24] Many child development specialists and learning theorists have shown the need for young children to feel a sense of belonging, empowerment, and self-efficacy in their learning environments.[25]

The second problem is that young children need psychologically safe, warm, nurturing, and supportive environments in which to develop, grow, and learn.[26] While some discipline and intervention approaches are supportive (see Chapter 7), many approaches, including interventions for children with various special needs, are punitive and use a deficit approach to target unwanted behaviors.[27] According to Gargiulo and Bouck, punishment is frequently used in educational programs to address inappropriate and undesirable behaviors.[28] Although punishment has been shown to reduce undesirable behaviors in children, due to its many negative side effects, most researchers and educators view punishment as ineffective and do not recommend its use for reducing undesirable behaviors.[29]

According to Ormrod, punishments can have severe negative effects on children.[30] One such effect is negative emotional responses like anger, anxiety, and aggression. Another is the creation of classically conditioned stimuli in children—i.e. between anger and the teacher, anxiety and school (school phobia), fear and learning, and even a variety of avoidance behaviors. For example, some intervention models require the child to be deprived of their favorite activity as punishment for displaying inappropriate behaviors.[31] A deficit approach to early education—focusing on what children cannot do, or are at risk of not being able to do—is counterproductive, and can cause children to feel inadequate and incapable. This can lead a child to feel early on that they are no good and cannot learn.

The third problem is that there is an increasing body of data showing that during their later school experience, many boys still struggle more when compared to girls. Some of this data on boys during the later school years—after third grade—indicates that:

- more boys are diagnosed with various learning disabilities, are involved in bullying (as victims or bullies), or are suspended from school;

Notes from the Field

From Enthusiasm to Reluctance: A Young Boy's Story

A few years ago, I received a copy of a letter sent to the editor of an early childhood publication from the mother of a four-year-old boy. In this letter, the mother recounted her son's first few weeks in preschool. Her son was a typical, active four-year-old who was energetic, curious, fun-loving, and messy. He had enthusiastically anticipated his first early childhood experience—to make friends, expand his world, and enjoy exploring and learning.

After a few weeks in the program, the mother realized his enthusiasm was gone. Then he became reluctant to go to school. This surprised her, as he had always loved learning, being with other children, and having new experiences. His mother insisted he keep attending, believing this was just a temporary situation that would pass. But it did not, and he seemed more and more upset. Finally, she called the teacher and arranged for a conference.

The conference took place about six weeks after the boy had started the program. The mother expected the teacher to discuss ways the school and family could work together to address any issues interfering with her son's learning and him benefiting from this new experience. The mother was willing to work with the school to make sure her son was successful. After all, this would set the tone for the rest of his school experience, which she wanted to be positive.

However, the teacher immediately informed her that her child would not be allowed to return, that he had ADHD and Oppositional Defiant Disorder (an emotional and behavioral disability), and that the mother should also have him tested for possible "autism spectrum disorder." No formal assessment had been conducted, and no specialist had been consulted to make these diagnoses.

Expulsion:
An All Too Common Occurrence for Young Boys

A student in one of my community college classes reported that the mother of a four-year-old boy had contacted her because she runs a family day care program. The mother was desperately looking for a place for her child who had just been expelled from a program—for the third time! Apparently, the boy had been doing well in the program, as the teacher and her assistant had learned how to work effectively with him, and everyone seemed to get along well. Then the teacher moved to another program.

The new teacher was much stricter, and did not tolerate any of the behavior this little boy typically displayed. One day, the teacher got very upset and tore up the boy's discipline chart. As a response, the boy threw something at the teacher. The mother went to the school to address the situation and to find out how she could work with the program to address the problem. When she arrived, the administrator of the program had already expelled her child.

- more girls have better grades, fewer discipline problems, and graduate from high school and go on to college;

- boys are less engaged in academic school activities, they view school as less important to their futures, and have poorer study habits;

- more boys drop out of school; and

- today, more women are admitted into college and graduate from college.[32]

Research shows that these challenges among many boys can continue through their formal education years, and in many cases they actually get worse. This can include dropping out of school entirely, which can lead to lasting negative consequences.[33]

Early Childhood Should be a Positive Experience

There is a large body of knowledge that argues for early childhood programs and elementary schools to provide multicultural opportunities that match each student's culture, learning styles, language, and competencies. It is understood that these children need school experiences—activities, curricular content, classroom materials, and adult-child interactions—that provide them with the best possible opportunity to succeed.[34] It only makes sense that these school experiences also optimally match their learning styles, behaviors, competencies, and dispositions.

It is likewise important to ensure that the early education and elementary years are positive experiences for boys—experiences where they feel successful and empowered; experiences that prepare them to resolve both social and academic challenges in later school years; and experiences that teach boys *self-efficacy*. According to Bandura, self-efficacy is the belief that with a certain amount of effort and persistence, one is capable of executing behaviors successfully like learning specific skills, tasks, or concepts.[35] For children, this is the belief that they can learn under the right circumstances.

From Challenges to Solutions: A Historical Perspective

Throughout the history of early care and education, there have been times when problems of one kind or another came to a head, and major changes were required to address them. My view is that we are now at a similar time when a paradigm shift in early childhood programs and elementary schools is needed. All of the historical movements described below resulted from historical, political, and/or pedagogical situations that cried out for change. The changes that resulted from these movements provided long-lasting improvement in the education of young children. Now is the time for another such radical change. As pointed out earlier, a disproportionate number of boys com-

Notes from the Field

Observations from a Head Start Program: Where Do Boys Play?

For 10 years, I was the director of a Head Start program in an industrial city just north of Denver, Colorado. Head Start is a federal program for low-income three- to five-year-olds and their families. Our program served primarily Hispanic and White families, although there were quite a few Vietnamese and Hmong families, as well as African American families.

One day, I was talking to my special needs coordinator, who worked with classroom teachers to address the needs of students struggling in the classroom. This might be due to discipline challenges, emotional struggles, social conflict, or attachment issues. She showed me a list of students she was working with, and then pointed out that almost two times as many boys were on her list.

This bothered me, and did not seem to make much sense. I thought the list should have been about even between boys and girls. I decided to do a formal, extensive observation of my classrooms and the following is what I discovered.

- The teachers—all female—were either working at the tables in the dramatic play or art areas. The teachers were standing or sitting on chairs.

- The girls were mostly working at the tables in the dramatic play or art areas.

- Most of the boys were either in the block area or playing on the floor with blocks and wheeled toys. They were either moving around or sitting on the floor.

- Most of the discipline issues and social conflicts were with boys.

- Several times the boys who were "acting out" were punished by being kept inside while the rest of the class went outside to play.

- All of the dramatic play props were typical traditional female objects—women's clothes, shoes, and hats; child-size ovens, sinks, and tables; cooking utensils and imitation food; and dolls.

- The books provided in the reading area were mostly things girls typically like such as fairy tales, baby animals, and pets.

- In the classroom, most of the physical activities were fine motor—puzzles, art, games, and table toys—with very few gross motor activities such as dance, movement, or woodwork.

I also knew from previous interactions with my teachers and their manager that at the beginning of each school year, the teachers would lobby hard to get as many girls and as few boys as possible in their classrooms.[36]

pared to girls are suspended or expelled from early childhood and elementary school programs; far more boys than girls are identified with developmental delays or special needs, including ADHD and specific learning disabilities; and more boys than girls struggle with behavioral issues in our programs—often resulting in the use of punitive discipline methods. For many young boys, the early childhood experience is not a positive, empowering one. Too many are suffering, and we need to make major changes at every level of the field—from expectations, the environment, instructional approaches, and discipline methods—to policies regarding school readiness and special education. Rather than seeing these changes as simply reacting to the current early childhood practices, we need to view them as needed improvements to everything we do with young children, especially boys.

Friedrich Froebel's Kindergartens, John Dewey's progressive education movement, Jerome Bruner's report and recommendations from the Woods Hole Conference,[37] and the creation of the seminal book, *Developmentally Appropriate Practice*[38] are all relevant examples of major changes to the way we care for and educate our young children.

Froebel's Kindergartens

Friedrich Froebel was the product of the educational approach of his time—Europe in the early 1800s: strict discipline, adult-centered instruction, sitting on hard benches and desks, and everyone learning the same thing in rote fashion. He hated his school life, and would escape to nature and its soothing influences.[39] At age 15, he became a forester, and eventually used his love of nature to develop the *Kindergarten* (children's garden) philosophy.[40]

Froebel's original ideas focused on the use of the outdoors; designing environments to maximize the natural development of each child; and the use of play, the arts, and music and games. He also emphasized the important role of the home and society; and the value of hands-on learning, freedom, and nurturing individual potential.

Dewey's Progressive Education

In the late 1800s and early 1900s, John Dewey developed his vision of education in the U.S.[41] His views became known as *progressive education*, and greatly influenced the Bank Street approach to early childhood education, the alternative school movement of the 1970s-80s, and the Reggio Emilia early childhood philosophy.[42]

Dewey rejected the traditional view of education prevalent at that time, which focused on a top-down approach of knowledge and skills, and the need for schools to teach immigrant children how to become true Americans. Instead, he focused on learning by doing (experiential learning), child-centered curricula and activities, and the creation of classroom communities.

Bruner's Concept Learning

Maybe the most famous response to a problem in the approach to public education in the U.S. was the Woods Hole Conference of 1959. This conference was a high level, multidisciplinary examination of the perceived failure of education and an exploration of needed changes. While focusing on K-12 and college education—both curriculum and instruction, especially in science—some of the ideas generated from the conference not only apply to approaches for young children, but also specifically to boys.[43] One major recommendation Jerome Bruner made was to move away from rote learning towards approaches that use real experiences and exploration to learn about concepts and contexts in-depth.[44]

Developmentally Appropriate Practice

In 1987, the National Association for the Education of Young Children (NAEYC) published the influential book *Developmentally Appropriate Practice*.[45] A central purpose of this book was to respond to the growing trend toward more formal, academic instruction for young children, created by the push-down of the public-school curriculum.[46] Early childhood programs at that time focused on rote learning, whole group instruction, and teaching

narrowly defined academic skills. Testing, placement of children in different level programs, and retention were also the norm for programs serving young children.[47] *Developmentally Appropriate Practice* was created as a reaction to programs, policies, and practices that many felt to be inappropriate for young children. The theoretical basis for the publication included well known early childhood theorists—Froebel, Piaget, Montessori, Erikson, Bruner, Bandura, Bronfenbrenner, Vygotsky, Dewey, and Gardner.

All of these radical shifts in our approach to early care and education are examples of the way our field responds to problems, changes direction, and addresses the changing needs of children, families, and society. In the same vein, it's time to challenge many of the normative practices used today in early childhood and elementary education, and to implement a variety of changes in what we do in these programs. This is required to make sure our programs provide maximum support for the development and education of young boys. Not surprisingly, many of these changes are similar to those proposed by Froebel, Dewey, Bruner, and the creators of *Developmentally Appropriate Practice*.

Chapter Review

This chapter outlined the challenges faced by many young boys in organized early childhood and elementary education programs (those that serve children birth to eight), and provided research data and several different real-world observations to support this claim. The chapter emphasized that these challenges are a valid problem that needs to be proactively addressed throughout the early care and education field. Several examples were given as evidence of radical shifts in the country's approach to child care and education that directly resulted from dissatisfaction with the status quo. Finally, this chapter suggested that now is an opportune time to begin making another one of these shifts, embarking on a new, radical approach to how we care for and educate young boys.

Questions to Ask Yourself

- Have you noticed that certain boys struggle academically in your program or classroom?

- Do you feel a radical change is needed for how we educate young children or will a few small tweaks work?

- How is your current classroom or program different from your own early childhood education experience?

- Are more boys than girls asked to leave your program?

CHAPTER 2

Causes: How Did We Get Here?

If we reflect on the experiences we had during our early years, many of them are probably very different from what young children experience today. My early years were spent on a farm in the beautiful lowland border country between England and Wales—picking strawberries, harvesting potatoes, and chasing sheep. Even when I was in an early childhood program—and later in an elementary school—many of my experiences involved games, hiking across the countryside, art, music and dance, acting in simple plays, doing woodwork, and growing vegetables in the school garden.

Certainly, many of today's adults did not grow up on a farm, but they still had experiences that were dominated by hands-on activities, play, exploration, and the arts, whether at home or in some kind of early childhood program that they attended. Many of the activities they engaged in were what we now call *whole-child activities*. This chapter examines the transition from the traditional approach to early education to the current reality. Although I am not suggesting that we go back to "the good old days," I do believe the following:

- the early childhood experiences of young children in this country today are radically different from those experienced by children 40 years ago; and
- many of these changes negatively impact the development and learning of young children, particularly boys.

This chapter identifies major events that have caused this change to how we care for and educate children, and which have ultimately brought us to our current situation. Each of these significant events resulted from sincere efforts to improve the lives of children, families, and communities in this country. These events were the *War on Poverty*, which led to the creation of the Elementary and Secondary Education Act (ESEA) and Head Start; standardizing early childhood programs and schools; zero-tolerance policies; and special education.

The War on Poverty

The War on Poverty is another name for President Lyndon Johnson's Great Society programs. It included a variety of efforts targeted at reducing poverty in the U.S. including the ESEA and Head Start. While many of the Great Society programs have not survived, ESEA and Head Start are still prevalent and continue to influence how we work with young children, and are contributing factors to why boys struggle in early childhood and elementary programs today.

Elementary and Secondary Education Act

The intent of the ESEA was to provide direct federal support for low-income and minority schools—particularly elementary schools. Passed in 1965, the federal money was sent to the states under ESEA's Title I provision: to fund schools serving a significant number of students under the poverty guidelines.[1] Fast forward to the No Child Left Behind Act (NCLB), which was the 2001 reauthorization of the ESEA under President George W. Bush. NCLB mandated a series of assessments in public schools to determine how well students were performing. These assessments evaluated student progress according to a variety of standards, focusing on literacy and math.[2] As a result of NCLB, public schools began to focus on preparing children to pass these tests, which concentrated on discrete academic and literacy standards, and ignored the arts, physical activity, social-emotional skills, and whole-child development.[3]

NCLB had a direct impact on public elementary schools, which were required to show annual yearly improvements.[4] As a result, schools shifted to the teaching of academic skills—often in a very teacher-directed approach, practicing test-taking procedures, and taking tests. After the publication of *A Nation at Risk*, many schools began to decrease and even eliminate recess.[5] This trend increased after the passage of NCLB, with its focus on academics and assessment (accountability).[6] Additionally, according to Jarrett, this cutback on recess most profoundly impacted low-income and minority schools due to the achievement gap—the discrepancy between the high academic achievement of White and Asian American students, and the low academic achievement of African American, Hispanic, and Native American students.[7] Further, not only was the reduction of recess much higher in low-income schools, it was also used extensively as a punishment, especially for boys.[8]

In a similar manner, the focus on academics and assessment led to a narrowing of the curriculum, particularly in low-income and minority schools. This meant a reduction of non-academic content, including physical activities and the arts.[9] NCLB also directly impacted public and private early childhood programs because schools tightened their school entry requirements. This meant that early childhood programs focused on teaching the required academic skills, while reducing play, the arts, social and emotional development, and physical activities.[10] Parents also picked up on this pressure, insisting that early childhood programs prepare their children to be successful in the more rigorous, academically oriented elementary schools.

Some young children thrive while under these tight academic standards and expectations, however, many struggle, especially boys. It appears that young boys are generally less mature than girls in both social and emotional development, and academic learning.[11] Further, as a result of increased academic expectations, more and more boys are being diagnosed with a variety of developmental delays and other forms of special needs, especially ADHD and specific learning disabilities.[12] Thus, it is quite logical to expect that as academic and behavioral expectations from K-12 programs are pushed down to three- to five-year-olds, more children will be assessed and then placed in special education.

The Evolution of Head Start

In 1965, the first Head Start program was created as a summer program for low-income children and their families. Soon, it became a year-round program for children the year before they entered formal education in the local school.[13] Head Start is a comprehensive program that includes nutrition, physical and mental health, education, and a variety of services for families including skills training, teaching parenting skills, and providing employment training and job opportunities. The belief of the original architects of the program was that this combination of comprehensive services would help create a "head start" for the children and their families, enabling children to be successful in K-12 programs; providing parents with the skills needed to support their children's journey through the K-12 school years; and helping parents get out of poverty.

At that time, it was believed that *social competence* in young children was the best predictor of future school success, and therefore, the Head Start curriculum focused on developing social competence. Social competence involves the skills and self-knowledge children use when they interact and learn from others. It enables children to function effectively with peers, family members, and the community at large. According to Gordon and Browne, children with high social competence have emotional regulation, social knowledge and understanding, specific prosocial skills, and positive social dispositions.[14]

As a result of pushback from the report, *A Nation at Risk* (a report published in 1983 of U.S. public school results), and the increasing size of the federal budget for Head Start, policy makers began to change the overall goals of Head Start.[15] Due to political pressure and the direct impact of NCLB, Head Start's view of school readiness radically changed to a much more specific set of academic and behavior skill expectations and outcomes.[16]

In 2007, the Improving Head Start for School Readiness Act was passed, making it a top priority for local programs to directly contribute to the school readiness of all children they serve. As the document, *School Readiness Goals for Preschool Children in Head Start Programs* states, "as programs work to contribute to children's learning and development, Head Start leaders must clearly identify the goals and skills children demonstrate when they are 'school ready.' A clear articulation of these goals and skills allows Head Start staff to choose and implement the most effective curriculum, assessments, and teacher-child interactions."[17] Local Head Start programs are also now required to align their curricula to each state's standards and frameworks.[18]

This move to an academic and behaviorally based readiness approach by Head Start has greatly impacted the overall early childhood field. Head Start used to be viewed by the field as the leading-edge prototype for quality early childhood programs in the U.S., especially for low-income students. Much of that reputation was based on a whole-child, developmentally appropriate approach to education and school readiness. However, now this is no longer the case.[19] Head Start must implement the same outcome-based approaches to behavior and learning that other early childhood programs and schools must follow, an approach that many criticize as too simplistic and narrow, and not culturally or developmentally appropriate.[20]

Standardizing Early Childhood Programs

While federal involvement in early childhood actually started during World War II,[21] Head Start reintroduced the importance of early education into the minds of politicians, educators, and the public alike. Since the inception of Head Start, there has been an increased call for universal preschool, and a stream of reports and papers about the importance of early education and its benefit for later school achievement.[22]

Although those who care for and educate young children are happy to see the rest of society catch up with their understanding of the value of these programs, this recognition has come with some fallout, especially for boys.

The problem is that when it is recognized that the early years are critically important for the development and education of young children, especially in terms of their later school success, then everyone wants a say in what should be included in these early years. Unfortunately, in most cases, this means the downward extension of the K-12 curricular content into the early childhood ages.

A push-down of the K-12 curriculum forces teachers to use teacher-directed instructional approaches that do not match up with the developmental needs of many young children, especially boys. The issue here is not the rigor of the curriculum or even its content. It is the approaches used to teach young children, which tend to be dictated by the curriculum. This idea of the relationship between curriculum and instruction is what other countries call pedagogy. The pedagogy used in our programs must match the way boys develop and learn (see Chapters 3, 6, and 7).

Learning Standards

According to Bowman, there are several different kinds of standards.[23] Program standards define the quality of a program: adult-child ratios, activities, environments, and training and staff qualifications. NAEYC's accreditation standards and Head Start's performance standards are examples. Standards for professional development specify what teachers should know and be able to do to be effective teachers and to achieve state licensure or certification. Learning standards are the skills, concepts, and content to be learned (and demonstrated) at each specific stage of learning. Essentially, they stipulate what children should know and be able to do, which are then validated by standardized assessments. Kindergarten entry skills that must be demonstrated by children entering school is one example; another is the standards that are assessed by the standardized assessments used in schools throughout the country (made popular by NCLB) at the end of specific grades. According to Kagan et al., 89% of kindergarten standards focus on literacy and other cognitive skills, 7% on social-emotional development, and 1% on physical and motor activities.[24] While learning standards are the norm in K-12 programs, state departments of early childhood have developed guidelines, frameworks, and other documents that also focus on learning standards.

In 1983, the report *A Nation at Risk: The Imperative for Educational Reform*, painted a dismal picture of public education in the U.S., especially when compared to public education in Asian countries.[25] This report propelled politicians and educators into action. One of the first responses was the enactment of the Goals 2000: Educate America Act in 1994.[26] The Act presented eight national goals for public education. These goals later morphed into standards that became a central component of NCLB. While NCLB has been replaced, this idea of standards was adopted by the Core Curriculum Standards, which is incorporated in all state early childhood standards and frameworks. Additionally, Goal One of Goals 2000—that every child should enter school ready to learn—drives the current focus on academic skills and behavioral expectations for school readiness.

These learning standards result in placing extreme importance on the early acquisition of academic skills and concepts at the expense of play, art, music, physical activities, and a whole-child approach to early development and learning. Often this leads to direct instruction teaching approaches that require students to sit still for long periods of time. These expectations and approaches tend to work against young boys, and as such, many are labeled as having behavior problems or special needs; are held back a year before kindergarten enrollment; or are expelled/suspended from school.[27]

Chapter 2: Causes: How Did We Get Here? **OH BOY!**

Figure One

Goals 2000

Goals 2000: Educate America Act set forth the following benchmarks to be achieved by the year 2000.

- All children in the U.S. will start school ready to learn.

- The high school graduation rate will increase to at least 90%.

- All students will leave grades fourth, eighth, and twelvth having demonstrated competency over challenging subject matter including English, mathematics, science, foreign languages, civics and government, economics, the arts, history, and geography. And every school in the U.S. will ensure that all students learn to use their minds well so they may be prepared for responsible citizenship, further learning, and productive employment in our nation's modern economy.

- American students will be first in the world in mathematics and science achievement.

- Every American adult will be literate and will possess the knowledge and skills necessary to compete in a global economy and exercise the rights and responsibilities of citizenship.

- Every school in the U.S. will be free of drugs, violence, and the unauthorized presence of firearms and alcohol, and will offer a disciplined environment conducive to learning.

- The nation's teaching force will have access to programs for the continued improvement of their professional skills and the opportunity to acquire the knowledge and skills needed to instruct and prepare all American students for the next century.

- Every school will support partnerships that will increase parental involvement and participation in promoting the social, emotional, and academic growth of children.[28]

Zero-Tolerance Policies

As a response to rising rates of juvenile crime and a feeling that young people were becoming increasingly dangerous, zero-tolerance policies developed.[29] In 1994, the Gun-Free Schools Act was passed, requiring schools that received federal funds, such as through the ESEA and special education funds, to pass laws to suspend or expel students who bring weapons to school. The 1999 massacre at Columbine High School in Colorado, and the continuing curse of bullying in schools, increased the use of these practices.[30] *Zero-tolerance policies* soon covered a vast array of misbehaviors, many much less harmful than carrying a gun to school.[31] These rules triggered instant suspension, expulsion, or other severe punishments for any behavior by a child in school—or even around the school—viewed as possibly leading to, or symbolic of, violent acts. Often school personnel had little control as to whether a child was to be disciplined by this approach.

All schools and early childhood programs must be psychologically and physically safe places for all students, and they have a responsibility to maintain the safety of their students. However, zero-tolerance policies in K-12 schools have produced a variety of negative results.[32] Research shows that out-of-school suspensions and expulsions increased everywhere as a result of these policies, and in some places, dramatically. Further, nationally, Black middle school students were four times more likely to be suspended when compared to White students; Latino middle school students two times as likely. Of all secondary school students expelled, boys were expelled twice as much, and students with special needs were three times as likely to be expelled when compared to a student without special needs.[33] Suspensions and exclusions have extreme negative impacts on the lives of students, from repeating grades and dropping out, to disengaging with the education process.[34]

These rules also trickled down into early childhood programs, especially those connected to K-12 schools. As a result, the appropriate physical and sometimes aggressive behaviors of young boys, such as rough-and-tumble play, playing with sticks on the playground, and typical impulsive behaviors, are often penalized by these rules. Even children engaging in pretend play involving swords, guns, and other imaginary weapons are punished.

Zero-tolerance policies—both in K-12 schools and early childhood programs—do not allow program staff to consider student behavior on an individual basis, or to use young children's actions and even aggressive behaviors as a way to teach children more prosocial behaviors. Such policies also tend to penalize young boys for behaviors that they typically engage in for a variety of developmental reasons. The policies make adult assumptions about the consequences of certain children's behaviors that in many cases are not true.

A child using a stick as a pretend sword is not necessarily a potential killer; a child who inadvertently pushes another child out of the way to get her toy is not necessarily a potential bully.[35] Active, aggressive, and even "unkind" behaviors are simply a natural part of young children exploring their physical potential, discovering social limits, and learning appropriate social skills.[36] Clearly, one of many possible results of these zero-tolerance policies is that more young boys end up being labeled with ADHD and other developmental delays, being identified with behavioral and emotional disabilities, and subject to various discipline actions, including expulsion.[37]

Special Education Policies and Processes

Gargiulo and Bouck use the term, "exceptional children" to describe children with special needs, and define them as those who differ from societal or community standards of normalcy due to any number of factors.[38] Many of these children require customized educational programs to meet their unique needs. However, according to Gargiulo and Bouck, "We must remember that exceptionality is always relative to the social or cultural context in which it exits."[39]

As a direct result of several court cases brought by parents of children with disabilities, the Individuals with Disabilities Education Act (IDEA) was passed, which guaranteed that all children, ages six to 18, have access to free, appropriate education in a *Least Restrictive Environment* (LRE).[40] The law has since changed many times, and now covers children, birth to age 21.[41] IDEA applies to children who attend public schools and public school early childhood programs; however, children identified with special needs who attend private programs are also eligible to receive some services.[42]

These mandated provisions for children with a variety of disabilities are a tremendous benefit for children who struggle with many challenges that could affect their educational success. Further, the LRE requirement, which enables students to be educated with same-age peers as much as possible, also benefits children with disabilities along with normally developing children. Like the Civil Rights legislation of the 1960s, the IDEA law has placed U.S. schools at the forefront of equal educational opportunity for all students.

The purpose of special education is to address the unique needs of children with disabilities.[43] IDEA makes sure children with disabilities have a free, appropriate education; that local schools provide for the unique educational needs of these children; and that there are plans in place—an *Individualized Education Program* (IEP)—to effectively educate each child. While some of these children will never be able to function at the level of their peers in the area of their delay or disability, their IEP is expected to target areas in which they can improve.

The implementation of IDEA, especially for children over three years of age, has often resulted in problems for young boys. First, IDEA is a *deficit model*—an approach that focuses on what a child has difficulty achieving, and then the development of a plan, or IEP, to address these deficits.[44] A second problem is that the current approach of identifying and treating young children with a variety of disabilities does not work well with all children, especially many boys.[45] This is because developmentally appropriate behavior of boys is commonly misidentified as a disability by people who do not understand the wide variability of young boys' development, resulting in misdiagnosis, especially of ADHD and specific learning disabilities.[46] Here are some additional problems with IDEA.

- It focuses on what children cannot do or what they struggle with doing correctly.
- It results in labeling children with a developmental delay or a specific disability.
- It creates the concept of "normal" and "abnormal" children.
- Many of the methods and techniques used with children who have disabilities are behavioral approaches that use what the child is good

at doing as a reward, or withholding this as a punishment (known as the *Premack Principle*). For example, a child who struggles to read (as a specific learning disability) might be rewarded for completing a pre-reading worksheet by being allowed to play in the block area with his peers. However, this means he will be punished by not being able to play in the block area until the worksheet is finished, if at all.

- It often increases a parent's anxiety and sense of helplessness about their child.

- Most early childhood staff are not trained in recognizing typical developmental variables, especially those caused by cultural and other factors, as well as abnormal or inappropriate behaviors. Therefore, staff in early childhood programs are sometimes too quick to recommend a child be assessed for a possible disability and to label a child with a disability.[47]

- Local school districts are responsible for evaluating children for delays or disabilities, a process called Child Find. Special education personnel and school psychologists are trained to work with K-12 students, which means that they are often not familiar with the developmental milestones, typical developmental profiles, or all of the assessment tools for young children, ages three to five.[48]

Reasons Many Young Boys Are Misdiagnosed with a Developmental Delay or Special Need

Assessment of disabilities in children is notoriously difficult, and subject to biases and various forms of invalidity.[49] Some of the challenges of identifying students with disabilities are linguistic and cultural incompatibilities between teachers, test givers, and the child (and the child's parents); use of instruments that have not been validated on the populations that they are now being used for; and test givers who may not be trained to give specific assessments. Another challenge is the fickle nature of children themselves who often do not give their best performance for a one-time assessment. These challenges increase with younger children, due to natural developmental variability in all young children; often immature linguistic, emotional, and social development; and poorly developed and validated instruments.

There is a disproportionate number of boys identified with special needs in many of the 13 *federal disability categories*.[50] These discrepancies are for children six to 18-years-old (we do not have good statistics for younger children with special needs, for a variety of reasons). It is appropriate to conclude that these discrepancies are even larger with young boys, birth to age six, due to some of the assessment issues addressed above. Additionally, according to Gargiulo and Bouck, boys tend to exhibit disruptive, asocial, and emotionally immature behaviors differently than girls, and the academic and behavioral pushdown of the curriculum into early childhood can naturally result in more "school related academic and behavioral" expectations on the part of teachers and administrators.[51] The following are a few possible reasons for these large discrepancies, including the diagnostic criteria used to identify children, and the question of what is typical and atypical growth and development.

Diagnostic Criteria

There are three to four times as many boys as girls diagnosed with ADHD.[52] These statistics do not include children under age six. Why the difference? One reason is because the criteria used to identify children with ADHD involves typical behaviors more commonly seen in boys than girls, and more typically seen in younger than older children. This criterion comes from the *DSM-5*, which is a document published by the American Psychiatric Association and included in checklists commonly used to diagnose children with ADHD.[53] For example, here are some of the items on one of these checklists.

- Difficulty sustaining attention on tasks or while playing.
- Easily distracted by extraneous stimuli.
- Difficulty waiting in line for his or her turn.

- Acts without thinking; impatient.
- Excessive running or climbing.
- Difficulty organizing tasks or activities.
- Schoolwork is often messy and disorganized.
- Difficulty engaging in quiet leisure activities.
- Fails to complete tasks.[54]

To me, this sounds like a typical young boy! Further, many of these items require judgment on the part of the observer, which can be easily skewed by someone who already believes that the child is hyperactive, and thus simply fulfilling expectations.

Boys are diagnosed with specific learning disabilities two to four times as often as girls.[55] A *specific learning disability* is defined as "a discrepancy between a person's ability and academic achievement" in the areas of literacy and math.[56] Thus, a specific learning disability is focused on a child's proficiency in math and literacy.

As we will see in the next chapter, when compared to girls, the intellectual development of many young boys—especially in literacy—is delayed.[57] Girls tend to acquire language at the early end of the language milestones, while boys tend to at the later end. Further, more boys than girls exhibit a variety of language difficulties—a 2:1 to 3:1 difference between boys and girls. Finally, research shows that young children with language delays often need targeted intervention to catch up to their peers, and are at a greater risk of reading difficulties.[58]

Typical Child Development

Supporting the optimum development and education of young children rests greatly on an understanding of typical child development. This complex concept has at least three components: 1) important milestones for the average child; 2) the natural variability for each of these milestones; and 3) how various cultural characteristics (e.g., not speaking English) can impact these milestones.

Unfortunately, as a result of focusing on children with disabilities and on the increasing academic and behavioral standards and frameworks already discussed, we have created the misguided notion that any child who struggles to meet these standards must be deficient in some way—abnormal—as opposed to exhibiting typical developmental variance, or struggling due to cultural, linguistic, or other barriers. When a child struggles, we automatically see the child as deficient rather than questioning the standards, examining the way the learning materials are presented, critiquing the competency of the teacher, or wondering about the objectivity of the tester. It is always the *child* that must be fixed.

To "fix" the child there are really only three options: implement a discipline plan that might eventually result in expulsion, place the child into special education, or delay the child's entrance into the formal school program. In all cases, boys are much more likely to be placed in one of these options than girls.

Chapter Review

This chapter provided a discussion of a variety of policies and practices developed over the years that have led to our current approach to caring for and teaching young children. While each of them was created with good intentions, the net result is an approach to caring for and educating young children that is not conducive to the success of many young boys. The chapter began with a discussion of the War on Poverty, and two specific programs, ESEA and Head Start. The establishment of ESEA enabled the federal government to directly influence policies and rules in local public schools; Head Start is a federal program to prepare young children for success in K-12 schools. However, as a response to the report *A Nation at Risk*, Head Start's approach to school readiness changed from one of teaching social competence, to one that now focuses on academic skill and behavioral expectations. *A Nation at Risk* also inspired the development of Goals 2000 and NCLB. As a response to school violence and bullying, zero-tolerance policies were established, and became conditions for receiving federal funds for K-12 schools. In 1975, the federal government passed the first of a series of laws guaranteeing equal access to schools for children with a variety of disabilities. This chapter discussed how these programs, in various ways, have increased the challenges many young boys face in our early childhood and elementary school programs.

Chapter 2: Causes: How Did We Get Here? **OH BOY!**

Questions to Ask Yourself

- Why does the author suggest that some of the changes in the way we provide early care and education have a negative impact on boys?

- Some people believe that the push-down of academic and behavioral standards into early childhood is so that all children can succeed in school. How does this view short change many young boys?

- Why do you believe far more young boys are placed into special education programs than young girls? Does this statistic suggest there is a problem in how we identify children with special needs?

- Why do so many politicians see investing in the early childhood years as the solution to problems with U.S. public education? How can this focus end up negatively impacting the early education of young boys?

- Is it reasonable and defensible to expect all young children—i.e. all boys and girls—to learn the same things at the same time/same age?

CHAPTER 3

Young Boys are Unique

Young children function very differently from school-age children. This is one reason that early childhood programs are generally separate from K-12 schools; colleges and universities are organized into separate early childhood and education departments; and each state has a child care and education agency. The fundamental reason for these differences can be divided into two important areas: 1) how children develop; and 2) how children learn.

Young children develop in a whole-child manner with each area or domain being directly influenced by development in all other domains.[1] As stated in *Developmentally Appropriate Practice*, "All domains of development and learning—physical, social and emotional, and cognitive—are important, and they are closely related. Children's development and learning in one domain influence and are influenced by what takes place in other domains."[2] For example, when a child begins to crawl, their mobility influences their feelings of autonomy and cognitive development. As a child learns to talk, this has a direct, positive impact on their social development, which in turn, enhances further language development and usage. Social and emotional factors also closely impact a child's academic development—not to mention their understanding of appropriate behavioral expectations.[3] This interaction and interdependency of the development of domains leads to a whole-child approach to the development and learning of young children, and to a whole-child approach to teaching them.

According to Gordon and Browne, the whole-child approach is based on the principle that all areas of human growth and development are interrelated—they are intertwined and mutually supportive.[4] For example, a child with hearing loss may also develop a language delay or disability; a child with poor social skills and emotional development may be unhappy and struggle to benefit from math activities taught in small groups.[5] By the same token, growth and learning in one domain often enhances growth and learning in other domains. Teachers working with young children must consider how development and mastery in one area, or lack of development and struggles in one area, might interact with one another: does a child's physical development affect how they feel about themselves; how does the child's cognitive development and social and emotional development impact language, and vice-versa?

Thus, young children are also *whole-child learners*. For example, when engaging in an art activity of painting birds, the child needs to have developed the fine motor skills to hold the paint brush, must have the cognitive information about different kinds of birds, needs to have the language skills to be able to listen to and understand the instructions of the teacher, and needs to feel competent in her ability to paint. Further, the child must have developed the emotional regulation to persist at the task until its completion.

Not only are young children whole-child learners, they are also concrete, hands-on learners. Young children are either in Piaget's sensory-motor stage (birth to two) or preoperational stage (two to seven). The sensory-motor child learns through interactions with the physical world using all of his senses; the preoperational child learns through many direct interactions with the social and physical environment.[6] As a result, a variety of real-life, hands-on experiences are critically important for children this age.[7] They need to manipulate, explore, use all of their five senses, build, create, discover, take apart, experience, and engage in constant trial-and-error. This enables them to learn the basic properties of objects and materials, how things work together, and the nature of complex ideas such as floating and sinking, gravity, liquids and solids. This, in turn, builds a foundation for later, more complex, abstract, and higher-level thinking and learning, self-regulation, and symbolic or representational capacities.[8] It is imperative that people who work with young children clearly understand the value of providing lots of hands-on learning experiences before moving to more complex and symbolic activities.[9]

Just as young children develop and learn differently than school-age children, there is an increasing body of research showing that young boys and girls develop and learn differently. Often schools and teachers are not only unaware of these differences, but sometimes interpret the natural ways boys learn and develop as oppositional, lazy, or defiant.[10] This would account for some of the overrepresentation of boys in special education, expulsion and suspension statistics, and zero-tolerance discipline results discussed in the previous chapter.

There is an indication that, on some level, the ways young girls learn are easier on the physical and emotional disposition of teachers, than the ways young boys learn. Young girls tend to paint, play in the dress-up area, enjoy books and literacy activities, and interact socially with teachers; young boys tend to prefer to play in the block area, on the floor, or in the outdoors on the playground.[11] The prevalence of rough-and-tumble play with boys when compared to girls is just one example.[12]

Why do boys develop and learn differently than girls?

Causes of Gender Differences in Behavior and Learning

Beginning in the 1960s, there was a strong movement associating gender differences in children with social and cultural values, expectations, and norms.[13] Later, the view shifted to an exclusively genetic view: the varied behaviors and learning approaches of young children are based on inherited, sex-linked genetic differences.[14] This perspective begins with the understanding of the basic biological difference between boys and girls that begins to appear with the 23rd pair of chromosomes, known as the sex pair: XX for girls; XY for boys. These chromosomes trigger the development of hormonal differences between boys and girls.[15] While boys and girls produce many of the same hormones, boys produce far more testosterone than girls, and girls produce far more estrogen. This increase in testosterone seems to be linked to behavior that is typically associated with young boys including:

- risk-taking;
- exploring;
- accidents;
- impulsive behavior;
- inattention and distractions;
- hyperactivity;
- many behavioral and learning disabilities;
- more childhood illnesses;
- short attention spans; and
- the need to use more space for many activities.[16]

These hormonal differences impact brain development in both boys and girls. Young boys, on average, seem to have a less mature and well-developed *pre-frontal cortex*, the part of the brain that controls behavioral regulation and controls and directs learning; and many boys have less mature language areas of the brain compared with girls.[17]

However, the pendulum has shifted a third time, and we are at a place now where many believe that the learning and behavioral differences of young girls and boys are based on an interaction between biology and the physical and social environment. For example, if a child is genetically more apt to move while he learns, an environment that encourages and supports kinesthetic learning will enhance the child's learning, as opposed to one that punishes the child's movement. I call this approach a *goodness-of-fit*, a concept that originated from the research on temperament by Thomas and Chess, although, this approach has always existed within the overall philosophical construct of developmentally appropriate practice, as well as Vygotsky's *zone of proximal development*—matching the range within which learning occurs in each child.[18]

Goodness-of-fit is the idea that parents—and other caregivers—need to modify their attitudes and behaviors toward individual children, based on the child's temperament.[19] This concept has been extended to suggest that optimum development occurs when a child's social, emotional, cognitive, and

physical development is matched by the appropriate social and physical environment. When the physical and social environment matches how the child develops and learns, then there is a goodness-of-fit; when the physical and social environment does not match, and even punishes how the child optimally develops and learns, this is a poor goodness-of-fit.

Cultural Expectations

Culture plays a large role in the way that boys and girls develop and learn. It has a significant function in why young minority boys—especially African American, Hispanic, and Native American boys—struggle in our programs.[20] "Boys will be boys" is an expression that is often heard when adults talk about boys. It is an expression that communicates the belief that boys are expected to behave in certain ways—often more active, more impulsive, louder, less social, and with more energy—than girls. This expectation of young boys, however, can be a double-edged sword.

While boys can sometimes get away with more rough, aggressive, and asocial behavior than girls, they often will be automatically disciplined simply because they are boys, and assumed to be engaging in—or soon to engage in—inappropriate behavior. This is the result of two conflicting sets of social expectations: boys are "naturally" more aggressive, physical, and asocial than girls, while early childhood teachers are expected to teach all of their students to be cooperative, socially proactive, and compliant, according to basic school readiness requirements.[21]

Gender-specific behaviors are culturally expected and reinforced. Each culture teaches girls and boys to behave in a certain way, what is termed *gender-role socialization*. Most adults in each culture behave according to these roles, and reinforce certain behaviors of young boys and girls. Female teachers have been raised with different gender-role socialization than young boys, and this can cause a mismatch between the culturally prescribed behaviors of the teachers of young children—most of whom are women—and the culturally-taught behaviors of boys.[22]

The Female Culture of Early Education Programs

It is clear that the early childhood field is a female-centered culture. Historically, in most societies, it was the mother's role to care for young children, while fathers were involved in hunting or farming, and making sure the family had a warm and safe place to live. According to the U.S. Bureau of Labor Statistics:

- 95.5% of caregivers are women;

- 97.2% of preschool and kindergarten teachers are women;

- 81% of elementary and middle school teachers are women;

- 64% of public elementary principals are women; 62% of K-12 non-religious private school principals are women; 75% of K-12 Catholic school principals are women; and

- most support staff—social workers, school psychologists, health aides, etc.—in child care, early childhood, and elementary schools, are women.[23]

While these are U.S. figures, they reflect the same reality in other countries such as New Zealand, Canada, and England.

As pointed out above, one of the central concepts of this book is goodness-of-fit—all children need a goodness-of-fit between the physical and social environment and their unique needs, including those characteristics influenced by gender. One of these needs is that boys need men in their lives; and they need to engage in typical male activities and interests. However, more and more boys grow up in families without men, and more and more young children spend an increasing amount of time in early childhood programs that have few, if any, male educators. Early childhood programs have in many ways become a substitute for the home and a substitute for many of the things that used to occur within the home.

While there is obviously overlap, women often engage in activities that are of more interest to girls, and men often engage in activities of more interest to boys. The intent here is not to encourage programs to create prototype boys and men; both boys and girls should be encouraged to follow their interests and be given the opportunity to do so—whether that means playing with dolls or playing sports, or both. Boys and girls in early childhood programs need to be exposed to more men on a regular basis—both teachers and volunteers: fathers, boyfriends, and uncles, etc.

Men in Early Childhood Education

While both women and men can provide young boys with the kind of goodness-of-fit that they need for maximum development and learning, it is clear that in many ways this comes easier to men. Many men tend to be more accepting of boy's impulsivity, aggressiveness, and general disruptive behavior and challenges. It's not that men necessarily accept young boys more, but that they understand them better, and therefore, can help boys modify their behavior and help them appreciate why others do not approve of their behaviors. Men know what it was like to be a boy—including the frustrations of always appearing to be in trouble with authority. The issue is not that boys should only have male teachers; it's that a gender balance in early childhood and school classrooms is healthy for young children—both boys and girls.

However, beyond providing goodness-of-fit, boys need to be around men as healthy role models. Boys and girls live in cultures where gender differences are pronounced and emphasized; and boys and girls need to learn healthy gender-role socialization.[24] Children grow up both in the overall U.S. culture and the various individual cultures that make up the rich fabric of society. While we are all aware of the limitations of gender stereotypes, and the need to encourage boys and girls to challenge gender expectations, this does not alter the fact that our children grow up in cultural contexts where male and female expectations have a powerful impact on their development and identity. Young boys need to be around healthy men—at home, and in the early childhood program—to learn how to behave like men in the overall U.S. culture and in their own individual subcultures. In Chapter 9 we expand on this issue, discussing a variety of ways to increase the number of men in early childhood and elementary school programs, and exploring approaches to nurture the important role of men in our programs.

What Young Boys Need

It is now understood that for maximum growth, development, and learning to occur a goodness-of-fit must be made between all domains of each unique child and the physical, social, and emotional environments in which the child grows and learns.[25] The understanding of brain development in young children confirms why the idea of goodness-of-fit is so important. For boys, this means that early childhood and school programs need to tailor their expectations and approaches to meet the unique needs of each child, including boys.

Because young boys develop and learn differently than girls, they need different experiences. The following outlines some of the general needs of young boys. Later chapters will carefully explore specific approaches for working with young boys, including needed policies and procedures, curricula approaches and materials, instructional methods, and indoor and outdoor environments.

Lots of Physical Activities

Many boys seem to learn by using their whole body: they need to physically engage with the environment to learn. They learn through kinesthetic actions, learning by doing, hands-on learning, and real-life problem solving, and they need lots of opportunities for whole-body exploration and learning. Young boys benefit from frequent physical activity experiences where they can:

- move freely through open space;

- use the outdoors for optimum play and learning;

- experiment and mess around with all sorts of materials;

- engage in activities and interactions that don't have to fit an adult's view of order and neatness;

- make lots of noise;

- explore the concept of cause-and-effect in multiple ways;

- take a variety of physical risks;

- physically engage with other children in many different ways;

- participate in all sorts of constructive and manipulative activities that help develop fine motor skills;

- explore different ways to communicate their emotional needs; and

- push physical and social limits safely: rules, people's patience, the capacity of the physical environment, the use of certain materials, and how things work and don't work.

The challenge for caregivers, teachers, and various early childhood specialists, is to know when to allow these whole-body, messy, very physical behaviors, and when to realize a child needs help to make sure the activities do not get out of hand, become destructive, and asocial. It is important to remember that this is the natural way boys learn and interact with the physical and social environment; they are usually not deliberately trying to be destructive and to push the patience of the adults caring for them.

Rough-And-Tumble Play

Research shows that children across all cultures engage in *rough-and-tumble play*—but especially boys.[26] Many believe rough-and-tumble play has a very specific role in the social development of young children; it enables children to play with others without physically hurting the other person, thereby developing a variety of important social skills.[27] In rough-and-tumble play, children do not set out to hurt each other; that is not the intent—and usually not the result. The intent is to engage in play-fighting in which children reverse roles, with the good guy changing to be the bad guy, thus allowing children to share powerful roles, while also experiencing being the victim.[28]

Children, especially boys, engage in rough-and-tumble play with siblings and peers. More boys than girls engage in this kind of play, across all cultures.[29] Male teachers are often pounced on by boys the minute they enter a

Notes from the Field

Boys and Girls Playing Outside

For a year I taught kindergarten in rural Pennsylvania. At the school, we had a large outdoor area with woods, streams, and ponds that we used every day, weather permitting. For many of the activities the children experienced outdoors—feeding the chickens and collecting eggs in the community barn, picking up sticks, checking deer rubs on tree trunks, and looking for bird nests in the spring—the boys and girls behaved in a very similar manner. However, when we stopped off at the large pond for free play, gender differences suddenly appeared.

First, the boys and girls played in separate groups, and rarely moved into each other's group. The boys went immediately down to the pond's edge, scrambled on the large rocks set in the shallow water, threw objects into the water, explored the intersection between the land and water, and created dams on the small streams that entered the pond. They also always had something in their hands—on one occasion, every boy held a stick. Some were using the sticks to poke at objects in the water; others were pretending to fish in the pond. The boys tended to play by themselves in a loosely-configured group, although they sometimes imitated what other boys were doing.

The girls on the other hand, collected around the picnic table under a large maple tree away from the water. They used buckets to collect moss, leaves, and other materials to make beds under the table; created little houses for dolls and imaginary figures; and generally cleaned up the area around the picnic table—cleaning away twigs, sticks, leaves, and stones. When flowers were blooming or autumn leaves scattered on the ground, they would make bouquets and garlands. The girls tended to play together, in twos and threes, or in the whole group. They were also much more organized.

The school served children from a religious organization much like the Amish. These families celebrate gender differences through dress, occupations, and specific family and community roles. In this case it was interesting to note which play activities followed these typical gender stereotypes and those that did not.

classroom, eager to engage in rough-and-tumble play. According to recent research by St. George, Fletcher, and Palazzi, while both parents engage in rough-and-tumble play with their children, it's the father's favorite form of play.[30] They believe men's preference for rough-and-tumble play is linked to evolution. Males—teachers, volunteers, and administrators—also often seem more accepting of children engaging in rough-and-tumble play than women. As a result, increasing men in the early childhood program would create more of a goodness-of-fit for young boys.

With many families becoming smaller, and more families where there are no men present, often the only place children can experience rough-and-tumble play is at the early childhood program or elementary school—during the organized day or in an after-school program. For this reason, it is imperative

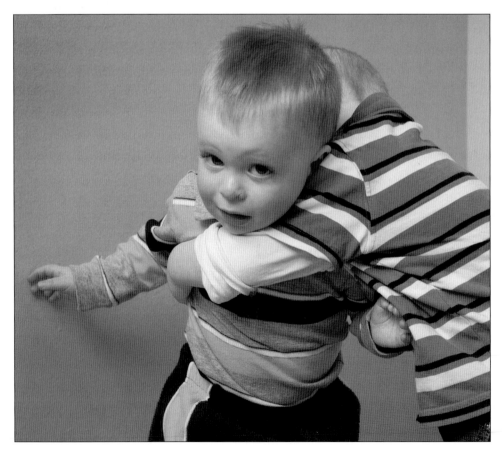

Photo by John Mayer (https://flic.kr/p/64kwCB) licensed under CC by 2.0

that schools and early childhood programs allow this kind of play and recruit as many men for their programs as possible: volunteers, teachers, other staff, fathers, and grandfathers.

Hands-On Learning

Girls are generally more verbal than boys and girls' language development as a whole is more advanced when compared to boys of the same age.[31] It makes sense then that girls can often verbally explain what they need, or describe to an adult an activity they are engaged in, while boys are much more prone to physically demonstrate how to do something or what they want—and to become frustrated when peers and adults don't understand.

It is critically important that teachers remember that young children are *concrete learners*, and need meaningful concrete learning activities before engaging in more complex, abstract, and intellectually higher-level pursuits. It appears that some young boys need these hands-on, concrete experiences even more than girls do, particularly those who struggle with learning and behavioral expectations. With the focus on literacy and academic standards in today's programs, it is even more important that teachers fully explore hands-on, concrete learning before engaging in academic pursuits. Boys' predisposition to construct, create, and manipulate objects; joy in woodworking; and engagement in building forts and tree houses, all need to be honored as legitimate ways to learn important social and academic skills and concepts.

Initiative and Industry

Erikson's third psychosocial stage of development is *initiative v. guilt* (three to six); his fourth is *industry v. inferiority* (six to 12).[32] In both these stages, children learn to do certain tasks, master doing these tasks, and enjoy showing others—adults and children—how to become proficient in the skills needed to accomplish these tasks. During these two stages, children develop a sense of their own identity and self-worth through what they can initiate and what they can do well. This can be a physical skill like riding a bike, an academic

Notes from the Field

My Initiative and Industry

When I was a young boy, I struggled greatly with all of the required academic tasks; I did very poorly at schoolwork throughout the elementary grades. I much preferred being outdoors on the farm, helping feed the animals, and care for and harvest the crops. However, I was very good at art. My parents and teachers encouraged my artistic activities and did not punish me for my academic struggles.

I felt good about my success in art and I enjoyed the recognition I received. While I was upset that I could not read, and my writing was very poor compared to the other students, my artistic skills and recognition of those skills carried me through until early adolescence when I finally learned to read and my writing blossomed.

During my elementary years, my artistic successes matched Erikson's view of initiative and industry. I was able to achieve these important developmental tasks, even though I struggled in traditional school-related pursuits and achievements.

skill such as reading, or an artistic skill such as playing an instrument or painting a picture.

Because many boys struggle with traditional school expectations, especially behavioral and academic ones, they desperately need to be validated in a variety of other activities and skills in the program. Unfortunately, many discipline approaches and special education methods used with young children prevent these children from engaging in the activities and tasks that they are good at and that they like to do. To this end, early childhood programs and elementary schools need to find ways to provide supportive activities and opportunities to all children, but especially for boys.

- Find something each child can do well, and is competent in performing. While it is ideal for this activity or skill to be within the program's curriculum, it may not be.

- Encourage children to try out new challenges, tasks, and activities even if they do not appear to have any valuable end result. This is particularly important when working with perfectionists.

- Provide opportunities for children to demonstrate their unique skills and proficiencies, both in front of peers and adults—parent social activities, art displays in local businesses, and musical and dance performances.

- Give all children—including those who struggle physically, mentally, socially, and/or emotionally—opportunities to be liked by their peers, especially peers of their same gender.[33] And make sure children with social challenges are not isolated from social activities with peers, i.e., are not pulled out of group activities for individual therapy.

- Never withhold an activity a child enjoys and is good at performing as punishment (or use it as a reward) for something he struggles to master.[34]

- Support each child's efforts to try out new activities and to be competent and successful in activities other children excel at doing, even if these activities do not appear to have school-related value.

- Relax control. All children want to have as much control as possible and need a deep, internal sense of empowerment: "look what I did all by myself!"

- Be particularly concerned that children diagnosed with a developmental delay or special need are not labeled by the school, and are not viewed by peers and adults as incompetent or lacking in proficiency. Make sure these children have many opportunities for success and for demonstrating success to peers.

The Arts

As someone who struggled in school, but excelled in art, I am a huge proponent of the arts in early childhood and elementary programs—drawing, painting, ceramics, dance, sculpture, music, and woodwork.[35] Ever since the work of Froebel, Montessori, Steiner (originator of Waldorf education), and Dewey, the arts have always been central to the early childhood and elementary school curriculum. More recently, the Reggio Emilia model and the Project Approach have emphasized a variety of artistic activities to document learning, and three of Gardner's eight learning styles—visual, musical, and kinesthetic—focus on the arts. Below are some of the reasons the arts are considered so important at this age.

- **The arts provide a unique way for children to process information.** Artistic activities provide an ideal medium for manipulating concepts, putting experiences into one's mind, and expressing feelings and emotions. And since young children are not verbally sophisticated these processes are very important to development and learning.

- **The arts teach children how to create and accept their own realities.** To handle the constant and often conflicting stimulation of the external world—peers, parents, teachers, television, electronics, books—children need to be able to create their own secure, internalized world. Children paint pictures of the way they see the world; they play rhythms on a drum that meet their internal satisfaction; they make objects on the workbench that represent their ideas, concepts, and wishes.

- **The arts empower visual, kinesthetic, and musical learners.** The arts give children with these learning styles legitimacy, positive self-esteem, and a medium through which they can learn a variety of academic and other skills and concepts. This is particularly powerful for children who struggle using the traditional learning styles to learn and feel competent.

- **The arts facilitate young children's enactive and iconic memories.** According to Bruner, when processing new information we use three modes of representation (memory): enactive, iconic, and symbolic.[36] Enactive representation is muscle memory—remembering how to ride a bike, perform a dance, or swing on a swing; iconic memory is the use of pictures to process information—the face of a friend, the color of a house, the shape of a bird; and symbolic representation is numbers and words. Also, according to Bruner, young children are quite adept at enactive and iconic representation, while many struggle with symbolic processes. Unfortunately, most learning experiences in our early childhood programs and elementary schools focus on symbolic processes, and many young boys struggle with these activities. The use of the arts enables young children who may struggle with traditional learning activities to learn complex skills, tasks, and concepts.

- **The arts encourage creativity and innovation.** Creativity involves children producing ideas, inventing and making something for the first time, or coming up with unique ways to express their thinking.[37] The arts legitimize this process: it empowers children to be creative and to embrace their own creativity.

- **The arts encourage messing around.** Piaget believed children need to constantly manipulate the real world in order to progress intellectually and to learn.[38] The arts involve hands-on interactions with the environment: bodies, props, clay, paint, paper, wood, play dough, wax paper, musical instruments, tools, wood, glue, and dramatic play props.

- **The arts develop self esteem.** Art activities are an activity in which children control the whole process—from selecting the media and subject, to deciding when the creation is finished. It is their creation; they own it and can feel proud of it.

- **The arts develop creative thinkers and problem solvers.** As the world becomes more and more complex, we need to develop creative thinkers and problem solvers. The arts teach problem solving by using trial-and-error, testing alternative solutions, and experimenting in a low-key, risk-free environment.

- **The arts help children deal with feelings and emotions.** Often children have difficulty expressing their emotions in words. The arts give them an outlet for their emotions and enables them to deal with a world that often makes little sense to them. Because some young boys struggle verbally, the arts are a wonderful alternative way to express their feelings.

- **Supporting the arts develops a lifelong appreciation in children.** One of the richest rewards in life is the appreciation of the arts—plays, concerts, art exhibits, music festivals, and dance presentations.

The arts therefore, should not be considered "specials"; they must be part of the core curriculum. All children must have access to the arts, but especially those who struggle in school: children in special education and/or who have behavioral challenges. For various reasons, the arts are especially effective for children who struggle with traditional school-related expectations. These children can use the arts as an outlet through which they can demonstrate their own competence, genius, and exceptionality. There are few right answers and many opportunities to be creative and unique.

The arts also use several of Gardner's learning styles, which may match the learning style(s) of the child who struggles to learn in the traditional manner.

The child often gets to impose their meaning and structure on the art activity or enjoys mastering a method or technique that is meaningful to them, but not imposed by the teacher.[39] The arts enable the struggling child to receive needed positive feedback from peers and adults, something they would not otherwise receive since they struggle with learning traditional skills and content.

As was already discussed, the arts are very hands-on. They involve manipulating and imposing one's will on the environment with hands, sticks, the body, and instruments. The arts are unstructured enough that the child can impose his or her own meaning of the world on the project; in other words, they can follow their own desires, dreams, and motivations rather than follow the view or instructions of others. When the arts are taught correctly, the child gets to judge the value and mastery of their own work against their own standards and criteria, and not compared to the work of other children. Because the finished product—a picture, dance, woodwork construction, pot, or mask—is a unique individual product, it has value by itself and the child has value in creating it.

Nature

Nature is an ideal environment in which young boys can develop and learn. In recent years, there has been a renewed interest in exposing young children to nature. Nature is soothing and accepting; it provides a blank slate upon which the child can interpret their own reality; and it inspires creativity by challenging the child to use all of their senses and full imagination.[40] Nature-filled environments are places where young boys can:

- make lots of noise;

- be very messy and use a lot of space;

- interact with the fascinating natural elements of the environment—soil, sand, water, stones, sticks, mud, leaves, insects, and bark;

- change elevation by getting low in a pretend fox hole or crawling through a tunnel; getting high on a giant tree stump, fallen tree trunk, or large rocks;

- build with branches, ferns, bracken, twigs, leaves, plant stalks, and sticks;

- find private spaces to get away from other children or simply play hide-and-seek;

- throw all sorts of things like sticks and loose pieces of tree bark into the stream, mud on the bank, stones down the hill, snowballs at a tree, plant seeds into the air (e.g., dandelions); and

- climb on trees, rocks, and banks.

For young children, nature also has two central elements that make it fun: it's a fantastic place for exploration and discovery; and it is always changing—as a result of the weather and the seasons—both in growth and decay. In natural environments children also learn about the fascinating world in which they live and grow: birds, animals, weather, seasons, changing length of the day and night, erosion, growth, death, insects, and plants. Early childhood programs and elementary schools need to explore a variety of ways to include as many natural elements as possible within their playgrounds, including gardens.[41]

Appropriate Approaches to Discipline

Because many young boys struggle with emotional regulation due to immature brain development, poor social skills, and a lack of fit between their development and the expectations of early childhood programs and elementary schools, boys get into trouble and struggle to behave according to the rules and expectations of the program. Some also struggle at home. What these young boys need is appropriate approaches to discipline that are warm, nurturing, and supportive; scaffold desired outcomes; and help them become important members of the classroom and school community. What they do not need is harsh punishment, exclusion from their peers, and eventual suspension and expulsion. We look at appropriate approaches to the discipline of young boys more closely in Chapter 7.

Self-Efficacy

For optimum learning and development to take place in young children, a goodness-of-fit must exist for each child, and the child needs to learn *self-efficacy*. Self-efficacy is the view that people are more likely to engage in certain behaviors when they believe they are capable of executing these behaviors successfully.[42] Self-efficacy addresses the question: "How will I do such and such?"—the learner's belief about their competency in completing a specific act or task.[43] Specifically, we are interested in self-efficacy for learning—"I can learn this if I set my mind to it."

The central factors that impact the development of self-efficacy for learning are one's own previous successes and failures, the messages that others communicate, and what is learned by observing others.[44] Once children have developed self-efficacy, when they encounter small set-backs, they learn that sustained effort and persistence are key ingredients to success.[45] However, when a child meets with constant failure in learning a particular task or skill, they have little confidence in their ability to learn; each new failure reinforces this belief. Students with a history of success in learning have higher self-efficacy than those with lower success; students with various delays or learning disabilities often have low self-efficacy regarding learning and academic success.[46]

Children's self-efficacy can be enhanced when others praise their performance or assure them that success at a particular task or at learning a particular task, albeit with effort and persistence, is possible. While this positively impacts self-efficacy, its impact is short lived if the child's effort is ultimately unsuccessful.[47] Teachers who directly show students how to improve are enhancing self-efficacy because they show them that they have faith the child can learn. However, providing more assistance than is needed communicates "I don't believe you can do this without my help."[48]

Children also learn about their self-efficacy by observing the success and failure of others, especially peers with similar abilities. Seeing a classmate model a task successfully is often more effective than watching an adult. Further, watching a peer struggle to accomplish a task or learn a skill shows others that success does not come easily, and that effort and practice are needed.

The best way to develop self-efficacy is to provide a goodness-of-fit between how young boys develop and learn, and the program's expectations and the social and physical environment. Based on the discussion presented in this chapter, the following are some ideas to help accomplish this.

- Provide a range of activities that develop the child's whole being, focusing on integrating all domains and understanding how development in one domain impacts performance in other domains.

- Have children engage in concrete, hands-on activities and experiences that build a solid foundation for future, more complex learning: risk taking, experimentation, trial-and-error, building, taking apart, and messing around with a variety of materials.

- Be very careful before placing a child into special education. Change the environment, adjust to different learning styles, and increase or decrease the difficulty of the tasks—before recommending the child for special education services.

- Increase the involvement of men in the early childhood program and school—parents, uncles, boyfriends, volunteers, teachers, and classroom aides (see Chapter 9).

- Provide lots of opportunities for physical activities: indoors and outdoors, gross and fine motor, including rough-and-tumble play, exposure to nature and the outdoors, and opportunities to build.

- Focus on opportunities for children to be successful, especially children who struggle with the program's academic and behavioral expectations. For these children, try offering learning opportunities that use visual-spatial, musical, and/or bodily-kinesthetic learning styles, and build activities on what children already like to do and can do well.

- Use discipline approaches that focus on the natural and logical consequences, and that are developmentally appropriate; avoid punitive, negative discipline approaches, and never deny a child access to what they can do well because they struggle academically or behaviorally.

- Find ways to empower boys to impact their environment, to control their own learning, and to be successful.

- Provide positive role models, real and symbolic; show positive male role models succeeding academically and/or behaviorally in the program, in books, on TV, and in video games.

- Integrate the arts throughout the curriculum and daily activities. All children need opportunities to experiment with various materials, and to express themselves through the arts. For children who struggle with more traditional activities, or with behavioral expectations, determine whether the arts can be used to teach the same concepts, skills, and outcomes.

- Treat each child individually and make sure each child achieves success based on their own abilities, experience, and skills. Do not compare children's behaviors and academic success to each other; especially, do not compare boys to girls.

- Set behavioral and academic expectations within each child's zone of proximal development and to fit each child' temperament, personality, skills, and abilities. Treat each child as a unique individual.

Chapter Review

This chapter provided a detailed discussion of the needs of young boys. It began with an explanation of the differences between young boys and girls, both biological and cultural. Next was an explanation of what young boys need, which is a goodness-of-fit between how boys develop and learn, and the social and physical environments in which they develop and learn. To achieve this, boys need lots of physical activity, hands-on learning, rough-and-tumble play, and engagement in the arts. They also need many opportunities to explore nature, respond to appropriate approaches to discipline, develop self-efficacy, and be around men, both at home and in early childhood programs and elementary schools.

Questions to Ask Yourself

- What do we mean when we say that development and learning in one domain affects the development and learning in other domains?

- What do we mean when we claim that young children are "whole-child learners" and why is this particularly important to remember when teaching young boys?

- How does exploration, trial-and-error, and "messing around" with many concrete objects and materials create a solid foundation for a child's future academic success?

- Do you believe men bring a different and unique dimension to caring for and teaching young boys compared to women? How so?

- What are constructive ways to increase the involvement of men in early childhood programs and elementary schools?

- Why should early childhood programs, in general, provide more physical activities for all children, inside and outside?

- What are some reasons the arts should be a central part of an early childhood curriculum for young boys specifically?

- More and more experts are suggesting that rich, frequent exposure to nature is critical for the healthy development of young children. Why?

- Why is it critical for every child to experience some form of success, especially children who struggle with traditional learning and appropriate behavioral expectations?

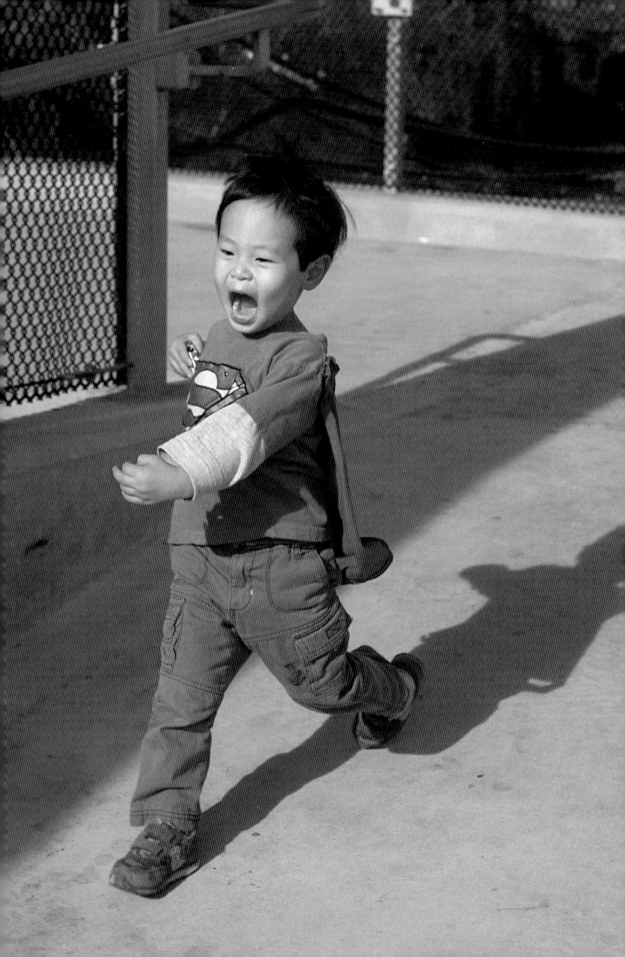

CHAPTER 4

The Solution: Theoretical Underpinnings

This chapter will explore a variety of well-known child development and learning theories to help better understand gender differences in young children, and to suggest ways to help care, nurture, and support the development and learning of young boys.

Figure Two

Principles of Child Development and Learning That Inform Practice

The following 12 principles of *Developmentally Appropriate Practice* provides the basis for the ideas discussed in this chapter.

1. All the domains of children's development and learning—physical, social, emotional, and cognitive—are important and they are closely related. Children's development and learning in one domain influence, and are influenced by, what takes place in other domains.

2. Many aspects of children's learning and development follow well-documented sequences with later abilities, skills, and knowledge building on those already acquired.

3. Development proceeds at varying rates from child to child, as well as at uneven rates across different areas of each child's functioning.

4. Development and learning result from a dynamic and continuous interaction of biological maturation and experience.

5. Early experiences have profound effects, both cumulative and delayed, on a child's development; and optimal periods exist for certain types of development and learning to occur.

6. Development proceeds toward greater complexity, self-regulation, and symbolic or representational capacities.

7. Children develop best when they have secure, consistent relationships with responsive adults and opportunities for positive relationships with peers.

8. Development and learning occur in and are influenced by multiple social and cultural contexts.

9. Always mentally active in seeking to understand the world around them, children learn in a variety of ways; a wide range of teaching strategies and interactions are effective in supporting all of these kinds of learning.

10. Play is an important vehicle for developing self-regulation, as well as for promoting language, cognition, and social competence.

11. Development and learning advance when children are challenged to achieve at a level just beyond their current mastery, and also when they have many opportunities to practice newly acquired skills.

12. Children's experiences shape their motivation and approaches to learning such as persistence, initiative, and flexibility; in turn, these dispositions and behaviors affect their learning and development.[1]

Brain-Based Development and Learning

Over the last 30 to 40 years, our knowledge of how the brain develops and supports learning has been truly revolutionized. This has occurred as the direct result of two major advancements: new methods to record brain functions and the use of technology. Now, we can observe brain functions of living people as they process information, engage in various mental activities, and respond to stimuli. This new understanding has radically changed our knowledge of how children learn and about the kinds of approaches that enhance or inhibit learning.² Here, we explore the ways this new information can guide and assist the care, support, nurturing, and education of young boys.

Because the early years are a critically important period for optimum brain development that establishes a solid foundation for later growth, development, and learning in all domains, it is very important to provide activities, experiences, and environments that are best suited for maximum brain development.³ Specifically, for young boys, this means the following.

- Encouraging activities and environments that create positive emotions. Positive emotions occur as a result of a sense of mastery, accomplishment, and success. These produce deep, meaningful learning. Young boys also need many opportunities to overcome challenges and to master new skills and accomplish new tasks. These opportunities need to be within the child's zone of proximal development, challenge all their domains, and involve whole-child learning—often these activities occur through play.

- Avoiding activities and environments that cause stress, anxiety, and a sense of failure. Stress produces the hormone, *cortisol*, which retards brain development. Stress also increases the synaptic connections in the brain that increase vigilance and sensitivity to fear. Stress, anxiety, and fear can be caused by harsh punishment, threats, fear of failure, and lack of a consistent, nurturing environment, high-stakes assessments, and inappropriate competition.

- Providing constant, appropriate, and responsive stimulation in all domains. This stimulation must match each child's unique development, and correspond with critical and sensitive periods. For example, during the period of language development, young children need to be exposed to a variety of rich language stimulation that matches their development. Young boys need all sorts of physical activities; opportunities for whole-child learning; warm, positive interactions; and environments that encourage exploration, risk-taking, and the acceptance of failure.

- Providing lots of deep, rich, meaningful human relationships that build important neural networks in the brain. In general, the prefrontal cortex, which regulates behavior, learning, and judgments, is less developed in young boys than girls. This can affect both the development of emotional regulation in young boys, along with behaviors that influence a child's ability to direct and control their own learning. All young children need human relationships, which can often come easily for most children, but can be lacking for those children who struggle academically and behaviorally, i.e. many young boys. This is because other children often avoid interacting with these children (especially when it is commonly known that they are difficult or have a special need), and adults in authority tend to be directive, punitive, and controlling with them. It is critical to remember how important frequent, positive human interactions are for the optimum brain development of young boys.

- Movement enhances brain development in young children, especially young boys. To encourage this development it is important to provide many movement opportunities such as:

    - rough-and-tumble play;

    - physical exercise;

    - outdoor learning activities;

    - group games;

    - individual play;

    - cooperative play;

    - constructive play;

    - walking and hiking; and

    - exploring the outdoors.[4]

Froebel's Kindergarten

Friedrich Froebel is the father of the Kindergarten, which was originally developed in Germany. The first American Kindergarten was created in 1855 in Watertown, Wisconsin. The word Kindergarten translates to "children's garden," and this symbolizes his philosophy: the extensive use of nature and the outdoors, and a belief that, like flowers and other plants, children should be allowed to develop and mature at their own unique pace. Froebel's philosophy stressed the integration of the arts including music, dance, and drama, and the extensive use of the visual arts. He invented a series of educational materials, which included balls, cubes, mosaics, puzzles, and small blocks called "gifts," and created a set of educational activities or "occupations" that used these materials in a variety of creative ways. Froebel believed that the early years set the foundation for later school success and were a unique educational level in their own right. He also involved mothers in the education of their children. Today's kindergartens show little resemblance to the original philosophy.

Specific ideas for the care, development, and education of young boys that stem from Froebel's original philosophy include:

- using the outdoors to explore, experiment, touch, feel, manipulate, mess around, impact, control, and create; studying and learning about important scientific skills and concepts such as the changing seasons, the impact of the changing length of the day on plants, birth, growth, decay and dying, survival, ecological balance, migration; and using the natural world for important learning materials—water, sticks, stones, trees, leaves, bark, dirt, and mud;

- regular use of the arts, especially music, dance, and singing;

- engaging a whole-child approach, developing all of the child's domains in an integrated manner—cognitive, language, arts, physical, social, and emotional;

- providing continual opportunities throughout the day for movement—Froebel deeply understood that children need to move to grow and learn;

- encouraging the use of Froebel's gifts and occupations, which are three-dimensional, concrete objects and hands-on skills that teach a variety of important Science, Technology, Engineering, and Math (STEM) related skills and concepts, and which provide an excellent goodness-of-fit between how many young boys learn, think, and interact with the environment; and [5]

- including play, exploration, and games throughout the curriculum, which many young boys enjoy and are good at.[6]

While language development and learning are not ignored in the application of the Froebel approach, they are not as important as interacting with real objects, physical activity, involvement with the arts, and movement activities.

Piaget's Cognitive Theory

Understanding Jean Piaget's first two stages of cognitive development is helpful because this knowledge shows us that young children learn in very qualitatively different ways from that of older children and adults.[7] And as already suggested, there is a tendency to push young children into learning modes more appropriate for older children. This temptation can be especially difficult for many boys who struggle academically and/or behaviorally.

In the *sensory-motor* stage (birth to two), infants and toddlers learn through activities that combine physical activity with sensory input. For example, an infant sees an object, grabs the object, puts the object in his mouth, and then tastes it. These actions help the child learn about the world.[8] They continue this circular activity, known as a *scheme*, developing a repertoire of repeated actions that begin to build basic memory in the child's mind.[9]

Preoperational children (two to seven or eight) learn by manipulating the physical environment—pouring, stacking, constructing, playing, sliding, digging, and transporting. They do so to develop new schemes about how the world works. To Piaget, preoperational thought meant "before operations"—that is, before having the ability to think abstractly with words and numbers. While children this age can think symbolically, Piaget believed they learn most effectively by manipulating a variety of concrete materials.[10] Approaches to the education, care, and development of young boys that are consistent with Piaget's theory include:

- interacting with the physical environment in a child-directed, whole-child manner;
- using cognitive expectations that do not exceed preoperational thought (this does not preclude challenging activities);
- developing a love of learning and discovery;
- using math manipulatives and pattern blocks when learning math concepts;
- using the outdoors as a laboratory—in all sorts of different weather conditions—when learning science concepts;

- interacting with people of different backgrounds and races, who speak different languages, and have different cultures, when learning about human diversity; and

- providing lots of opportunities to mess around with an array of materials, concepts, ideas, and solutions; children need to be encouraged to explore and discover, as opposed to following a linear, step-by-step approach to problem solving.

Vygotsky's Sociocultural Theory

Lev Vygotsky's sociocultural theory provides two powerful ways for working with young boys: social learning and scaffolding. Vygotsky believed that children learn a great deal from others—both peers and adults, and viewed much of learning as social. This is particularly the case when the adult or peer is an expert in whatever a child is trying to learn—or at least knows more than the child does.[11] For example, if a child is trying to hammer a nail into a piece of wood on a workbench, a peer who already knows how to do this can show him that he needs to secure the piece of wood with a "C" clamp, hold the nail in such a way that he won't hit his fingers, and then show him how to use the hammer properly.

Young boys need lots of opportunities to be around peers, and to learn from them in a variety of healthy, prosocial activities. They need to be included in all group activities and not be removed for individual interventions, either to improve academics or for special education therapy. Young boys also do not benefit from discipline approaches that isolate them from their peers.

In Vygotsky's view, children learn from other children and adults through a process known as *scaffolding*. Scaffolding is joint problem solving and learning between the learner and expert—an adult or peer. The learner is an active participant, while the expert structures the activity ("first do this, then this"). The structuring is usually verbal, but can include modeling, or both—making language a critical component in assisting young children in learning.[12]

Initially, the language is provided by the expert, but later can be used independently by the learner, what Vygotsky called *private speech*. Young children's private speech is not private—it is spoken out loud. Only as children get older are they able to internalize this speech to meet social expectations. Young children must be allowed to use language scaffolding out loud, and because boys often struggle with verbal communication, this caution is particularly relevant when working with them. Some suggestions for applying Vygotsky's concepts to the care, development, and education of young boys include:

- providing lots of opportunities for cooperative learning, including in mixed-age groups, and not excluding children who struggle socially from these opportunities;

- providing lots of small-group activities;

- having male teachers, volunteers, aides, and even older elementary school mentors in the classroom as some boys are more open to modeling by men than by women;

- encouraging children to use private speech to regulate their behavior such as repeating classroom rules when needing discipline assistance, and repeating the scaffolding of teachers or older children when problem solving;

- allowing private speech to be vocal;

- using each child's learning style to help them develop language and to use language to communicate with peers and adults;

- making sure behavioral expectations are within each child's zone of proximal development; and

- introducing new skills and tasks that fit within each child's zone of proximal development.

Gardner's Learning Styles

According to Howard Gardner, a *learning style* is the preferred or best approach a child uses to process information and solve problems. Today, our early childhood programs and elementary schools—both for instruction and assessment—tend to almost exclusively use the verbal-linguistic and logical-mathematical learning styles. While both boys and girls can exhibit any of these learning styles, young boys who struggle academically and behaviorally often prefer to learn using one or more of the other learning styles. This section presents several learning styles that are often very helpful in teaching young boys: bodily-kinesthetic, naturalist, visual-spatial, musical, and interpersonal. Note that most children have several learning styles, not just one.[13] Each of these learning styles needs to be integrated within the overall curriculum and instructional approach, and not taught simply as a "special" or an add-on content area.

Bodily-Kinesthetic Learning Style

A *bodily-kinesthetic learning style* is the ability to use one's body for self-expression and physical performance through a combination of physical activity, muscle control, sensations, reflexes, coordination, and movement. Body-kinesthetic learners can pick up rhythms, repeat choreographed sequences, and master athletic skills such as kicking a ball or hitting a ball with a bat. Maybe of all the learning styles, this is the one that most closely matches the prevailing learning need of many young boys to be on the move, and are sometimes disruptive and even aggressive in doing so.[14]

> *Figure Three*
>
> ## Gardner's Learning Styles
>
> - Bodily-kinesthetic: learning through the use of whole-body movement.
> - Naturalist: learning from nature, interested in ecology, and enjoys the outdoors.
> - Visual-spatial: use of pictures, graphics, designs, and maps to learn.
> - Musical: learning through singing, playing an instrument, and participating in a choir or orchestra.
> - Interpersonal: use of social skills to organize, negotiate, and mobilize others.
> - Intrapersonal: learning through introspection, insight, and a personal philosophy.
> - Linguistic: learning with words—both oral and written—reads and writes well.
> - Logical-mathematical: uses math and a linear, logical approach to learn; does well in traditional math and science activities.[15]

Boys need opportunities to build forts and to play with blocks, play in sand and water, climb on playground equipment, play physical games, dance, and learn physical skills such as riding a tricycle and swinging on a swing. These activities need to be viewed as valuable learning experiences and not simply diversions from real academic learning. Teachers need to understand that when boys are eating, reading, painting, and so forth, their whole body moves. This is the way they are!

Photo by Scott Bilstad

There is growing evidence that suggests physical activities actually increase cognitive abilities.[16] Intervention studies for students who struggle with behavioral issues in their programs recommend adding physical activities to learning experiences; physical movement helps develop positive emotions through role play, drama, dance, and art.[17] Early childhood programs and schools need to work closely with parents to convince them of the value of physical activities, and to help them find opportunities in the community for their children to engage in these activities, including sports teams, recreation centers, and the use of outdoor playgrounds. In Chapter 8 we discuss ways that the community can be used to support young boys' physical activities.

Notes from the Field

Learning Folk Dances

I have taught folk dancing to young children, and unlike older boys (nine and above), young boys have no resistance to dancing, and enjoy it as much as girls (when taught at the appropriate developmental level).[18] Engaging in dance provides boys with an acceptable outlet for physical activities they love, but are often punished for doing: jumping, stamping, leaping, hopping, swinging, pulling, and playing roughly.[19] They can also engage in these behaviors as a group, and thus, no one is singled out as being inappropriate, asocial, or simply, "bad."

Like songs and classical music, folk dances are very repetitive, have a regular beat, and require the child to anticipate upcoming sequences, formations, and steps. Many of these skills prepare students for future learning, especially math. They also teach important physical skills, balance, and coordination.

Folk dances can be used to celebrate various cultural events. For example, in a Head Start program I worked for in Colorado, the teachers taught the children Mexican folk dances that were then performed by the children for their parents at a Cinco de Mayo celebration.[20]

Naturalist Learning Style

A child with a *naturalist learning style* is fascinated by nature; can make distinctions between different birds, animals, and plants; and delights in exploring the rich, natural world. Learning experiences should focus on exploration, discovery, observation, cause-and-effect, and most importantly, active, whole-child engagement with the natural environment. Here are some ways to encourage naturalistic learning.

- Provide a year-round garden where young boys can prepare the soil, and plant and harvest vegetables.

- Have a variety of animals that young boys feed and care for.

- Hang bird feeders in the playground and outside the classroom window.

- Set up wind measuring instruments and rain gages in strategic places on the playground.

- Visit parks, green spaces, and bird and animal refuges.

- Visit outdoor museums that include a variety of farm animals and plants, and provide demonstrations involving the care of these animals and plants.

- Visit a fish hatchery.

- Invite naturalists and park supervisors to give classroom presentations.

- Invite bird sanctuary experts to display some of the birds they work with.

- Visit city greenhouses where plants are prepared for city parks.

- Participate in tree planting activities with your local city government, school district, or nonprofit agency.

Visual-Spatial Learning Style

Visual-spatial learning style involves thinking about objects in different spatial orientations, being able to "see" objects from different points of view, organizing objects in space, understanding and explaining how objects are arranged in space in relationship to each other, and using visual images to enhance memory, information processing, and retrieval. Many current scholars see the visual-spatial learning style as a key component in the discipline we now call STEM and in the arts.[21]

Many boys are visual-spatial learners.[22] Research also shows that boys score higher in visual-spatial learning assessments than girls. For boys, the use of visual-spatial learning is important, especially for those who struggle with the traditional linguistic and logical-mathematical approach to learning and assessment. It legitimizes the time boys spend in the block area, building and construction activities—including woodwork—and the extensive use of the arts throughout the curriculum and daily activities.[23]

Visual-spatial learners enjoy drawing, design, maps, architectural and technical drawings of buildings, diagrams of locations, geometric shapes, and woodwork.[24] It is also important that art, in all of its variety and rich possibilities, is taught in a developmentally appropriate manner for visual-spatial learners. Young children's art develops through distinct stages, and any art activities and instruction, including those integrated in other disciplines or used to record projects and design activities, must align with these stages.[25] To expect a child to perform art at a level beyond the child's developmental stage will cause frustration and create in the child a sense of failure. Here are ideas that can encourage visual-spatial learning in young boys.

- Provide a variety of large-format, colorful books on how to design, how to make things, architectural drawings, maps, photography, and abstract art.

- Make sure all children, including young boys who may struggle academically and behaviorally, have the opportunity to engage in a variety of art activities every day (i.e. children are not punished by being removed from art activities).

- Provide a well-equipped woodworking bench in each classroom for children three years and older.

- Encourage play and learning in the block area, and when the weather is nice, bring large, hollow blocks outside. Integrate other disciplines such as social studies and math into block play.

- Use a variety of documentation techniques for projects and other activities—digital photography, drawings and diagrams, and three-dimensional models.

- Teach students how to use drawings to plan projects such as building a fort, creating a garden, or adding to the playground; display these drawings in the classroom.

- Display children's artwork throughout the program or school (not just the classroom) where everyone can see the value of art.

- Have local artists and designers—especially men—visit the classroom to demonstrate their techniques and display their work.

- Arrange for the exhibition of children's artwork at local venues—banks, airports, city halls, or community colleges—and provide an official public opening for the exhibitions.

- Provide lots of opportunities for outside art projects such as using large chalk on the sidewalk, or painting on wooden fences with water paints and large house paint brushes. Children might even be involved in painting outdoor murals in areas that need to be brightened up such as concrete walls and culverts.

Musical Learning Style

Starting in prenatal development, a fetus begins to become aware of sounds and voices, and is conditioned by the rhythms of his mother's heartbeat. After birth, the infant soon discriminates a variety of sounds, pitches, inflections, and rhythmic patterns, many associated with language, but others developed through exposure to lullabies and access to music. Children with a *musical learning style* can easily repeat complex rhythms and melodies, enjoy listening to music, learn to play an instrument—or several instruments—and excel in singing and dancing. They are also sensitive to the vast richness and variety of environmental sounds.[26]

Notes from the Field

Red and Blue Horses

As a young child, I struggled with math and learning to read. But I enjoyed art: I was a visual-spatial learner. I greatly enjoyed the artwork of German artist Franz Marc, who painted red and blue horses (I grew up on a farm surrounded by Welsh ponies and Clydesdales). As I grew older, I began to enjoy the colorful and whimsical artwork of the Swiss artist Paul Klee.

Visual-spatial learners enjoy books that have colorful and graphic displays of all sorts of art, patterns, and three-dimensional diagrams; and detailed drawings of how things are constructed: castles, suspension bridges, tunnel networks, and complex machinery. They also enjoy books of photography and abstract art. The publishing company Dorling Kindersley offers many large-format colorful books on these topics. All early childhood programs and elementary schools need to make sure they provide a variety of these kinds of books, along with the more typical children's books.[27]

Music provides learning opportunities for boys who may struggle with the traditional logical-mathematical and linguistic learning styles; it also offers opportunities for hands-on learning (playing an instrument) and social engagement (participating in a choir or orchestra). These activities in early childhood programs are also great for young boys because they involve whole-body movements, using simple instruments, whole-child learning, and social interactions—all things many boys enjoy.[28] Ideas to encourage musical learning include the following.

- Provide music lessons to the whole class. There are several programs designed specifically for young children, including those of Kodaly and Orff.

- Teach folk dances.

- Provide opportunities for creative dance. Children can "act out" familiar stories, use props, and interpret their favorite music (one of my favorite pieces for creative dance is Darius Milhaud's jazz piece, *The Creation of the World*).

- Songs—beginning with babies and toddlers—should be a central part of the curriculum, including the use of ethnic lullabies. While some songs are used to teach specific skills or reinforce certain behaviors, singing for the sake of singing must be included. Many songs involve body movements, such as clapping hands and "putting your left foot in." Some Waldorf and Froebel schools also use "singspiels," which are complex forms of singing and movement. As we have said, young boys love physical movement.

- Expose children to a variety of different music. Music is one of the best ways to learn about other cultures and nationalities—from jazz, Mexican dance music, cowboy songs from Argentina, African American spirituals, Native American music, and classical pieces that are based on authentic national folk music from around the world.

- Encourage children to learn to play an instrument.

- Challenge stereotypes in music. There are famous African American opera singers, White hip-hop artists, African American and Hispanic composers of classical music—men and women.

- Take children to music performances in the community such as orchestras, brass bands, Andean folk music groups, Mariachi bands, Native American powwows (where traditional music is played to accompany the dances), church choirs, and high school orchestras and choirs.

Interpersonal Learning Style

A central task of development for young children is to learn to understand other people and to be sensitive to their moods, actions, and feelings. Some children are more adept at this ability than others. Children with an *interpersonal learning style* are good at listening, cooperating in group tasks and projects, seeing things from the perspective of others, and organizing and negotiating group activities.[29] They have natural leadership abilities. In fact, leadership is one of the four areas of giftedness and is defined as "an unusual ability to inspire, guide, direct, or influence others."[30]

The challenge of working with young boys who have an interpersonal learning style is that their involvement, organization, and leadership of other children may not always be viewed in a positive light—young boys' group leadership may not be a match with teacher or program goals. Nevertheless, boys with interpersonal learning styles must be given lots of opportunities to lead. Here are some ideas to facilitate this process.

- Encourage young boys to direct projects and activities.

- Help them join a variety of group activities.

- Support young boys when other children select them as group leaders.

- Include young boys in small groups that organize classroom and school-wide activities such as parent nights, community events, and culmination activities for the Project Approach and Lifelike Pedagogy.

- Scaffold young boys' interpersonal skills to produce positive rather than negative results.

- Recognize and acknowledge the leadership skills of young boys. It is important that programs make sure boys who have leadership skills, but who struggle academically or behaviorally, are not excluded from leadership roles in the classroom or school.

Erikson's Psychosocial Stages

Erik Erikson's theory of eight lifespan stages proposes that an important task of development must be achieved at the end of each stage; if it is not achieved, the person will struggle to complete the next stage.[31] Understanding Erikson's first two stages: 1) *trust versus mistrust* (birth to one); and 2) *autonomy versus shame and doubt* (one to three) can help in meeting the unique needs of young boys.

Trust versus Mistrust

The goal of this stage is for the child to develop a belief that the world can be trusted and is basically a good place. This disposition is developed through warm, responsive, sensitive, and human interactions that respond to the unique needs of the infant. Infants that are relatively easy to care for produce positive responses from caregivers, while irritable and difficult infants can produce impatience, restrictions, and punishment—often severe.[32] Young boys, who are often more difficult to care for as infants, are more at risk of abuse than girls.[33] The following are some ideas for supporting young boys during this stage.

- Treat every infant as an individual with his own needs, wants, and unique characteristics.

- Use every possible opportunity to deeply engage with the infant and develop rich, human relationships.

- Respond to the child's needs—physical, social, emotional, and cognitive—as soon as is reasonably possible. This includes the child's need for play, stimulation, and challenging cognitive activities.

- Provide advice and parent training to help parents understand how each of their children is different and that children who are difficult need extra patience, warmth, care, and attention—but not punishment.

- Never compare infants to each other and help parents understand the negative results of doing so.

- Make sure there is a cultural match between the home and the behaviors and expectations used in the home and those used in caring for the infant in the early childhood program.

- Give shy and slow-to-warm children plenty of time to respond to change, support them in understanding and anticipating difficult changes, and help them learn about new environments, including new people in their world.

- Feed and change infants according to their unique schedules and not based on an arbitrary schedule imposed by time or convenience.

- Hold infants as much as possible. While infants are beginning to move to the autonomy stage they need the warmth, stimulation, and heartbeat of close proximity to an adult.

Autonomy versus Shame and Doubt

Anyone who has worked with toddlers is very familiar with this age: it's all about *me* and about *my* control, as toddlers strive for independence and try to do everything themselves. Toddlers need to feel empowered by their autonomy, even though adults must provide very close care and supervision to protect them from accidents. For young boys, the challenge is that many get into all sorts of problems by typical age-appropriate risk-taking, trying out new things, practicing skills they have not mastered, and getting into conflicts with other children due to immature emotional regulation and poor social skills. To put it mildly, the toddler's desire for autonomy far exceeds his ability to actually be autonomous!

Caregivers and teachers need to make sure they provide toddlers with as much freedom and autonomy as possible, while maintaining safety and a semblance of order. One secret is to remember that it's all about the child's perception of his autonomy, and not about real freedom and actual independence. Here are some activities that support young boys as they progress through this stage.

- Provide many acceptable choices, such as choosing clothes to wear (give them two choices), food to eat, and toys to play with.

- Provide opportunities to experiment with new materials. Remember, for young children, materials such as sand, soil, mud, stones, leaves, wood, plastic, bubble wrap, sand paper, cardboard, wool, silk, straw baskets and hats are all new sensations that they love to explore and engage with.

- Allow a young boy to do as much as possible on his own such as dressing himself, washing, and eating.

- Scaffold activities and tasks in a way that the child can see what they are doing on their own and how they can continue to master other parts of the activity.

- Remember that regardless of what they are doing, young boys need to move their whole body.

- Limit competition and the need to get something right; let them enjoy a variety of options and results.

- Stress cause-and-effect—help young boys see the results of their actions and behaviors, but avoid punishment.

- Stress mastery of almost anything—language, physical skills and coordination, and even toilet training. But remember that mastery involves trial-and-error, mistakes, and lots of practice to get something right.

- Limit "no" and don't." Instead, try: "you can do it this way," "try it this way," or "have your tried…?".

- Remember that in many areas, young boys are slower to mature than girls. Interpret developmental milestones with this in mind.

- Provide multiples of the same toys so that when children play together, they are not competing for the same toy. At this age, sharing is not an appropriate expectation.

- Limit verbal instructions. Young children have poorly developed language and reasoning skills; young boys even more so. If words are used, use only one demand or instruction at a time and model what you want the child to do.

Dewey

There are four important concepts from John Dewey's extensive scholarship that assist us in meeting the developmental and learning needs of young boys: meaningful learning, using each child's unique experiences as the start of the curriculum, learning by doing (experiential learning), and viewing the classroom as a community.[34]

Meaningful Learning

The idea that learning is easier and more effective when it is meaningful to the learner is a powerful teaching concept. Some ways to encourage *meaningful learning* with young boys include:

- soliciting ideas from parents about activities their child likes to do at home and things he always wants to do when he has a choice;

- asking children what they would like to learn, things they are interested in, and what they do at home to occupy themselves;

- carefully observing children's play, activity choices, books they read and look at, what they do on the playground, and other personal interests;

- webbing curricula ideas by first selecting a theme that is of interest to children in the class, based on observations and asking them, rather than simply adopting the theme listed in the curriculum;

- visiting many field trip sites in the neighborhood that are of interest to young boys: farms, fire stations, construction sites, outdoor museums, green spaces, fish hatcheries, auto repair garages, wild animal refuges, road repair projects, quarries with huge trucks, and water works projects;

Photo by Widhi Rachmanto (https://flic.kr/p/cwDYR7) licensed under CC by 2.0

- providing a variety of books throughout the program or school on topics boys are interested in: wild animals, monsters, construction sites, cars and airplanes, huge trucks and earth-moving equipment, and fantastic adventures;

- developing a science area filled with all sorts of things to fix: old typewriters, cake mixers, old telephones, mechanical toys, and car parts; and

- inviting a parent or other important relative to visit the classroom and demonstrate—and maybe even teach—a hobby, skill, or activity that they enjoy doing at home. In this way you can see what is important to the child's family.

Using Each Child's Unique Experiences as the Start of the Curriculum

Designing curricula around each child's unique set of experiences requires teachers to build on the foundation each child brings with them to the classroom. Just as young boys seem to have many different interests than girls, they also bring a body of unique and different experiences to our programs. These interests should be used as the foundation for their learning. Therefore, much of the curricular content will be different for boys than for girls. However, fundamental basic skills, concepts, and outcomes in each learning domain can be taught through a curriculum that originates with each child's unique experiences. The way curricular content is taught depends, of course, on the developmental age of the students. Here are some ways to begin the curriculum with each child's unique experiences.

- For a child from a farm, or a child who has pets at home, a curriculum could begin with exploring different kinds of animals, such as working dogs and their different uses around the world.

- For a new immigrant from another country, the curriculum might begin with a map of the world, showing all of the countries where Americans have come from and the language spoken in each country.

- A child whose parent is a local artist might start his curriculum by studying different art movements and then creating examples from each movement.

- For a child whose family belongs to a religious minority in the U.S. such as Jewish, Muslim, or Quaker, the child could study the movement towards religious freedom and reasons why the U.S. differs so radically in this belief when compared to other countries.

- A child from a family that celebrates his French heritage and history can begin by studying the history and culture of France. He can visit local French organizations and schools, and invite French people to visit the classroom and talk to the class.

- A child whose family is involved in the social issues important to his Black community can begin his studies by examining the Civil Rights movement of the 1960s and then invite local Civil Rights leaders, educators, and historians to visit the classroom.

- A child fascinated with dinosaurs can visit the local natural history museum, arrange a field trip to a local dinosaur fossil site, and begin to study the various historical periods.

Learning by Doing

Learning by doing (experiential learning) means that learning experiences are built around a real task or activity. Because these are real activities, the various tasks involved have meaning and purpose, so long as children can see the big picture. By engaging in real-life activities, children learn a variety of specific skills, along with developing self-esteem and learning responsibility. In the past, young boys would engage in these activities by doing tasks on a farm, helping with their parents' small business, or assisting adults in the community on projects. Young boys thrive at learning by doing because it is a whole-child, multisensory approach to learning, and because it often requires children to move, engage in activities, and take risks. Suggestions for learning-by-doing activities include:

- caring for a group of laying hens, from baby chickens to collecting the eggs;

- joining a community garden and caring for vegetables, from planting seeds to selling vegetables at a local farmers' market;

- selecting a local senior center to visit on a regular basis and interacting individually with the seniors;

- for grades one to three, matching up with preschool-age children in a local early childhood program and working with the children on a variety of activities and projects;

- caring for the neighborhood where the school or early childhood program is located—picking up trash, cleaning, and covering over graffiti;

- looking after animals at a local farm or outdoor museum: horses, pigs, cows, sheep, or goats;

- working with a group of parents and community volunteers to redesign and rebuild the program's playground; and

- inviting a parent, grandparent, or volunteer to regularly visit the classroom to work on their skill or hobby such as making jewelry, repairing instruments, knitting blanket squares, or carving wooden toys.

The Classroom as a Community

The idea of the classroom as a community means that we must value each member of the classroom, and make sure that each child's contribution is acknowledged. Classrooms and schools need to be supportive, safe, and caring communities. Children need to be free to make mistakes and fail without the fear of humiliation, punitive judgment, or exclusion.[35] Boys who struggle should not be excluded from activities; boys who need one-on-one therapy should not be removed from important group activities for these sessions; and boys who have special needs should not be labeled and viewed as less competent or valuable than others in the classroom. Failure should never be a choice. As much as possible, young boys should be able to see themselves as important members of the classroom, school, and community.

Chapter Review

This chapter explored a variety of theoretical frameworks that can be used to help us understand gender differences in young children, and provide opportunities and conditions under which young boys can be successful in our early childhood programs and schools. It began by describing the *Principles of Child Development and Learning that Inform Practice*, which provided the framework for the rest of the chapter. The chapter then explored some of these concepts and theories, beginning with brain-based learning and Froebel's Kindergarten, and continuing with a discussion of Piaget's cognitive theory, Vygotsky's ideas of scaffolding and private speech, and Gardner's eight learning styles. The chapter concluded with a description of two of Erikson's psychosocial stages, and Dewey's ideas about learning, curriculum, and creating a learning community. After each discussion of a concept or theory, we provided specific suggestions for various ways each of these perspectives can be used to help enhance the care, nurturing, development, and learning of young boys.

Questions to Ask Yourself

- Which of Gardner's learning styles do you believe should be encouraged and fostered in your classroom or program to support boys?

- Why, according to Vygotsky, do all children, including those who struggle academically and/or behaviorally, need lots of opportunities to learn from peers?

- What are safe and healthy ways to enable toddlers to experience Erikson's stage of autonomy?

- What are some ways you can support young boys by using the outdoors to implement a developmentally appropriate curriculum?

- How can we find ways to accept more movement by young children, especially boys, during their early childhood and school experience?

- If most future school learning involves words and numbers—abstract symbols—why is there a need for young children to use concrete materials to learn new information and solve problems? Is this not simply delaying the inevitable?

- Is it possible to support a child with a special need without others in the class knowing of his disability? How so?

- Why is it important for every child—including young boys who may struggle academically and behaviorally—to be an important part of the classroom and school community?

- What are different ways an early childhood or elementary school classroom can be made into a nurturing, supportive, and psychologically safe community where everyone belongs?

CHAPTER 5

Policies and Program Practices

This chapter identifies several program policies that negatively impact the success of young boys and offers solutions on how these policies can be altered to help accommodate the unique needs of boys. This examination of program policies may seem far removed from the daily activities of child care providers, teachers, specialists, and administrators, including their interactions with boys and the families of boys. But it is clear to me from my own experience teaching and working in early childhood and school programs that these policies have a direct impact on the daily experiences of young boys. Further, after listening to the concerns and frustrations of my community college early childhood students, it is apparent that many of these policies and program practices often inhibit their ability to provide the rich kinds of experiences they know and believe their children need.

Early Childhood Is Not School Readiness

Many children who enter kindergarten are not ready for formal academic classes and the kinds of behaviors needed to pursue these activities. This "readiness concept" is an even greater issue with younger children because developmentally young children exhibit such a large range of maturity and experience. Early childhood programs—especially those serving children birth to kindergarten—should not be viewed as the first rung of the educational ladder (formal education should begin in the first grade). The driving force of school readiness today is the belief that early childhood programs should help children develop the skills, dispositions, and knowledge that are the first rung of the linear school curriculum ladder, leading eventually to college entrance. This ladder is dictated by college entrance requirements, and thus the standards for each rung are predetermined by external expectations and not the child's development and learning.

Instead, programs that serve children birth to age six should focus on the view of school readiness popular *before* the current focus on academics, and characterized by the idea of developing social competence as a major goal for preschool.[1] The foundation for this approach is the belief that each individual child's natural development and predisposition to learning should be at the center of everything we do. This should be supported and embraced by a nurturing environment with educated, sensitive, and well-trained staff. It's an approach that is directly guided by the developmental profile of each child. The main purpose for this paradigm shift is to enable young boys who currently struggle in our programs to be viewed as successful children progressing through the normal and appropriate stages of growth, development, and learning.

The following will discuss a variety of broad, overall approaches to the early childhood years beneficial to young boys. For young boys to thrive and succeed during these early years, programs should focus on play, exploration of the arts, creating a classroom community, extensive use of the outdoors, movement, and the use of integrated approaches to learning.

While the approaches discussed below cover the early childhood age range (birth to eight), the hope is that they will also extend upward beyond third grade, positively impacting K-12 curricular and instruction (pedagogy) in a variety of ways. The intent is to make sure that every school and educational program is ready for every child—academically, physically, emotionally, culturally, and socially. The end goal and ultimate outcome of school should be high school graduation, and then successful entry into a trade, career, or college program. That's the time for specialization, not before.

Focus on Play

Traditionally, play was at the heart of the early childhood curriculum.[2] This was no accident. Not only does play match up well with the overall developmental needs of all young children, but it allows boys to engage in experiences that help them develop and learn in a natural, developmental manner: whole-child learning, movement, exploration, trial-and-error, hands-on, messy, and the extensive use of their imagination. Play encourages the child to explore the social and physical environment, without the imposition of strict rules or externally imposed expectations. It places the child at the center of the activity, allowing full control—except for issues of health and safety—in their hands: choices of who to play with, what to play with, how to play, and the very nature of the play activity and its direction and duration.[3] For boys, play is hands-on, self-directed, under their full control, and uses all domains in a whole-child learning approach. It's the ultimate goodness-of-fit for young boys! See more in Chapter 8.

Figure Four

A Different Way Is Possible:
Early Childhood Programs in Finland

Students in Finnish schools consistently score high on international rating scales such as the Programme for International Student Assessment (PISA) and consistently outperform students in the U.S. in math, reading, and science.[4] In fact, by age 15, Finnish students surpass all but a few countries on international assessments.[5] In Finland, children do not start formal schooling until age seven, and yet, the vast majority of students arrive in school with solid reading and math skills.

In Finland, every child under age seven has a right to child care and preschool by law. Further, Krista Kiuru, Finland's Minister of Education says: "Early childhood teachers all have a bachelor's degree, and we trust our teachers and that is very, very important."[6]

Finnish early childhood programs—up through the end of kindergarten (ages six or seven)—focus on social skills, developing self-sufficiency, and play and play-based learning.[7] In general, academic pursuits do not begin until first grade.

Finland's kindergarteners spend a sizable chunk of each day playing, not filling out worksheets.[8] Play includes constructive play such as building forts on the playground; arts and crafts activities in the classroom; and dramatic play, as illustrated by children re-enacting a pretend ice-cream shop where ice cream is sold to classmates. Some is pure free play, e.g., building a fort; and some involves skillful scaffolding of higher order skills by teachers such as helping the ice cream seller figure out the amount of change to give a customer.

Reinikka, who directs several preschools in Kuopio, Finland said that kindergarteners rarely sit down to complete traditional paper and pencil exercises.[9] And there's no such thing as a typical day of kindergarten. Instead of a daily schedule, the week is divided into no more than several major activities per day: Mondays, for example, are dedicated to field trips, ballgames, and running, while Fridays are for songs and learning centers.[10]

Not only is play emphasized within the curriculum and daily activities, but its importance is actually enhanced in the new national curriculum, which was rolled out in the fall of 2015. What's more, Holappa, who leads the development of the country's core curriculum, said that play is being emphasized more than ever in the latest version.[11] In fact, the country's early childhood education program places a heavy emphasis on the concept of "joy," which along with play, is explicitly written into the curriculum as an important learning concept. It is believed that when children learn with joy, it is more meaningful and effective.

In Finland, there is also a national program to train all teachers who work with young children. Teachers help kindergarten children to read "if he is willing and interested"—often by using a play-based literacy method that integrates a variety of literacy activities throughout the daily play of students.[12]

Exploration of the Arts

Froebel, Steiner (Waldorf approach), and Montessori all believed in the value of the arts during the early years. Dewey was also an advocate of art education.[13] The arts are totally hands-on whether it be finger painting, playing an instrument, working with clay, or building something on the woodworking bench. And, as we have said, boys are very much hands-on learners. They love to hold objects, preferably in both hands, bang sticks on pots and pans, mess with mud and paints, learn to use tools to make things, and find a variety of ways to impact their immediate environment. Central to the arts is the creative process: making things and changing the environment. This is all about control, and young boys strive for control as they learn to adjust to the social expectations of home, school, and community. Since young boys are often delayed in learning social skills and in their development of emotional regulation, the exploration of the arts throughout the day is needed at this age.[14]

Create a Sense of Community

Dewey believed that a school and a classroom must become a healthy community where everyone belongs and everyone has an important role to play.[15] All students in the school and classroom, including those who may struggle academically and behaviorally, should be viewed as important parts of the whole. All students should be involved, to the extent that they can developmentally, in structuring and maintaining the classroom environment by: creating and reinforcing rules, having input into the schedule and individual expectations, and maintaining the safety and cleanliness of the classroom and school.

This means that adults—teachers, volunteers, administrators, and specialists—must be very sensitive to the classroom climate, and the impact of their actions on this climate. Individual students should not be excluded from group activities; all students should be given multiple opportunities to learn from other students; and no student should be excluded from favorite activities or isolated—even for therapy or tutorials. All students should be empowered to assist those that struggle. Since young boys tend to have more problems with engaging in appropriate social skills and developing emotional regulation, this approach is particularly relevant to them.

Use of the Outdoors

What makes the outdoors so attractive to young children—and young boys—is that it has its own set of rules, laws, and realities that must be followed in order to enjoy it. The challenge then is to determine how exactly the natural world works: what happens when you dam up a stream, water the vegetables too much, or when a baby bird falls out of a nest? Is it always bad when the woods are burnt down? What happens next? These rules and realities are not arbitrary ideas imposed by teachers or parents; they are real consequences of the natural world, and thus make sense to a child figuring out how the world works. See more in Chapter 8.

Move, Move, Move

There is no research or theory in the vast early childhood body of knowledge that supports the view that children can only learn while sitting down quietly. In fact, there is growing research that suggests movement is positively associated with learning.[16] Young children need to be encouraged to move throughout the day, both indoors and outside. This movement needs to be viewed by teachers, administrators, and specialists as a very positive learning process, as opposed to an impediment to learning or something that needs to be controlled.

Young boys love to move, and seem to be preprogrammed to do so.[17] Punishing this natural predisposition may well cause them to develop a sense of guilt, and view this natural need as somehow going against the norms of society and of the school.[18]

Physical play, dance, hands-on learning, mastering physical activities such as riding a bike and kicking a ball, skip rope, and hop scotch, are all excellent ways to encourage movement in young children.

Teach Academics in an Integrated Manner

Earlier we stated that many young children, especially young boys, are not ready for the push down of academic tasks and expectations common in preschool and kindergarten today. Technically, this is not true; what they are not ready for is how these academics are usually taught. Young children are fascinated with language, science, math, art, geometry, music, and other traditional school disciplines, but at their own unique developmental level. And this level is what we call an integrated learning approach.

How do these disciplines affect the world around them, and how can they explain and measure that world? If a child wants to know which chicken lays the most eggs, the child has to count the eggs and then compare them. If a child wants to know if it rained more today than last week, the child will need to measure the rainfall and then compare it, and if he wants to know how to make a birthday card for his mother, someone will have to show him how to cut, fold, draw, and write. All sorts of rigorous academic concepts and skills can and should be taught at this age. But it must be in an integrated manner that makes sense to each child, and not in academic isolation.

Standards, Frameworks, and Outcomes

All professions need standards to define their field, create quality expectations, and develop training programs. However, what has occurred in early childhood programs and K-12 education is that these standards have shifted from quality program-related standards, such as Head Start's Performance Standards, to learning standards that exclusively evaluate students' behavior, development, and academic achievement against a predetermined standard or outcome (and then blames the child—and intervenes—when these standards are not met).

Learning standards are based on an additive, sequential approach to college entry—both for "school readiness" and then for tracking children's progress in the elementary years and beyond. They are "…written descriptions of the skills and knowledge that children should know and be able to do at specific ages or grade levels. … Learning standards—also referred to as academic or content standards, outline what students are expected to learn, not how they should be taught."[19]

These learning standards, frameworks, and outcomes all presume that the only goal of U.S. education is entry into college; college entrance is the top rung of the sequence for everyone. Concerns have been expressed that the focus on standards and assessments narrow the curriculum and create a curriculum based only on the areas assessed by these tests. Thus, art, music, physical education, and social and emotional development tend to be de-emphasized.[20]

Further, one of the more negative results of this approach has been the use of inappropriate, *high-stakes assessments* of young children that take away valuable time, energy, and resources from real learning; teach children school anxiety; and interfere with the ability of caregivers and teachers to develop positive, nurturing relationships with each child. Many children struggle with this learning standards approach including many minority children and young boys.

Program standards, on the other hand, are program requirements established by funding sources, government oversight agencies, and regulatory agencies, and cover all aspects of the program, from teacher qualifications and health and safety regulations to curriculum, parent involvement, and child-teacher interactions.[21] Unfortunately, programs that serve young children have generally shifted from a program standards approach to the exclusive use of learning standards—at least in assessing the educational component of the program.[22] For example, when the No Child Left Behind Act of 2001 (NCLB) was passed, reauthorizing the federal Elementary and Secondary Education Act (ESEA), it relied heavily on specific learning standards and high-stakes assessments to provide the accountability for achieving these standards (see Chapter 3).[23]

A paradigm shift is needed. We need standards, frameworks, and outcomes that focus on:

- all aspects of the child's development equally, including physical, social, and emotional development;

- the typical variability of young children from a variety of different cultural backgrounds as the norm, meaning that the natural variability of the growth and development in young children is the standard, not the exception;

- a process approach, and not an outcomes and objectives approach—the *Principles of Child Development and Learning That Inform Developmentally Appropriate Practice* presents this idea well: there is variability between individual children's development and between domains within each child;[24]

- quality human relationships between teachers and caregivers and the children;

- creating and maintaining a positive relationship between the program and the child's family;

- recognizing, supporting, and affirming cultural attributes that may be invisible to the greater society and may be missed by traditional developmental milestones, while being sensitive to milestones that reflect child development in the dominant culture;

- performance standards—everything from the layout of the classroom and the design of the playground to classroom materials and curricular activities; and

- eliminating all high-stakes assessments. The use of assessments during the early years should only be for: medical purposes; to identify true developmental delays based on the normal development of all young children including boys, minorities, and new immigrant children; to collect information to help design appropriate curricula, develop experiences, and select materials; and/or to evaluate the effectiveness of the curriculum and learning activities. These assessments need to be naturalistic, authentic, and culturally appropriate.[25]

Figure Five

Recommended Approach to Revising Federal Education Programs

The U.S. government plays an extremely important role in early care and education, nationwide. Its main function is to enforce civil rights legislation guaranteeing educational equality regardless of race, ethnicity, language, gender, and disabilities. IDEA, ESEA, and Section 504 of the Rehabilitation Act, are examples of these important federal programs. By law, these programs are reauthorized—revised and updated—on a regular basis. Unfortunately, in the past, many of the revisions to these acts have resulted in some very destructive policies, especially for young boys.

When changing these laws in the future, the federal government should avoid imposing universal, standards-based approaches to all programs and for all children. Rather, funds and expertise should be used to support local early childhood programs and schools. They should be directly targeted to local initiatives that improve the care and education of students who struggle most in our schools—minorities, those with special needs, and boys—especially approaches that challenge the traditional, standards-based assembly-line approach to curriculum and learning. They should fund, support, and encourage innovation, experimentation, research, and change.

Special Education Policies

The idea of educating children with a variety of disabilities within early childhood educational settings is supported and embraced by most educators. However, specific aspects of the application of the Individuals with Disabilities Education Act (IDEA) have come under considerable criticism.[26] Concerns include a disproportionate number of young boys (67%) in special education and a disproportionate number of Black, Hispanic, and Native American students identified with special needs.[27] Labeling young children with a disability is also criticized by many, and some of the approaches to instruction and behavior modification we have already discussed are viewed as inappropriate for young children, and can be counterproductive.[28] It is time for the law to undergo major changes. Two changes are recommended here.

One Continuous Program to Administer IDEA

Currently, children (birth to three) are served by Part C of IDEA, which is administrated by a local non-profit. At the age of three, the child must transition to Part B, which is administered by the local public school. The central problem is that just as families are becoming used to working with one community agency, they then have to turn around to transition to working with another community agency—their local public school.

Clearly, young children are different from older children. However, what is needed is one continuous program for children birth to graduation from high school, with many of the ideas and approaches used with the younger children incorporated into this new approach. One idea that should be included is much more of a family orientation in working with children with special needs. Another is a more whole-child approach to developing the child's individualized education program, as opposed to a school-centric view. More training is needed for educators and administrators that focuses on incorporating the development of young children into the culture and institutional values of local public elementary schools.

No Labels

As we discussed in Chapter 2, to qualify for IDEA a child must be given a disability label. Further, because IDEA is a deficit program, these labels focus on areas in which the child struggles—usually developmentally, academically, or behaviorally—and which need additional intervention, instruction, and attention. For children ages birth to three (and often children up to age eight, depending on the state), the general category, *developmental delay* is used.[29] What this means is that at the onset the program labels a child with a disability that will follow the child for as long as he is in a special education program. This reliance on the use of labels is one the most controversial aspects of the IDEA program. According to Gargiulo and Bouck, these disability labels have negative impacts on children in a variety of ways:

- they can stigmatize or even lead to stereotyping of children;

- they tend to focus the attention of the early childhood program or school on the limitations of a child instead of the child's strengths and capabilities;

- sometimes they become an excuse to not hold high expectations of the child—both by the program and by the child himself;

- they contribute negatively to a child's self-concept and self-esteem;

- they can cause exclusion from certain activities and programs in the school and community that are enjoyed by other children; and

- they may suggest a disability is both permanent and always limiting when this is not always the case.[30]

In addition, for young children a major developmental task is the creation of their own unique identity. Identity involves the interaction between a child's inner self and the response to the child from the outside world—especially peers, family, and the school program.[31] A child who is labeled at an early age with a disability will naturally incorporate the label into his identity. And since these labels are negative—areas where the child struggles—and the outside world responds to these negative labels, they will contribute to a deficit perspective of the child's identity.

Here is an alternative. To fund schools, the program would operate in the same way Title I schools are now funded, through direct funding to the school and the district, based on the overall percentage of children with special needs in the school at the present time. All children enrolled in district schools and early childhood programs would have an *Individualized Education Program* (IEP). (IDEA requires an *Individualized Family Service Plan* (IFSP) for children birth to three; and an IEP from three to 21).

Many schools already follow this best practice, calling it an *Individualized Learning Plan* (ILP). This plan would be continually updated via information from classroom teachers, school psychologists, and other experts using a variety of authentic and performance-specific assessments. This plan would also include the child's areas of strength. Given the use of technology in today's schools, it would be easy to update and use these plans for activity and program planning. One example of this process is CATs—computerized adaptive tests—which create a custom test for each student based on their progress on the content covered by the standardized assessment.[32]

Children who struggle would also receive additional help, based on need; those who excel would receive activities tailored to their talents through a variety of approaches. However, the focus would be on working collaboratively with parents and teachers to help each child succeed in the classroom in all domains including physical activities, the arts, and practical skills. Children will not be deprived of certain activities in order to focus on other "more important" areas.

Notes from the Field

IDEA Services in a Private School

At age eight, my son was still struggling to read. My wife and I decided to have him assessed to see whether he would benefit from special education services. At that time, he attended a private French International School. We contacted the school district where we lived and arranged for him to take a series of assessments. These results showed that my son had a problem with auditory discrimination, and therefore, could not discriminate letter sounds. Additionally, he lacked basic organizational skills. The results of these assessments were then discussed at a staff meeting at the local elementary school.

An IEP was developed with appropriate interventions for these two deficits—provided at the local school (within walking distance from the private school). Ideas were also provided for how teachers at the French school could assist in these areas. An additional recommendation from the staffing committee was that we remove my son from the French school, due to a belief that the bilingual environment interfered with his ability to learn to read English (this is an example of special education focusing only on what are believed to be important skills that directly relate to school success). We rejected this suggestion.

My son would walk from the private French school to get services once a week from the special education teacher. He enjoyed these sessions, and we were grateful that he could receive these services while attending a private school. His reading and organizational skills improved and he went on to graduate from high school and college.

Zero-Tolerance Policies

As discussed in Chapter 2, zero-tolerance policies were initiated in the late 1980s as a response to increased juvenile crime, bullying, and a view that young people were becoming increasingly violent.[33] In 1994, the Gun-Free Schools Act was passed, requiring schools that received federal finds to expel or suspend any students who brought a gun to school.

By the 1996-97 school year, 79% of public K-12 schools across the country had adopted some form of zero-tolerance policy.[34] And as is often the case, these policies also trickled down into early childhood programs below kindergarten—especially those connected with public K-12 programs. The idea behind these policies is that schools and students benefit when destructive students are removed from the school setting. Zero-tolerance policies provide punitive, predetermined sanctions for a vast range of violent behaviors, bullying, and aggressive activities in school. There is little room to negotiate; staff cannot make individual judgments or use professional discretion in applying these policies.

The results of these policies in K-12 schools included increases in out-of-school suspensions and expulsions throughout the nation.[35] Further, in many schools, students were suspended and expelled for behaviors that fell well outside of the state's zero-tolerance policies. Nationally, Black and Latino students were expelled at a much higher rate than White and Asian students; boys were twice as likely to be punished as girls. Also, more students with disabilities were disciplined than students without disabilities.[36] But maybe the most severe result of these policies was on the students who were disciplined. They experienced lasting negative effects that included low academic performance and dropping out of school.

While detrimental to all students, these policies are particularly problematic for young boys. As has been pointed out, young boys tend to exhibit a range of behaviors that can be interpreted as aggressive, violent, and asocial. Many behaviors of typically developing young boys such as rough-and-tumble play, full-body movement, aggressive play and the use of sticks as weapons, impulsivity, and extreme ego-centric behaviors can be misinterpreted by teachers and caregivers as inappropriate and unacceptable in an early childhood program or school setting. Additionally, the emotional regulation of many young boys—the ability to control these aggressive behaviors—is often poorly developed when compared to girls.[37] As a result, any zero-tolerance policies designed to cover all children in a program often do not reflect the developmental struggles of many young boys.

What young boys need—as is discussed at length in Chapter 7—is not punitive discipline, expulsion, or suspension, but rather a wide range of safe, supportive, compassionate opportunities to learn how to interact prosocially with peers. Teachers and caregivers need to be empowered to adopt and use a range of approaches in working individually with each student and his family, and to find ways to teach their students appropriate behaviors and interactions.[38]

According to Kang-Brown et al., today there is a growing consensus that zero-tolerance policies are not effective in creating safe schools, and the most effective way to address school safety is by using a case-by-case basis that matches individual situations and needs.[39] This suggests that discretion be used in each unique case. One approach is to use positive behavioral support, fairness, and productive student-teacher relationships. Some school districts are using restorative justice practices. This is an approach that views crime as a harmful act against an individual and a community, as opposed to opposition to the state, school, or school district. In this approach, the offender is held accountable for the damage done and a process of mediation and resolving problems is implemented between the offending student and teacher involved.

Other school districts are focusing on prevention, intervention, and ways to promote positive behavior in the school. An approach called *Positive Behav-*

ioral Interventions and Supports (PBIS) is being used. This is a school-wide approach designed to teach and encourage prosocial skills and behaviors, such as all staff finding ways to be more engaging with students, and providing more productive learning environments. Many districts have also outlawed suspensions for "willful defiance."

Most of these approaches apply to K-12 schools and early childhood programs that are part of these organizations—public and private. However, other early childhood programs will also be positively influenced as the overall attitudes towards discipline and school safety are radically changed. Plus, many of the concepts discussed throughout this book focus on engagement; meaningful learning activities; whole-child, integrated learning; teaching prosocial behaviors; individualization; and healthy, engaging student-adult interactions. These have all been shown to improve school safety and discipline. In Chapter 7 we discuss a number of specific discipline and behavior approaches that extend this discussion.

Chapter Review

This chapter provided suggestions of ways to change policies and program practices to better serve the needs of young boys. It started by recommending that the early years—birth to kindergarten entrance—should not simply be a time to get children ready for starting school, but rather a way to develop a solid foundation for future learning. Next, the chapter deconstructed standards and frameworks, arguing that the development of young children should not be dictated by these external factors, but rather by the true developmental needs of each child. It then proposed that special education should be changed to an affirmative program that supports whole-child development and the learning of all young children, without using labels or isolating some students. Finally, zero-tolerance policies were examined and their detrimental effect on young boys was discussed. Alternative approaches to addressing school safety were then described.

Chapter 5: Policies and Program Practices   **OH BOY!**

Questions to Ask Yourself

- Should all students begin kindergarten at the same place academically or should we expect that children will be at various places when they enter kindergarten, and thus adjust our curricula to meet this reality?

- Why do you believe that many early childhood programs and elementary schools insist on children sitting and being quiet when research shows that movement has a profound positive impact on the development and learning of young children—especially boys?

- How would you create educational policies that focus on the developmental needs of young boys—birth to age eight—while at the same time providing them with the needed foundation to be successful in school?

- What are some possible ways to provide special education services and support to young children without using a deficit model and labels?

- Why is a zero-tolerance approach to the discipline of young boys not only ineffective, but may be counterproductive in helping them develop appropriate prosocial behaviors?

CHAPTER 6

Curricular Approaches

Chapter 5 explored the idea that the early childhood period should be a separate program focused on whole-child development for all children, with an emphasis on physical development and social competence. Programs with children this age should not focus on preparing children for school entry, and should not be the first rung of an educational ladder leading to college entrance. At first grade, its appropriate for schools to involve more formal curricula, introducing children to a variety of academic concepts, hands-on skills, and vocational disciplines. This chapter will explore two concepts: 1) what exactly is a curriculum?; and 2) what are the best curricular approaches for young boys?

What Is a Curriculum?

There are probably as many definitions of curriculum as there are people! It is one of those terms that is used by everyone, yet seems to lack a common definition. All curricula have three components:

- what to teach—the content of the curriculum (*scope*);
- when to teach the content (*sequence*); and
- how to teach it (*methodology*).

In the U.S., that last piece—the methodology—is often separate (usually called instruction). In the rest of the world, it is part of an overall concept known as *pedagogy* that covers all three components. In Chapter 5, much of the criticism of the current standards approach to curriculum focused on the content and scope as both negatively affecting the development and learning of many young boys.

But why?

The other day, I read an advertisement for a very popular early childhood curriculum. It stated, "input equals output," meaning that whatever content is in the curriculum will be learned by the students—information, skills, and dispositions. This, of course, is the mechanical model of the current K-12 curriculum. Here are some of the many problems with this approach.

- It doesn't work very well (for example, in Colorado, one-third of high school graduates need remedial help before they are ready to take college level classes).[1]

- It contributes to the high dropout rate in our schools.

- It doesn't work well for many minority students.

- More and more boys—of all ages—are struggling with this approach.

- It totally ignores the child's development—brain development, overall physical development, emotional and social development, and cognitive development.

- There is a lack of agreement as to what exactly the input (content) should be in the curriculum.[2] For example, the recent priority of STEM as the focus of both K-12 and early childhood curricula.

Not surprisingly, one of the more popular criticisms of the curricula design process is that while focusing expertise on the scope and sequence, child development and the many complex ways children learn is not a priority.[3]

Early Childhood Curricula

The early childhood field is rich with a variety of interesting, innovative, and well developed early childhood curricula including Montessori, Waldorf, British Infant/Primary Schools, Banks Street, HighScope, and Reggio Emilia. However, many of these approaches are now being infiltrated—and greatly altered—by state standards and assessments. These standards and assessments are a result of the push-down K-12 curriculum and a strict adherence to school readiness standards and expectations. Today, the central focus of the early childhood scope and sequence is to prepare children for entrance into kindergarten.

Further, early childhood curricular approaches—especially those used in public early childhood and Head Start programs—are now required to *align* with the state's K-12 curriculum.[4] This essentially means that the mechanical-ladder approach to curriculum is now the official approach to early childhood curricula.

Elementary School Curricula

As pointed out, traditional K-12 curricula used in U.S. schools are defined by scope and sequence. The scope of the typical elementary school curriculum used today focuses on teaching literacy, math, and now STEM. For those who do well in these areas, they can also get "specials"—art, music, and physical education. For those who struggle—often boys and minority students—these "specials" are replaced with remedial work—called recovery—and targeted special education intervention, often called *Response to Intervention* (RTI). In some schools, recess has been reduced or even eliminated. Children who

struggle also can lose recess time as a punishment or because they have to go work with a specialist.[5]

Common in today's elementary schools is the idea of the "earlier the better" sequence, and, of course, this now includes early childhood curricula. Both content and skills/concepts are pushed down to lower and lower grades. Often the sequence makes little educational sense.[6] One example of this focus on the "earlier the better" is the need for every child to be able to read by third grade, a canon that the education profession deeply believes. However, for this to be accomplished, all children—but especially those who are at risk of having reading problems—need intensive literacy instruction in early childhood.

Curricular Philosophy: The What and How We Teach

I have four children. During their early childhood years they were cared for in a rich variety of early childhood settings including at home, by other mothers in their own homes—including a wonderful Sikh caregiver—and in a variety of traditional early childhood programs; during their early school years they were home-schooled, and attended private (international/bilingual), religious, and public schools.

The point is that since children learn and develop differently, their learning and developmental needs differ, and therefore, so do their curricular needs. Some children excel in rigorous, highly structured curricula; others do not. This brings us back to the concept of goodness-of-fit: the fit between how a child develops and learns and the structured curricular frameworks in which he develops and learns.

All curricula are based on a *curricular philosophy*—the what and how of teaching.[7] This philosophy establishes the framework for the entire educational program—curriculum, instruction, and environment. A philosophy that is conducive to the optimum development and learning of young boys is based on the idea that boys need opportunities to:

- engage in hands-on activities in order to be successful;
- experiment and take risks;
- make mistakes and learn from those mistakes in a safe, non-punitive environment;
- control their own learning;
- engage in integrated learning through the use of lots of projects;
- make a mess and to "mess around" with ideas, concepts, words, and all sorts of materials—mud, water, clay, wood, paint, play dough, sand, papier-mâché;
- learn a variety of specific skills such as making things on the woodworking bench, painting, writing, and dancing;
- be encouraged to develop socially and emotionally at their own developmental pace, not at the pace of a predetermined formula;
- be around teachers and caregivers who are skilled at nurturing their development, challenging their learning, and scaffolding their activities;
- be surrounded by books and other curricular materials that include subjects that boys typically like to do and are interested in: machines, sports, insects, monsters, constructions, yucky and gross ideas, superheroes; and
- engage in learning using all of Gardner's eight learning styles.

The foundation for this philosophy is the idea that the natural development and learning of boys is the norm; it is what is to be expected, and will be nurtured, encouraged, and supported (with the obvious need to develop prosocial skills in all children, when they are ready). It's time the traditional approach be radically changed. The following are some curricular approaches that demonstrate this philosophy and are particularly responsive to young boys.

Emergent Curriculum

The philosophical roots of *Emergent Curriculum* include Dewey, Piaget, Vygotsky, and Erikson. It is an approach that operates much like it sounds; it emerges. This approach relies on extremely talented and knowledgeable teachers who can help children select areas to learn, design learning activities, and scaffold learning. It also relies on teachers being able to "see the world from the child's unique viewpoint."[8] The heart of this approach is Dewey's view that curriculum must begin with each child: their experiences, emotional temperament, home and community life, and "view of the world." Curriculum is also what happens—it is fluid, active, and dynamic.[9]

Emergent Curriculum Begins with the Child

Emergent Curriculum begins with the interests, experiences, attitudes, and enthusiasm children bring to the classroom.[10] It is then formed into learning activities, instructional opportunities, and a variety of rich and interesting projects by the teachers with continual input and involvement by the students. These learning activities and experiences provide children with an array of opportunities to not only learn basic skills of literacy, math, and science, but also to paint, dance, make things on the woodworking bench, and construct models and life-size replicas. The following is one example of the use of Emergent Curriculum.

Jonny comes to school on Monday morning full of excitement. It has snowed all weekend and his house in the mountains outside of Denver is covered by six feet of snow. He wants to know if the snow will break the roof of the house—he is also quite concerned and scared about how his goats will find food and why the water for his goats is frozen. Other children catch his enthusiasm—and anxiety—as they too have watched the snow fall all weekend.

Before taking off their outdoor clothes and boots, four boys decide to make angels in the snow on the playground. One of the teachers watches the activity. After making their angels, a robust debate ensues: whose is biggest, whose is the smallest, and whose is best (based on some arbitrary criteria nobody quite understands). The teacher has the foresight to bring a camera and takes pictures of each angel thinking this might be helpful for a future project.

The classroom teacher tunes into the interests and enthusiasm of the class. She decides to begin the day with reading a book about the snow, snowflakes, and melting snow. Then her assistant goes back into the playground to help Jonny and his friends build an igloo, while the teacher stays inside to help other children fill the sand and water table with regular snow, to see what will happen when it melts. They also put snow into the refrigerator to see if it too will melt.

The teacher creates a matrix to record student predictions:

- will the snow in the classroom melt?;
- will the snow in the refrigerator melt?; and
- will the melted snow take up more or less space than the regular snow?

Some of the children can write their names on the matrix and record their hypothesis; others need help. Some of the children are interested in extending this activity by weighing the snow and then weighing the water after the snow has melted. They also predict which will weigh the most or whether they will end up the same.

The teacher also remembers that during a parent-teacher conference, Jonny's father told her that Jonny is very fascinated with the melting snow every spring. He wanted to know: "Where does the snow go?" "When the water goes into the creek where does the creek take it?" "If it ends up in the sea, why is it salty?" "How does the snow get into the clouds?" So the teacher plans to make a diorama with the children out of papier-mâché with mountains, streams, and rivers. And she will look for books and videos about the cycle of water.

The rest of the day is spent exploring snow, ice, and water; making art projects by cutting out snowflakes; feeding the birds on the birdfeeder; and recording the depth of the snow in the playground and writing it on a chart in the classroom.

Photo by Dion Hinchcliffe (https://flic.kr/p/HocaVZ) licensed under CC BY-SA 2.0

Getting Input for the Plan

Emergent Curriculum depends largely on responding to the interests of students in the class. One way to do this is to simply observe children and respond to their interests in a variety of innovative and creative ways. Here are some other approaches to initiating Emergent Curriculum.

- Sit down with small groups of children and ask them what they like to do and what they would like to learn.

- Solicit ideas from parents about what their children enjoy doing. Include this question on the initial application to the program, include the topic in regular student-teacher conferences; place a suggestion box in the classroom.

- Solicit ideas from staff who may have engaged in successful activities before or who have an interest or hobby they can share with the children.

- Carefully observe children's outdoor play and record their interests and activities, which can later be used to design interesting learning activities and projects.

Staff then use these ideas to plan activities and learning experiences for the students. One approach to this planning is the use of *webbing*. According to Jones and Nimmo, webbing allows staff the chance to explore the possibility of any material or idea in order to make decisions about its potential use: is it likely to generate developmentally appropriate activities?; does it suggest ways to enrich the activity with other materials or questions?; and does it offer insight to how long children's interests might continue?[11] Information from this exploration should be carefully collected and stored, and referred to as staff begin to develop new projects, ideas, activities, and plans.

> **Figure Six**
>
> ## Sources for Emergent Curriculum
>
> - Interests of individual children
> - Interests of teachers and caregivers
> - Reported interests of children by parents
> - The physical environment—both indoors and outdoors—according to the seasons
> - People in the social environment (in the program, family, and community)
> - Social issues in the program—conflicts, rules, caregiving, natural routines (e.g., eating/sleeping, feeding the birds, watering the garden, etc.)
> - Values of the school, family, and community[12]

Scaffolding Learning

Central to the full and productive implementation of Emergent Curriculum is the careful and intentional use of *scaffolding*. Scaffolding is a technique used by experienced and knowledgeable teachers to expand, extend, and integrate the curriculum content into more and more developmentally appropriate and rigorous learning activities and experiences. It is a teacher-student approach that works especially well with curricula that are flexible, creative, and encourage teachers and students to collaboratively design the learning activities and processes. In the case of Emergent Curriculum, the content is derived from the child's interests and personal experiences.

Scaffolding is an idea that comes from Vygotsky's sociocultural theory and involves structuring children's learning so that it moves from simple, concrete, and novel to more complex, sophisticated, abstract, and symbolic learning.[13] It's an approach that requires skilled teachers and caregivers to initially adjust to the level of each child's zone of proximal development, and then collaboratively move to higher order processes. Questions, modeling, demonstrating, and suggesting new and more complex possibilities and approaches are all forms of scaffolding. Children with more experience in the activity or skill also act as experts in scaffolding learning for other students.

The concept of scaffolding applies both to this discussion of curriculum and the discussion of instructional approaches covered in the next chapter. From a curricular perspective, scaffolding requires the curriculum to be designed in a way that children can learn from each other in a supportive environment, along with learning from experts in the field. Vygotsky's approach to learning is social, which is why it is imperative that all children, including those who struggle due to developmental challenges and/or special needs, are fully integrated into the classroom and outdoor activities. The Emergent Curriculum approach is grounded in a safe, supportive learning community that involves positive interactions between students, caregivers and teachers, family members, and the community.

The most important reason that the use of Emergent Curriculum is effective with many young boys is because it selects its content from what the boys in the classroom are interested in, have experienced, and/or want to learn. Specifically, this approach enables young boys to engage in hands-on experiences, take risks, learn through the use of projects, integrate many different materials, concepts, and skills in their learning, and develop socially and emotionally. Many of the important basic skills that the traditional curriculum focuses on such as literacy, math, and science can be taught through the use of Emergent Curriculum, but in a manner that matches more closely to the many ways young boys learn. In so doing, young boys feel successful, enjoy learning, and develop self-efficacy.

The Project Approach

The *Project Approach* is based on the same theoretical foundation as Emergent Curriculum. One of the purposes of this approach is to nurture in all children "dispositions for learning"—habits of the mind that children naturally use to learn. Helms and Katz, the authors of this approach, believe that these dispositions for learning are being "taught out of" children in our traditional approach to education. These dispositions include children:

- making sense of their environment;
- finding out how things work;
- determining cause-and-effect, especially of their own actions;
- persisting in finding out the resolution to a problem;
- predicting and caring about the wishes and feelings of others;
- theorizing, analyzing, hypothesizing, and synthesizing; and
- trying to be as accurate as possible.[14]

The Project Approach is especially effective for young boys because:

- it involves whole-child learning;
- it includes lots of hands-on learning;
- boys can use their strengths—such as art, computer graphics, modeling, woodwork, writing, and photography;
- boys can learn at their own pace while also practicing what they have learned; and
- children learn from each other.

Figure Seven

The Project Approach

The Project Approach is not a full curriculum. Rather, it forms an extended, in-depth learning opportunity around a single project pursued over a significant period of time. To successfully carry out a project, the following things are needed.

- A *permanent site* that shows significant change over time and that the children can visit on several occasions—such as a construction site, flower nursery, grocery store warehouse, or farm.

- The ability to arrange the classroom—and maybe the playground—for a variety of follow-up and research-related activities.

- A flexible daily/weekly schedule with large blocks of time.

- Recording and observation materials for children's use.

- A time and place for a final community celebration.

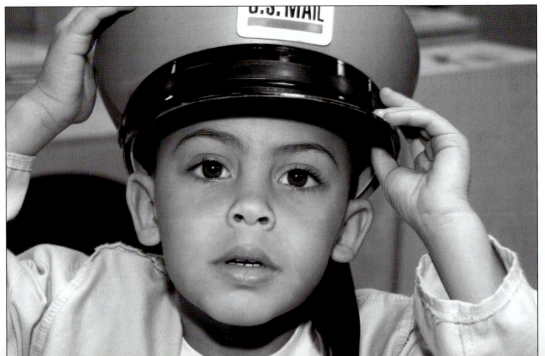

Using the Project Approach involves three distinct stages: getting started, investigation, and concluding the project.

Stage 1: Getting Started

This is the planning stage for the project. It begins with selecting a topic of interest to all the children and finding a site that can be accessed multiple times and is safe for young children to visit. A site that shows significant progress or change over time is best. Next, teachers need to determine what children already know about the topic, and then arrange the classroom (and possibly part of the playground) to put items from the site that children can explore and investigate further. Equipment to use on the site visits needs to be collected such as clipboards, cameras, tape recorders, baskets, and binoculars. Ways to include parents both on site visits and at the progarm or school must also be planned for. Finally, site permission should be obtained and site personnel apprised of ways to work effectively with young children.

Stage 2: Investigation

This is the actual project. Children visit the site on multiple occasions; they take pictures, make drawings, talk to the workers, pick up artifacts they can safely bring home, and record their observations on tablets and video or sound recorders. They then return to the classroom to further explore and investigate their experiences through play, art, reading books, building models, making objects on the woodworking bench (maybe with found objects they picked up on the site), asking teachers and parent volunteers questions, and calculating future progress and success. Younger children can build replica models in the block area, construct examples in the sandbox, and role play what they have experienced on the site. Parents can volunteer both to assist on the site visits and to work with students on their return to the program or school. A parent with specific knowledge and expertise on the topic is especially valuable.

Notes from the Field

An Example of the Project Approach: Raising Laying Hens

Getting Started. When I was teaching at a small school in the mountains of southwest Pennsylvania, I decided that my kindergarten class would benefit from a project. One possible site for the project was a barn within walking distance of my classroom. It housed sheep, goats, horses, and a few bantam hens, and stored the food for the animals.

I visited with Joe, the person in charge of the barn. He showed me around and then pointed out an empty area. "We are expecting newly hatched chickens next week. They will be raised into laying hens for the community." I had an idea: could my class be involved in some way in caring for and learning about these chickens? I took this idea back to my class, who enthusiastically agreed to help raise the chicks. The workers at the barn had worked with school children before so there was no need to educate them about working with my children. Joe was the father of one of the students so we had parent involvement built into the project.

Investigation. The class visited the barn before the chicks arrived. Joe and his workers showed them how to fill the food and water containers, and talked to them about ways to care for the young chicks. Before beginning the project, I checked with our librarian to get some books and magazines about caring for animals in general, and about chickens and laying hens in particular. I also obtained plastic buckets for the children to collect materials from the site; and clipboards, paper pads, and felt pens. Finally, I arranged the classroom to be able to display the artifacts from the site and added materials to help the children explore the project such as dress-up clothes and boots, large blocks, miniature farm animals, materials for the woodworking bench, and various art materials.

Once the chicks arrived, my students began to feed and water them on a regular basis. The children loved caring for the baby chicks and began to discover that as they grew older, they became less cute and more aggressive. They also ate more food and drank more water! The students learned to clean the water and food containers, and watched the workers keep the room clean with new straw and prepare the nesting boxes as the hens began to lay their eggs.

The workers showed my students how to carefully collect the eggs from the nesting boxes, and how to handle hens that did not want their eggs taken from them. They showed them how to carefully put the eggs in the buckets so that they would not break. The children were also told to let a worker know if a hen seemed sick or had an obvious injury. We found carts to use to take the buckets of eggs from the barn to the kitchen where they would be stored and then used.

The children discovered many found objects that they took back to the classroom including a variety of feathers (size, color, and texture); samples of grit,

food, and straw; materials used to make the nesting boxes; shells from broken eggs; and instructions about how to care for newborn chickens. I added pictures and information to the classroom about common predators including hawks and foxes, books about the variety of chickens worldwide, and recipes for making food with eggs. One of the mothers also visited the classroom on several occasions to show the children ways to use eggs in cooking activities.

Concluding the Project. The students' parents, Joe and his barn workers, the librarian, and others involved in working with the kindergarten and school were invited to dinner in the school's lunchroom. The dinner consisted of a salad, fresh rolls, and beautiful, brown hard boiled eggs. After dinner, my students gave the guests a tour of the classroom, describing all of the project's activities, displays, and research they had done on raising chicks and caring for laying hens. There was also a short presentation where students provided those involved in the project with certificates that the children had made, thanking them for all of their work with the students.

In evaluating the effectiveness of this project, I considered the students' involvement and sense of responsibility. Students not only eagerly anticipated their work with the chickens, but took their work very seriously. They wanted to make sure each chicken had enough food and water; once they began collecting the eggs, they were very careful to make sure none were cracked or broken. The students also developed questions while on the site that they would investigate on return to the classroom or that they would ask their parents when they went home.

Because the project involved caring for the chickens from the time they were brought to the barn, until they became laying hens whose eggs needed to be collected, the children's interest and fascination continued throughout the project. They did not get bored.

While I was able to scaffold many extended learning activities in the classroom, I believe I could have gone further, maybe inviting other farmers to the classroom, presenting a multicultural twist to the project (i.e. how Mayans in Guatemala raised their chickens outside, without a fence), and examining other domestic and wild birds.

Stage 3: Concluding the Project

A culminating activity is an opportunity to share the project with the early childhood or school community including parents, volunteers from the site, and the wider community. Students should decide with whom they want to share the project, and what products they wish to include. This can be a physical celebration where community members attend including a PowerPoint presentation, dance performance, art display, slide show, harvest festival, YouTube video, or oral presentation by students. Or it can be a presentation outside of the early childhood program or school: a display of art and models at a local bank, hospital, or airport. It can also be a combination of several types of presentations. This culminating activity places the children's learning front and center, and validates their efforts, dedication, planning, and involvement, regardless of their individual academic achievements, physical challenges, or behavioral issues.

A variety of authentic assessments can be used to determine the effectiveness of the project. One important aspect of the Project Approach is to evaluate how engaged students were in the project.

- Do children take responsibility for their work?
- Are children absorbed and engrossed in their work?
- Are children becoming strategic learners?

- Are the project's tasks challenging and absorbing?
- Do teachers facilitate, scaffold, extend, and guide the children's work?[15]

The use of the Project Approach is a particularly effective learning opportunity for young boys because it provides a structured approach to support children's natural learning through hands-on exploration and sensory integration.[16] It teaches children to value learning an array of important academic skills within the context of the every day world in which they live. Many young boys thrive on meaningful, integrated, whole-child, hands-on learning, which the Project Approach embodies. Projects enable young boys to use their favored learning style, especially those that are not normally used in traditional learning activities, and to experiment with learning styles that they find more challenging, in a low-risk, comfortable environment. When the topic and project site are carefully selected, young boys can explore a variety of topics, items, concepts, ideas, questions, and apparent contradictions that they are deeply interested in. The Project Approach makes learning relevant and meaningful; which is important for many young boys.[17]

Lifelike Pedagogy

Lifelike Pedagogy is a curricular approach I discovered being used in a school in São Paulo, Brazil. Lifelike Pedagogy has many similarities to Emergent Curriculum and the Project Approach. However, it is a full curriculum and places far more control of the entire learning process in the hands of the students, beginning with the selection of the theme. The focus of Lifelike Pedagogy is on the dynamics of the group process. Like the Project Approach, Lifelike Pedagogy is broken into three phases or stages. These include choosing the theme, exploring the theme, and planning and executing the final project.[18]

Phase 1: Choosing the Theme

The central content of the curriculum is determined by its theme, and thus selecting the theme is critical. In this approach, the children select the theme. They do so through the process of exposure, brainstorming, and voting.

Exposure. Teachers provide students with books, magazines, catalogues, drawings, videos, and other materials. Teachers select these documents based on things children have recently shown an interest in, at the children's developmental age, while screening out inappropriate content.

Brainstorming. Here, children begin to discuss possible themes and start listing their ideas on the board or a large piece of paper. Teachers help the students list the interests, but do not support one idea over another.

Voting. Once the list of themes has been compiled, each one is presented to the class by its sponsor. The teachers help each child, especially those who are shy or can't express their ideas clearly, while calming down the more aggressive students. The students then vote on the themes by the raising of hands, casting secret ballots, or combining positive and negative responses. Children cannot vote for their own themes.

Phase 2: Exploring the Theme

In this phase, children explore the theme they have chosen through the process of preparing the map, initial research, and choosing the final project.

Preparing the Map. A child draws a map—actually a web—with the theme in the center. Radiating out from the center is a list of things the children know about the theme—assumptions or hypotheses. For example, for the theme of pizza, they know it is round; can be made of olives, cheese, and sausages; and tastes good. Then they list things they would like to know: can pizzas be square?; can they be sweet? As the children become more familiar with the process, these maps become more sophisticated.[19]

Teachers scaffold the process but they don't contradict students' false assumptions or answer their questions. Let's look closely at a sample of a project on corn. Here, children wanted to know the following.

- Why does corn stand up?
- Does the corn fall off the plant (like nuts from a tree)?

- Why are the seeds so close together?
- How do the seeds grow?[20]

Initial Research. Children research their questions and hypotheses, using a variety of sources including computers and personal connections—teachers, family members, other school members, and members of the community. The teacher helps them find the information and helps them determine the validity of the sources they are using.

While the map is the initial framework, new questions and hypotheses are added during the research process. In this way, children learn how to do research: questioning people, writing down questions and answers, reading directions to get information, and using computer skills and interviewing skills. In the corn project, the students also determined from a member of the school that there was a small farm in the city close to the school that they then visited on several occasions (like the site in the Project Approach).

Choosing the Final Project. In Lifelike Pedagogy, the culminating activity is at the center of the curriculum. The teacher's role in choosing the final project is to make sure the project has the potential for deep, rich, meaningful learning, and demonstrates everything the students have learned about the theme. Some of the culminating projects developed by Brazilian students include:

- producing a video about sharks to send home to families;
- visiting an aquarium to observe sharks and learn from people who care for them; and
- building a lifelike, 3D model of a shark.[21]

Phase 3: Planning and Executing the Final Project

Development Stage. In this stage, students plan the final project, which involves scheduling activities, creating budgets, writing lists of things to be accomplished and who will accomplish them, contacting people (for example, to arrange for transportation to the aquarium). Teachers help keep this process on track, but do not do the tasks themselves. Often, fundraising is a needed part of this step. To fund one project, students created a CD of popular Christmas songs which they then packaged, marketed, and sold to parents and the school community.

Final Project. As with the culminating activity in the Project Approach, the final project allows the students to demonstrate everything they have learned, and enables the school community to celebrate with the students that through dedication and hard work, anything can be achieved. Some additional final projects were visiting the São Paulo Aquarium, assembling and stocking a fish aquarium, and creating a complex model of the human body.[22]

The Lifelike Pedagogy approach provides young boys with opportunities for social interactions and conflict resolution, planning, and meaningful, hands-on learning. Maybe of most importance, young boys have direct input in what they will learn—they pick the theme and control the project through its entirety.

By selecting the theme, children believe that their ideas matter, and that they have some control of their own learning. As Erikson so eloquently described, young children struggle with the issues of autonomy, power, control, and who is in charge; and as has been suggested, young boys in particular struggle with these issues.[23] Not only does this approach give children the control, but it requires them to work together to implement the project, thus developing the emotional regulation and social skills many young boys struggle to master. It also provides many opportunities for boys who learn best through the use of leadership skills, but who need to learn how to use this ability in a prosocial manner. Finally, it is a logical extension of the Project Approach for teachers who find the Project Approach works well and would like to use it more extensively.

Lifelike Pedagogy also matches up well with Erikson's 2[nd,] 3[rd,] and 4th psychosocial stages—*autonomy versus shame and doubt, initiative versus guilt,* and *industry versus inferiority,* which cover the early childhood age range after infancy.[24] Many young boys struggle with autonomy, initiative, and industry—they feel that the adults in their lives are always trying to control them.

Lifelike Pedagogy gives young boys opportunities to control aspects of their learning through a structured and predetermined framework. They feel they have autonomy, initiative, and industry.

HighScope Curriculum

In 1962, David Weikart developed the HighScope Curriculum in Ypsilanti, Michigan to address the educational needs of low-income, minority children in local public schools. The theoretical framework for the curriculum includes the work of Piaget, Dewey, Hunt, Flavell, Erikson, and Kohlberg.[25] Central to this approach is the learning environment and the 54 *Key Developmental Indicators*, which are curricula content and sequence rolled into one. According to Weikart, these describe "what children can do, how they perceive the world, and the kinds of experiences important to their development."[26] Key developmental indicators are goals, objectives, and standards—what drive the curriculum—and are grouped accordingly:

- approaches to learning;
- social and emotional development;
- physical development and health;
- language, literacy, and communication;
- mathematics;
- creative arts;
- science and technology; and
- social studies.[27]

Daily Routine

The heart of the HighScope curriculum is the plan-work-recall process (formerly plan-do-review), which includes all aspects of active learning: materials, choices, Key Developmental Indicators, and adult supervision.[28]

Plan. The planning process includes children creating a goal or goals, expressing personal intentions and interests, and modifying their plans as they progress. This planning process provides children with a sense of control over their learning; a child's capacity to plan depends on their development, but increases with practice. Teachers help scaffold the process through asking questions, helping them think about the space and materials needed, and the activities and the sequence of those activities.

Work. At this stage, children engage in activities they have planned. They change, adapt, modify, and expand their plan during the process. Children use a combination of play, exploration, and interactions with people and materials as they are involved in a variety of Key Developmental Indicators, thus constructing their own knowledge. Teachers support this learning in a variety of ways, helping children feel successful using their ideas rather than directing the activity.

Recall. This activity helps students make sense of their learning experience. Children remember, reflect on the activity, relate their plans to what actually occurred, discuss their learning experience with peers, and evaluate the process: what worked, what did not work, and what happened unexpectedly. This gives the students a sense of control and helps them develop powerful dispositions around learning, planning, evaluation, and discipline.

The teacher's role during recall involves providing a supportive, safe environment, active listening, scaffolding children's thinking and recall, and using props to help with the process.

A full HighScope curriculum also includes other individual, small group, and large group activities—some of which are discussed in the next chapter. However, the plan-work-recall model is at the heart of the HighScope curriculum and is what separates it from more traditional curricular approaches.

The HighScope curriculum works well for young boys because it focuses on helping children feel successful throughout their learning experiences. This is accomplished by helping children plan their various learning activities, and then helping them evaluate the success of these experiences. Children's successes are not determined by adults, but rather by themselves, with careful assistance and scaffolding of the teachers. The learning process itself is dominated by play, exploration, and meaningful interactions with other people and materials—all things young boys thrive at doing. Finally, the goals of the curriculum cover all domains of development including physical development, social and emotional development, and the creative arts, along with the more traditional academic areas.

British Infant/Primary Schools

In 1967, the British government produced the *Plowden Report*, which described a new movement in British schools known as British Infant/Primary Schools.[29] Joseph Featherstone, in a series of articles in the *New Republic*, brought this revolution to the attention of U.S. educators, and it became the foundation for the open/alternative school movement.[30] This new approach focused on the work of Piaget and Dewey.[31] Today, there are schools scattered throughout the U.S. and the world that use the *British Infant/Primary Schools* curriculum. Characteristics of this approach include the following.

- **The Integrated Day.** Children spend the majority of the school day pursuing activities of interest to them. In this way they learn a variety of specific skills and objectives in an integrated way. The day is broken into large blocks of time, giving children time to fully explore their projects and activities.

- **Mixed-Age Groups.** Classes are made up of children of different ages. The same teacher follows the child throughout their entire experience in the program. This enables teachers to develop a solid relationship with the child and the child's family.

- **A Focus on Problem Solving.** Problem solving that involves planning, working together, and developing individual responsibilities, is stressed. Students also work on developing self regulation as this can help them focus on problem solving and working productively with other students and teachers.

- **Elimination of the Play/Work Dichotomy.** Much of the learning occurs through play; and play and work (or learning) are not presented as two opposing concepts. Optimum learning results from integrating play and learning together.

- **Intrinsic Motivation.** This philosophy is based on the belief that children are preprogrammed to learn—if sometimes in nontraditional and unusual ways. They want to control, achieve, master skills, and develop competencies. They want to discover and find out how things work. The role of the school is to find ways to scaffold and support this natural motivation.

- **The Teacher as a Guide, Facilitator, and Supporter.** Teachers work in teams, dividing classroom responsibilities and capitalizing on each teacher's strengths and interests. Teachers operate more as guides and facilitators; they are given great leeway and responsibility by the administration to creatively implement the curriculum, and to design educational experiences for the students.

- **A Whole-Child Approach.** In this approach, the whole-child is taught: social, emotional, physical, cognitive, creative, and linguistic. Developing the whole-child is the ultimate goal of the curriculum. The child's overall interests are used to structure activities and to learn important skills and curriculum objectives.

- **An Emphasis on Creativity and Learning by Doing.** Children are given lots of opportunities to engage in a variety of creative processes: painting, writing, dancing, playing, making constructions, and manipulating materials. The child's unique personality and individual learning styles are nurtured and supported.

- **The Importance of the Environment.** Since this approach emphasizes individual, peer, and small group interaction, exploration, and learning, classrooms are designed with a rich variety of learning centers, a library and reading center, a cooking area, and places to display projects as children are working on them. There are no desks and few chairs. Some classrooms also include a piano. Intense human interactions are encouraged and noise levels are often quite high.[32]

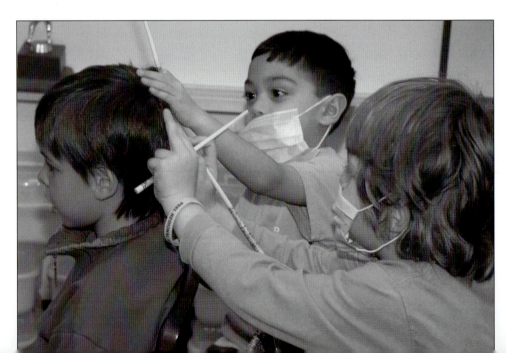

Figure Eight

Differences between Traditional U.S. Public School Approaches and the Stanley British Primary School*[33]

Traditional U.S. Public School	Stanley British Primary School
Children are grouped by age within the classroom.	Children are grouped in multi-age and multi-grade settings.
The curriculum is presented part-to-whole, with an emphasis on discrete academic skills.	The curriculum is presented whole-to-part, with an emphasis on integrated learning.
Planning of the curriculum and activities is based on federal and state grade-level standards. The curriculum is predetermined and must be carefully followed.	Planning of the curriculum is based on teacher enthusiasm, student's interests, past experiences, and needs.
Teachers begin with what the child does not know.	Teachers use children's knowledge as a springboard for future understanding, and to uncover new areas to study.
Instruction is mostly to the whole class, with small groups for reading, writing, and math.	When direct teacher instruction occurs, it is in small groups.
Children's learning is based on teachers' spoken instructions and rote learning.	Children are encouraged to collaborate with each other and to learn using each others' first-hand experiences.
Most of the time, learning is passive.	Learning is a result of active participation, with guidance, facilitation, and support from teachers.
The school day is scheduled in strict units of time.	The school day allows for long blocks of uninterrupted learning.
Assessment of learning is viewed as separate from instruction and is determined exclusively through tests.	Assessment of student learning occurs through teachers' observations of children's work, portfolios, and exhibits.

*The Stanley British Primary School is located in Denver, Colorado.

Young boys benefit from the British Infant/Primary Schools curriculum approach in a number of ways. The multi-age grouping reduces competition and students' comparing their progress, skills, and abilities with each other, and enables students to learn from knowledgable peers in a supportive way; the whole-child, integrated approach supports students learning in a more natural and age-appropriate manner; and boys thrive when engaged in active participation and involvement. The role of the teacher, along with the teacher following the child throughout his entire school experience, enables the student and teacher to develop deep, meaningful relationships. It also encourages the school and family to work together closely to meet the emotional, social, and academic needs of each child, including boys who may struggle with certain aspects of their school experience. The large blocks of time during the day provide students with opportunities to fully engage in their various learning activities; the rich environment encourages movement and hands-on learning, both attractive to many young boys.

Chapter Review

This chapter explored the topic of curriculum for young children and emphasized the importance of the curriculum for young boys in early childhood and elementary school programs. First, it discussed components of a curriculum; and repeated the argument that the current approaches to curricula in the early years (birth to eight) are often very destructive to the healthy development and optimal learning of young children, especially young boys. The chapter proposed a curricular approach that matches the development and learning needs of young children. This approach is based on the belief that the early childhood years constitute an important, separate stage in a child's development and learning, and that the overall purpose of an early childhood curriculum is to nurture and support whole-child development, encourage curiosity, mastery, competence, and develop a solid foundation for future growth and a positive disposition for learning. The curricular approach that is proposed in this chapter is grounded in a philosophy that focuses on physical activity, outdoor play, whole-child development and learning, the use of the arts to learn, and lots of exploration. The chapter then described several curricula that demonstrate this philosophy: Emergent Curriculum, the Project Approach, Lifelike Pedagogy, HighScope, and the British Infant/Primary Schools.

Questions to Ask Yourself

- What are important components of a curriculum in which boys succeed?

- If you teach in an early childhood program or elementary school, what curricular approach is used? How might you adapt it to meet individual student needs or must the curriculum be applied very rigidly?

- If you were charged with selecting a curriculum for your program, what criteria would you use to make sure the curriculum supports boys?

- How can young children provide input into the curriculum?

- Why is recall a central component of the HighScope curriculum? What is the educational value of this activity? How is this valuable to boys specifically?

- In what ways does a mixed-age group approach to a curriculum help young boys who struggle?

- Why is active interaction and learning, as opposed to passive learning, a central part of several curricula covered in this chapter?

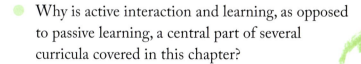

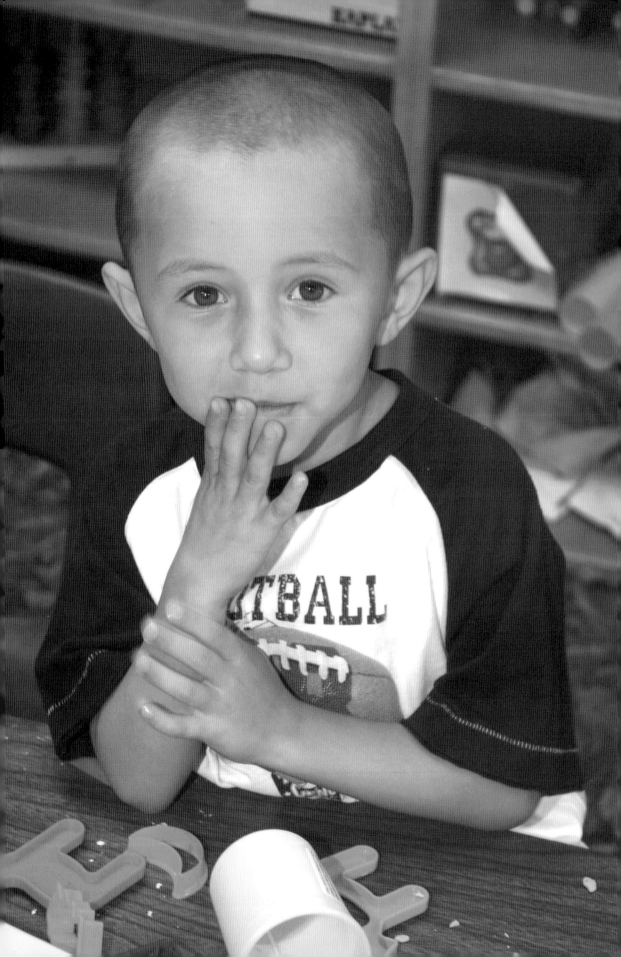

CHAPTER 7

Aspects of a Classroom

It is important to examine different ways the classroom environment can be arranged to maximize young boys' development and learning in a secure, nurturing setting. This chapter explores the indoor classroom environment (the outdoor environment is discussed in Chapter 8), educational materials, learning areas/centers, various instructional approaches, and guidance and discipline approaches that are supportive and responsive to boys.

The Indoor Classroom Environment: How It Can Encourage Development and Learning

Children learn by interacting with the environment: with people (adults and peers) and with things (materials and equipment). They stack blocks; create constructions on the workbench; and dress up as a firefighter with boots, a heavy coat, and hard hat carefully selected from the dress up area. The manner in which the indoor environment is arranged can enhance the way materials are used. Arranging paint, water, brushes, and paper so that they are easily accessible to students facilitates child-directed learning. The way the classroom environment is arranged can also increase the quality of human interactions. For example, a block area with enough room for several children to actively play together will increase cooperative learning; a cozy reading center with a rocking chair can encourage adults to read to children. While the design of the indoor environment is greatly influenced by a program's or school's curriculum, age of the children served, and length of the school day, a boy-friendly indoor environment should be safe, healthy, and support the following.

- **Whole-child learning.** Children are whole-child learners—they learn through their senses, emotions, language, and cognition all at the same time. Good environments encourage this kind of development and learning across all domains.

- **Multisensory learning.** All five senses should be used throughout the day in different combinations. Traditional environments tend to focus on learning through the use of sound—speaking and listening; boys thrive with input for all of their senses when learning.

- **Opportunities to control learning.** Young children need a sense of control in their learning. This can be achieved through collecting, creating, moving, building, designing, transporting, and constructing.

- **A variety of challenges, both in complexity and level of difficulty.** The environment needs to continually match the child's growth, development, and learning as the child becomes more experienced, sophisticated, and learns more.

- **Choice.** Children become empowered when they make choices; they gain a sense of control over their learning when meaningful choices are provided.

- **Peer interactions.** The classroom environment needs to provide many opportunities for peer interactions: playing with the blocks together, working on collecting materials, engaging in science experiments as a small group.

- **Opportunities to develop deep, meaningful relationships with adults.** Much of learning occurs though respectful child-adult interactions.

- **Separation from adults.** A child needs to be allowed to make mistakes, stumble, delight in freedom, and create his own social rules and his own rules of order. He needs some time every day to feel like his actions are not being observed and judged.

- **Soft and hard surfaces.** In general, all indoor environments need to include soft and hard surfaces, and those in-between. Soft surfaces are surfaces that respond to the child's body contours, and are supportive and relaxing for the child. Hard surfaces require the body to respond to them, and are tiring to the child. However, hard surfaces are ideal for certain activities and learning such as games using balls and skip ropes; these surfaces are also easy to clean (under paint easels and the tables where children eat). In-between surfaces are areas that are carpeted that provide both a stable surface for materials, but are less abrasive to the body than hard surfaces.

- **Lots of opportunities.** Opportunities for large and small muscle development and eye-hand coordination; opportunities to explore, experiment, and problem solve; and opportunities to be creative and engage in a variety of art activities.

- **Lighting.** A range of different lighting including natural lighting and uneven pools of light, at least for a part of each day.

- **Outdoor access.** Easy access to the outdoors throughout the day.

The indoor classroom environment should also have the following in order the encourage optimum learning and development for young boys.

Supply Plenty of Diverse Equipment and Materials

For young children, playing with and manipulating materials and equipment is one of the main ways they directly experience the environment of the early childhood program or school. Children are attracted to materials they find unusual, eye catching, and novel by their color, shape, texture, smell, taste, function, and sound. Equipment and materials for young children serve a variety of functions. In manipulating materials and using equipment, young learners develop a range of fundamental knowledge about the world and how it functions. For example, they learn that when stacking blocks, the blocks will fall if not carefully arranged; that round objects roll; and that the saw must be used in a very specific manner for it to cut a piece of wood. They learn to create, experiment, construct, order, control, and transform. They not only learn scientific and mathematical constructs and principles, but they also develop a sense of control, purpose, and mastery. And well designed and selected materials and equipment encourage a range of social interactions and cooperative learning.

Notes from the Field

Changes to My Head Start Classrooms

In Chapter 1, I described some of my formal observations at my Head Start classrooms. As a result of those observations, I made several major changes including purchasing woodworking benches and tool kits for each classroom. I then supplied wood scraps, nails, glue, and other items that could be used in woodworking. I also spent half a day training all of the teachers on how to make things out of wood—to be comfortable using the tools and helping children use them. The results of these changes included:

- more positive one-on-one interactions between teachers and boys;

- increased activity of boys in constructive play (e.g., making things out of wood);

- increased use of art materials and tools in the woodworking area by boys;

- a great increase of men volunteering in the classrooms—fathers, boyfriends, grandfathers—who were all very keen to show children how to work on the workbenches with the tools; and

- fewer boys having discipline problems in the classrooms and being referred for additional services.[1]

Recommended Woodworking Tools:

Having the most suitable tools makes a big difference and can reduce risk. Here are the four main woodworking tools.

Hammer: The best hammer is a "stubby" ball-peen hammer. These are now readily available. They are designed for adults to hammer in awkward places, but they are also a perfect weight for young children. They have short handles so they are more controllable and have a large hitting surface making it easier to hammer the nail.

Saw: Saws that cut on the pull stroke are so much easier for young children because they are more controllable and require less effort. There are many pull saws available these days. Use Japanese pull saws—light, thin bladed, and everyone who uses them is taken aback by how easy they are. These saws are used with both hands holding the handle.

Hand-drill: The best hand drills are those with enclosed mechanisms as there is no chance fingers can get caught in the exposed cogs. Ensure work is clamped when drilling. Short drill-bits are less likely to snap.

Screwdriver: Use a stubby Phillips screwdriver. Short-handled screwdrivers are easier to control and the Phillips "cross" shape means the screwdriver is less likely to slip out from the screw.

Some specific ideas for selecting classroom materials and equipment include the following.

- **Initial and prolonged interests.** A classroom environment must provide for two kinds of interests—initial interest (i.e., attractive because of colors, novelty, and potential use) and prolonged interest (i.e., that which holds the child's interest day after day), especially in programs where children spend many hours every day.

- **Open-ended and closed-ended materials.** Toys and other materials can be categorized as open- or closed-ended. *Open-ended materials* such as sand or water are those that children can engage with in many ways. *Closed-ended* or *high-structured play materials* can only be used in very limited ways. Jigsaw puzzles have one correct solution; realistic replicas of farm animals can only be used in one way.[2] Closed-ended materials can build a sense of mastery in children such as hammering a nail, or using an art or writing instrument in a specific way. But they require a high level of adult involvement, at least initially, and children can become bored and frustrated with these materials. There are also materials that fit between these two extremes, such as Legos and unit blocks. Individually, they have limited use due to their shape, but together, through the extensive use of constructive play, they provide for a wide variety of choices.[3] Programs should provide open- and closed-ended materials, and those that lie in-between.[4] However, open-ended materials and equipment give children a sense of control, and are well suited for young boys. These materials also enable children to engage with the material at their current level of development with interaction becoming more sophisticated as the child's development increases.[5] This continues to maintain the important goodness-of-fit between the materials and equipment, and the child's development and experience.

- **Concrete manipulatives.** Young children learn a great deal about their world through direct manipulation of the physical environment, and a good early childhood environment provides for a wealth of *concrete manipulatives*. Young boys love to play with unit blocks and other math manipulatives. However, many educators—and some parents—see this simply as "play" and not as an essential tool in learning math, engineering, vocabulary, architecture, and other basic concepts. And teachers often do not scaffold this play to help children learn evermore complex, abstract, and symbolic concepts as they interact with blocks. Concrete manipulatives include:

- wooden blocks of different shapes and sizes;
- wooden beads of different colors, shapes, and sizes;
- found objects such as buttons and tokens of different shapes, sizes, textures, and novelty;
- natural materials such as sticks, pieces of wood, leaves, and stones; and
- dried seeds of different shapes, sizes, textures, and colors.

- **Relevant materials that encourage dramatic play.** There are two kinds of materials that encourage dramatic play: real-life props such as hats, shoes, coats, and fire hats and hoses; and miniature items like farm animals and zoo animals, miniature people, and dolls. In both cases, the materials enhance play and learning by acting as a prop or stimulus. For young boys, they provide important clues to encourage all sorts of dramatic play including opportunities to extend and engage in ideas they bring to the program or school from their own family, community, and culture.

Organize the Space into Interest Areas/Centers

Typical early childhood classroom centers include a sand and water table, blocks, dramatic play, art, games and puzzles, books and writing, woodworking, music and movement, science, and computer.[6] Learning centers reflect the values and philosophy underlying the learning that is expected to take place in that space.[7] In each learning center there are a collection of carefully selected and arranged materials that encourage individual and small group learning and interactions that reflect the program's philosophy and curriculum. For programs that meet the needs of young boys, the centers should match the various ways young boys learn, behave, and interact. Here are some ideas on how to create learning centers that match the needs of boys.

- **Book and writing area.** Make sure that there are books that young boys find interesting: cars, trucks, constructions, animals, insects, sports, monsters, yucky things and gross events, superheroes, things that make strange and freighting noises. Some of these books should also be well illustrated with photographs and drawings. A computer should be included in this center as it can be used to extend writing activities, conduct research, and further explore topics.

- **Block area.** Include cars and trucks, miniature wild and domestic animals, Legos, signs, and other building materials, and pictures—including architectural drawings—of construction sites, houses, bridges, towers, highways, and natural elements.

- **Dramatic area.** Include props for activities that many men stereotypically do at home: barbeques, workbench, old car tires, briefcase, farm props, gas station props, carpentry, mechanical, and gardening tools. Include hardhats, firefighter's coats, fire hoses, police hats and badges, football helmets and baseball hats, and truck driver's tools.

- **Science area.** Include old typewriters, household appliances, bones, skulls, snake skins, stones, lots of different growing plants, decaying items, and things children bring in from the playground and field trips (obviously health and safety must be maintained). This is an ideal space to display items collected from the Project Approach site.

- **Games, puzzles, and math manipulatives area.** Games and puzzles should reflect themes that young boys are particularly interested in.

- **Woodworking area.** Include workbench, tools, wood, pieces of plywood and masonite, dowels of differing sizes, and other materials and attachments. Yarn, hinges, brackets, and decorative hardware can be added. This can be in the classroom, in an area on the playground, or in a transition area between the classroom and playground.

- **Art area.** In the art center, young boys can mess around with a variety of art material, experiment, try out new ideas, and create. In this area, it is OK to make a mess! Often art activities focus on process rather than product, which takes the pressure off young boys to always compare their work with other students. Because there are so many different art materials, instruments, and surfaces, this is a center that is easy to continually change and add to.

Photo courtesy of World Forum Foundation

All centers should continuously replenish their materials and introduce materials that support field trips, Project Approach themes, and other curricular units. Children should also be encouraged to integrate centers. For example, making road signs in the art area for constructions in the block area, using paint to enhance projects they make on the woodworking bench, and using the computer to print out puzzles to use in the puzzle and manipulative area.

Display Work Created by and of Interest to Children

Areas such as shelves, walls, and tables should be used to display examples of children's work in progress—art, emergent writing, photos, artifacts from field trips, lists, and finished projects. When children see their work and the work of others, they reflect on what they and their peers have done, while also helping them to expand and extend ideas and activities.[8] However, teachers should not compare different children's work when choosing items to display; it's about making the curriculum visible to children, parents, and teachers, not comparing children.

These displays focus on children's experiences and ongoing activities.[9] This enables children to work on projects over several days, and shows children and parents some of the exciting activities going on in the classroom. Information for parents and teachers about the display items should be posted in a separate area at adult level. Other items, such as books published by a child or the whole class should become permanent contributions to their related center.

Boys often need more time to complete projects and allowing them to do so beyond a set period of time gives them a sense of control. Being able to see concrete examples of what other students are doing is especially helpful for boys who are not primarily verbal-linguistic learners. By sharing their work with other students and parents, boys get a sense of being a part of the classroom community, which is especially important for boys who struggle behaviorally or academically.

Instructional Approaches

Chapter 6 described curricular approaches particularly conducive to the developmental and learning styles of young boys. However, regardless of the curriculum used by an early childhood program or school, certain instructional approaches provide a better goodness-of-fit for boys.

A great deal of learning involves instruction. Unfortunately, teachers often resort to some form of direct instruction when it is not always the most effective approach, especially for young boys. It is important to remember that *how* children learn and *how* they need to be taught is as important as *what* they learn and *what* they are taught.[10] A good instructional approach capitalizes on each child's unique motivation, finds multiple ways to engage the learner, and encourages flexibility in problem solving and learning.[11] Young boys also thrive in instructional situations where they feel they have some control, where they can make choices, and where they can achieve a sense of mastery.

In addition, a goodness-of-fit needs to be created between the child and his environment; in this case, between the learner and the instructional approach. Instructional approaches for young boys should center on whole-child, meaningful, hands-on, integrated learning; learning by doing; and the use of projects, the arts, and multiple learning styles. The following describes the kinds of instructional approaches that are not effective with young boys followed by specific instructional approaches that are ideal for boys including: three modes of representation, engaging multiple intelligences, scaffolding, and the use of manipulatives and other concrete materials.

What Does Not Work

Unfortunately, there are instructional approaches that do not work well with young boys—what Bruner calls negative instances.[12] These approaches include:

- direct teacher instruction;
- sitting still for extended periods of time;

- expecting all children to do the same thing at the same time;

- competition between students, comparing them to each other;

- focusing on external reinforcement (rewards);

- use of harsh punishment when failing to complete a task or learn a concept;

- use of high-stakes assessments;

- use of sarcasm, threats, and ridicule;

- expecting learning and behavior outcomes beyond the individual child's development and ability;

- placing children under constant pressure from parents and teachers; and

- use of the Premack Principle.

What Does Work

Instructional approaches that work well with young boys capitalize on their overall development, behaviors, characteristics, and learning styles.[13] An ideal instructional approach depends, of course, on what is being taught and the child being taught. That being said, in general, an effective instructional approach begins with a deep, respectful relationship between the teacher and child. For young boys, the approach must involve lots of movement, hands-on use of concrete materials, and learning by doing; it also needs to balance teacher-directed with child-centered learning, which is why scaffolding is so critical. While the content needs to be meaningful to each child—something they know and care about—the focus needs to be as much on the process (learning strategies) as on what is being taught and on the efficacy of learning. All of Gardner's learning styles should be used and many opportunities to include the arts should be provided.

It is also important to remember that not only should we teach to the individual child's overall Zone of Proximal Development (ZPD), but also to the child's ZPD that matches the content and behaviors being taught. A child might be advanced in math, yet struggle in emotional regulation. Critical to an effective instructional strategy is the social and emotional environmental context in which it occurs: relaxed, supportive, respectful, and challenging. In every instructional situation, regardless of the content being taught, there must be many opportunities for control, mastery, competence, and success for each child.

Providing an instructional goodness-of-fit for children with developmental delays, or who are *twice exceptional*, can be particularly challenging. Often these children benefit from direct instruction in specific areas, be they behavioral or academic. However, they also need to maintain a sense of control and a feeling of mastery and competence. It is critical that their ZPD in all areas of learning and behavior be carefully assessed so that they can be given adequate challenges in areas where they are more advanced and are allowed to take control of their learning in these areas. Just because a child may struggle in one area of learning and may need more direct, targeted instruction, does not mean he cannot engage in higher forms of learning in other areas including how to learn and meta-cognition.

The following looks at four instructional approaches that work well with many young boys.

Instructional Approach: Three Modes of Representation

Bruner's *three modes of representation—enactive, iconic,* and *symbolic*—constitute an instructional approach when they are used as a hierarchy to teach new concepts, skills, and behaviors. The hierarchy should be from enactive to iconic to symbolic.

According to Bruner's modes of representation:

- infants (birth to one) are predominantly enactive thinkers; toddlers, preschoolers, and young school-age children (one to seven) are mainly iconic thinkers; and children over age seven tend to be symbolic thinkers;

- learning becomes more complex as one moves from enactive to iconic to symbolic; and

- when faced with new challenges, even older students should progress from enactive to symbolic, and as Bruner has often cautioned, we tend to teach only using symbolic representation—specifically language—which can cause challenges for young boys.[14]

Figure Nine

Bruner's Three Modes of Representation

For many young boys, these modes should be followed in a progressive, hierarchical manner.

Enactive. This involves storing action-based information in our memory. One form is what we call muscle memory. For example, an infant remembers how to shake a rattle, a preschooler remembers how to kick a soccer ball. We can remember fairly complex things through enactive memory: riding a bike, typing, complex dance moves, and hitting a baseball.

Iconic. Information is stored visually in the form of pictures. Like all memory, some is conscious, some not. "I never forget a face" is an obvious example of visual memory. The effectiveness of iconic memory is seen by the way diagrams and illustrations are often used to help teach new concepts. Many know that iconic representation was a central part of Einstein's thought process.[15]

Symbolic. Information is stored through symbols such as words or numbers. Unlike enactive and iconic representation, symbolic representation is very flexible.

This approach works well with all young children, but may be especially effective with young boys. In particular, it is effective with boys because it supports multi-sensory and whole-child learning, and because children are encouraged to engage in hands-on learning and to use visual icons to remember and think, before moving to more complex, symbolic cognitive processes.

Instructional Approach: Engage Multiple Learning Styles

Contemporary instructional approaches in early childhood programs and schools are dominated by verbal-linguistic and logical-mathematical learning styles. However, many boys struggle with these two learning styles, yet excel in others. The multiple learning style instructional approach stresses the importance of exposing young children to a range of content areas so that they can have every opportunity to express themselves in a variety of ways, and develop their unique potential to the greatest extent.[16] This allows parents and teachers to discover and nurture the abilities of their children, beginning at a young age.

Use of this approach to instruction also enables teachers to use different methods to engage in in-depth exploration of important content and concepts, and to experience an array of different materials that lead to further development and learning. Another major strength of using multiple learning styles in instruction, especially when working with young boys, is that it is not a deficit approach, and instead, builds on each child's unique strengths giving them a sense of power, mastery, and self-confidence.[17]

However, in applying Gardner's theory, it is important to note that Gardner does not recommend just teaching students using their preferred learning style. Rather, he suggests using children's preferred style to teach new skills and concepts based on other learning styles. For example, many teachers encourage a child to draw a picture of something (visual-spatial), and then write a description underneath the picture (verbal-linguistic). I had a college student who used skip-rope routines (bodily-kinesthetic) to teach elementary students math facts (logical-mathematical).

Instructional Approach: Scaffolding

For boys, scaffolding provides a way to enter into an instructional relationship with the teacher that enables him to learn new information and gain more skills without giving up his own sense of power and control. Chapter 4 discussed the power of this approach, an essential element of Vygotsky's theory. Here, the focus is on Vygotsky's concepts of the *Zone of Proximal Development* (ZPD), *child-centered learning*, and *private speech*—all important components of scaffolding.

The Zone of Proximal Development. According to Berk and Winsler, the ZPD is "the distance between what a child can accomplish during independent problem solving and what he or she can accomplish with the help of an adult or more competent person."[18] The ZPD is unique to each individual child, and any attempt to teach a child outside the zone—too high or too low—is ineffective.

For this reason, the ZPD of each individual child must be constantly assessed and applied in all instructional activities. For young boys, maintaining their ZPD enables the teacher to mitigate naturally short attention spans, maintain intrinsic motivation, and continually challenge each boy's learning. Boys who are focused, engaged, and motivated are much easier to teach than those who are distracted and bored.

Child-Centered Learning. Scaffolding involves joint problem solving—engagement of children in an interesting, meaningful, problem solving activity with a peer or teacher.[19] The child must be actively involved in a task or in solving a problem. And this collaborative activity must involve *intersubjectivity*—a shared understanding between the learner and expert (teacher or peer).[20] When teaching young boys, this means that the child must be actively involved in an activity that is personally meaningful and is motivated to achieve a shared view of a solution with the teacher or peer.

Private Speech. Private speech is talking to oneself, initially out loud, to either regulate one's own behavior or to utilize scaffolding learned previously from an expert. For behavioral regulation, children use private speech to remind themselves of classroom rules, behavioral instructions, and techniques for emotional regulation. For learning, the child will use private speech to solve a problem by repeating the scaffolding used when they initially solved a similar problem. Research shows that using private speech for both activities is very effective.[21]

Eventually, private speech becomes inner speech: silently talking to oneself. Private speech can be very helpful—some children need to use it more than others and take longer to internalize it than other children.[22] By talking to themselves, children build a bridge between their own reality and the real world as they attempt to become competent and educated. For both behavioral regulation, something that many young boys struggle with, and learning new skills and concepts, boys should be encouraged to use private speech as long as it's helpful before transitioning to inner speech.

Programs use a variety of discipline approaches to address inappropriate and destructive behavior (see the section on discipline, below). Using private speech to repeat behavioral controls often works well because the child is the one repeating the rule or reiterating the important directive. Repeating learning strategies provided by a teacher or peer can help boys who tend to be impulsive and do not think before they act to structure their learning in a variety of effective ways, while also giving them a sense of control.

Instructional Approach:
Use of Manipulatives and Other Concrete Materials

The use of *concrete manipulatives* to teach basic math principles became popular in the mid-20th century with the introduction of the unit block, Cuisenaire rods, and colorful mosaic tiles, i.e. Froebel's gifts. Today, the use of concrete manipulatives is recommended by the National Council of Teachers of Mathematics.[23] Many teachers use colored beads, abacuses, blocks, stones, sticks, beans, geoboards, mosaic tiles, and other objects when teaching math. These manipulatives play an important role in children's development and in their struggle to understand a variety of math concepts including number, quantity, pattern, more and less than, shape, size, units of measurement, multiples, equality, fractions, non-equality, and geometric concepts. Further, research shows that boys are attracted to building materials such as Legos, Bamboo Blocks, unit blocks, and Magna-Tiles because they encourage exploration and creativity.[24]

With the advent of STEM, it is important that early childhood and elementary educators recognize how integral concrete manipulatives are in teaching math and engineering to young children. When children struggle with learning math, teachers should use manipulatives to help them; worksheets, calendars, drill-and-skill computer programs, and similar activities should never take the place of these manipulatives. And even when children are ready to learn more complex math skills, concrete manipulatives should be used as the basis to scaffold this learning.

While historically concrete materials have been used for teaching math, they are also very helpful in teaching a variety of other content because young children's initial understanding of the world is through real, concrete materials and experiences. In general, children's learning progresses from the concrete to the abstract—from real objects and materials (a wooden block) to symbolic thinking (a block representing a phone).[25] Field trips are not technically an instructional approach, however, the use of field trips either as a one-time event or as part of the Project Approach, provides children with concentrated real-life materials, objects, and events that set the foundation for more abstract processes. For example, when I recently took my seven-year-old grandson to an outdoor museum, we observed a male peacock using its display to attract females. This concrete experience can lead to later learning about reasons many male birds are more colorful than female birds and some of the differences between male and female animals.

Children can see and manipulate real materials such as sand, water, mud, and stacking blocks, and create various constructions that illustrate basic scientific principles and processes—post and lintel construction, cantilever, slope, balance, and stability. Young children can also engage with real materials during circle time reading by holding an object that is being described in the book such as a piece of clothing, bird's nest, loaf of bread, strawberries, or a bird feather.

There is a temptation by many educators to force children too quickly into the complex, organized, symbolic, and abstract—without the use of real objects. And many young children—especially boys—struggle when this transition is too rapid or when they have not had the concrete experiences on which the higher-order learning is based. Children with solid hands-on experiences of the real world are more likely to understand the complex ideas that are used to explain it.[26] For boys, playing, manipulating, and experimenting with real objects and materials provides them with a solid, meaningful foundation on which they can begin to learn complex scientific concepts. For example, young children need to engage in all sorts of activities with water—pouring, floating, sinking, making mud pies, creating waterfalls, damming streams, suction, and shooting a trajectory of water from a hose—before they learn about the complex scientific properties of water.

Instructional Approach: Utilize Meta-Cognition

At about age four, children develop a concept called theory of mind, which involves an understanding of their own mind and the minds of others—thoughts, beliefs, feelings, perceptions, and motives.[27] They realize that what they imagine and remember, in their mind, may in fact differ from the real world. Shortly after this realization, children begin to develop *meta-cognition,* which continues throughout their school years. Meta-cognition is a person's knowledge of their own learning and cognitive processes, as well as their ability to regulate these processes to enhance learning.[28] It is, in effect, thinking about thinking.

It is important to develop meta-cognitive skills in young children for two reasons.

- **Being an effective learner.** Meta-cognitive skills enhance a learner's efficiency and effectiveness—it is directly tied to school success.

- **Controlling one's own learning.** As children grow older, they begin to set goals for their own performance and to choose behaviors they believe will help them meet these goals. From a learning perspective, they learn how to control their own learning.

Both of these dispositions are important for boys because they enable them to learn more effectively as they become self-aware of how they learn, and because they increase their self-efficacy. The use of meta-cognition in the learning process is important for boys who struggle both with being effective learners and in controlling their own learning—physical and cognitive. Thus, developing meta-cognitive skills can be especially helpful and create a positive disposition for their future education.

Teachers can help young children develop meta-cognitive skills by asking specific questions: "What were you thinking about when you painted that picture?" "How did you remember that there were five pigs in the sty?" "What were your feelings when we read about the sick child?" "What do you like to learn and why?"

Discipline/Guidance in the Classroom

The reasons that a disproportionate number of young boys are in special education and involved in disciplinary actions are complex, often resulting from policies, procedures, best practices, staff training, and even the female culture of the early childhood field.[29] The program and classroom teacher can take action to address some of these issues.

Everything starts with the overcall climate of the classroom and program. A healthy climate is established by creating a community that acknowledges and supports the physical, emotional, and cognitive development and learning of young children—including boys engaged in developmentally typical boy behaviors.[30] The core of the community should be consistent, positive, caring, and engaged in responsive relationships between mature adults and children; among children; and between teachers, administration, and all staff. All members of the community need to make sure they contribute to each other's well-being and support the healthy climate of the program and classroom.[31]

Ideas for Reducing Discipline Problems

There are a number of actions that can be taken to reduce discipline problems for all children in the classroom.[32] Here, these actions are applied directly to young boys.

- **Let boys move their bodies.** Provide opportunities for physical activities throughout the day.

- **Conduct small-group activities.** Reduce the number of large group and sit-down lessons, substituting them for individual and small group activities.

- **Defuse conflicts.** Often situations are accidental, yet some boys seem to want to retaliate, so teachers should defuse conflicts and acknowledge and express emotions. For example, "Felix, Ephram didn't mean to knock over the tower. He feels badly about it."[33] Also, teachers should not assume the child is necessarily being cruel or vindictive; accidents do happen.

- **Use humor.** This tells boys that the adult is not uptight about the situation, and in turn, they don't need to get worked up either (especially about things that boys think will "trigger" negative adult reactions).

- **Avoid threats and embarrassments.** Threats set up power struggles that harm the teacher-child relationship. Instead, provide choices of acceptable options (however, never give a child a choice that is not acceptable to you).

- **Follow through.** It is critical to follow up with a boy after responding to unacceptable behavior. Children notice whether adults will do what they say they will do. If you decide to take an action, make sure you follow through each time.

- **Talk with boys about their emotions.** Considerable research shows that teachers often accept and talk to girls about their emotional responses to situations and ignore the emotional responses of boys, expecting them to cope without help. Boys also need to develop a large range of verbal labels for their emotions and be taught how to talk about them.[34]

- **Nurture boys.** Boys need the same kinds of acceptance, support, and nurturing as girls; they also need warm, caring, and nurturing teachers. Even if a child is defiant or hurts another child, he needs to know he is a fully accepted member of the class; it is his behavior that is unacceptable.[35]

Avoid the Use of Punishments and Rewards

There are two central problems in using punishment in the classroom and playground:

- punishments do not help the child learn how to behave appropriately; they do not provide the child with acceptable alternatives to his unacceptable behaviors; and

- punishments tell the child he is a loser, which not only destroys his self-esteem, but also tells the rest of the class of his status as a loser.[36]

As was discussed in Chapter 3, the Premack Principle is the concept that something a child enjoys doing (such as playing on the computer) can be used to reinforce something a child does not like to do (for example, his math worksheet). Young children can quickly be convinced to sit quietly and pay attention if they are allowed to play outside after being quiet and attentive.[37]

Chapter 7: Aspects of a Classroom   **OH BOY!**

Here are some of the major problems in using the Premack Principle with young boys.

- Boys who struggle with certain behaviors or academic achievements are denied the opportunity to engage in activities they enjoy—and that they desperately need to engage in to feel competent and empowered.[38]

- Children soon learn they have to earn the activities and tasks they enjoy doing and are good at. They begin to associate what they like to do—play and non-school work—with enjoyment, and what they don't like to do—school work—with learning.

- Again, this approach tells everyone in the classroom, and often the school, who are the winners and who are the losers.

Guidance Intervention Solutions

In the book, *Education for a Civil Society*, Dan Gartrell presents four different guidance strategies that can be used with young children:

- calm everyone down;
- use guidance talks with individual children;
- practice conflict mediation with disputing children in small groups; and
- use a comprehensive guidance approach.[39]

Each of these strategies is often used in different situations.

Calm Everyone Down

When conflict occurs, after checking for injury, the teacher calms everyone down, including himself or herself if needed. Calming everyone down reduces levels of stress, making it easier to address the situation appropriately. Calming approaches include:

- tell everyone to take deep breaths; model this approach;
- encourage children to choose their own approach: deep breathing, counting slowly, or sitting in a different area; and
- provide space and time for children to cool down by removing them from the conflict.

This approach, however, differs from the traditional *time out*, which is a classic form of punishment. Here, the purpose is for the child to regain composure. Sometimes the teacher might even need to stay with the child.[40]

Use Guidance Talks with Individual Children

Teachers use a five-level formula to talk with children about inappropriate behavior and possible consequences for that behavior.

1. Calm everyone down.

2. Help individual children understand how each person sees the conflict.

3. Brainstorm possible solutions—help scaffold this by providing possible suggestions and words, especially for children who struggle with language.

4. Agree on one solution accepted by all—and try it.

5. Monitor the results and provide follow-up information to those involved, especially those who need assistance with managing their emotions.

Practice Conflict Mediation with Disputing Children in Small Groups

This approach is appropriate when two or three children are involved in a conflict, and the teacher decides to become involved. The teacher is the mediator, leading the children through the process. The five-part formula above is applied albeit in a more structured manner. The mediation process reduces the power imbalance between the children. It also reduces the bully-victim syndrome that tends to be reinforced when the teacher punishes the bully and supports the victim.[41] Each time a teacher uses the mediation approach or any other conflict resolution technique, children learn important social skills and language used in conflict resolution. The eventual goal of the teacher is to move the mediation process from a teacher-lead approach to a place where children can solve their own problems.

Use a Comprehensive Guidance Approach

There are some children who struggle in group care and education situations, and are continually at odds with other children and/or staff. These children can benefit from a comprehensive approach to their social struggles. Like all the approaches mentioned here, the comprehensive guidance approach begins with a positive relationship between the teacher and child, and with ongoing communication between the program or school and the child's family.

Often a teacher will create an individual guidance plan with the help and support of a local resource team provided by the school district, Head Start program, company child care, or state—including expert staff, consultants, and other technical assistance.[42] The child's family should be directly included in this process. However, it is critical that the guidance plan aligns with the overall philosophy and climate of the classroom and program.

Before Recommending a Boy for Special Education

One of the dilemmas in identifying a child with special needs is the "*self-fulfilling expectation*" or "*self-fulfilling prophecy.*" Not only do many teachers and administrators expect boys to engage in inappropriate behaviors, but once someone suggests that a child should be screened for a possible special need, there is the temptation to find a special need: to fulfill the expectation.[43] For this reason, all programs that work with young boys should engage in a variety of proactive actions before recommending a special education screening. These actions include the following.

- **Talk with the child's parents.** Are there extenuating circumstances such as a recent divorce or a parent who has left to serve abroad in the military? Does the child's behavior occur at home? Does the parent use an approach at home to deal with this behavior that works?

- **Alter the environment, especially where the behavior occurs.** The environment has an extremely powerful influence on young children's behavior. For example, several young boys in one preschool classroom continually get into trouble for spilling paint, knocking over ceramic sculptors that are drying on a shelf, and brushing up against wet paintings. The teacher keeps reminding them to be careful and has tried punishment, but issues still continue. The problem is that the art area is right next to the exit to the playground, and the boys are so excited about going out to play or putting on their jackets before they can go to the playground that they forget to be careful. In this case, a simple solution is to switch the art center with the woodworking area. Before children go out to play on the playground, the woodworking tools are all put away, and the wood stacked in bins. So, there is nothing to spill, knock over, or brush up against.

- **Evaluate the child's feelings.** Does the child feel psychologically safe in the program? Does someone at his home tell him the teacher is a bad teacher; maybe the teacher has a negative history with his parents? It's important to determine whether any biases are present.

- **Assess whether the child is bored.** Many *gifted and talented children* are misdiagnosed with ADHD or a specific learning disability often simply because they are unchallenged and bored.[44]

- **Consider whether the child just "rubs the teacher" the wrong way.** We know that difficult children can produce very negative responses from teachers and other staff—what is commonly known as *bidirectional behavior*.[45] Once this occurs, it is often difficult for the teacher to change. Sometimes the teacher or the child needs to be assigned to another classroom.

- **Consider whether the child is only disciplined at home by men.** In some homes, a man is the authority figure and the one who disciplines the child. Unfortunately, when there are few, if any, men in an early childhood program this can make discipline difficult.

- **Look at whether the child's negative behavior is somehow being reinforced.** Often children engage in certain behaviors that are reinforced somewhere—by other children, parent volunteers, or even the teacher.

- **Determine if the child is confused.** Some children, particularly new immigrants, children who have not attended an organized program before, or children who have recently moved from another program are confused about expectations, schedules, rules, and hidden agendas.

- **Ask if the child is expected to "be bad."** Often, members of a family develop specific roles, which are then reinforced and expected in the home.[46] Some boys get a reputation at home of being "troublemakers" and so try to fulfill this role in the program or school.

- **Identify whether the child is a minority, especially Black or Hispanic.** While boys struggle in our programs for a variety of reasons, Black and Hispanic boys struggle even more. Additional staff training, workshops, and conference attendance may be called for. Working closely with the program or school's minority parents may be needed. Curricula materials used by the program and school must represent all the families in the program and school, and be well integrated within the overall program's instructional activities.[47]

- **Look at whether the boy has been taught to respond to conflict with violence.** Some boys are encouraged to be aggressive and respond to conflict, threats, and perceived insults by acting aggressively.

- **Determine if there is a conflict between how discipline issues are addressed at home, in the community, and at school.** Young children are capable of understanding that certain environments require different behavioral expectations, but these differences must be clearly defined and reinforced.[48]

- **Look at whether a language barrier is affecting the child's learning and social interactions.** There are many children in special education who have failed assessments not because of a cognitive or behavioral issue, but because they are not fluent in English.

- **Consider that overall cultural conflicts can produce problems.** Our programs are becoming more and more diverse, yet assessment tools, observational methods, and testing protocols are often not culturally sensitive.

- **Ask if the behavior is the result of a stereotype threat.** A *stereotype threat* is a reaction in which children from low-achieving groups perform poorly on tests and academic tasks because they know their group traditionally does poorly.[49] This can cause increased anxiety and reduced performance.

All of these issues need to be carefully considered and addressed before a child is recommended for special education services, including the initial screening.

Chapter Review

This chapter examined aspects related to the classroom. It began with the classroom environment, focusing on the basic elements of a quality classroom environment that supports the growth and development of young boys. It then described play and educational materials and various learning centers that are particularly effective for boys. Next, the chapter discussed some instructional approaches; first comparing those that don't work well with young boys to those that do, and then discussing a few specific examples: modes of representation, multiple learning styles, scaffolding, the use of concrete manipulatives and materials, and meta-cognition. A few approaches to classroom discipline, beginning with the need for the classroom to meet the physical and emotional needs of young boys, were covered. The chapter also examined problems with using rewards and punishments for discipline and looked at several effective guidance approaches. Finally, it listed a series of actions that should be taken before a boy is screened for possible special needs services.

Questions to Ask Yourself

- In considering the indoor environment, what are some essential aspects of the classroom to include that match the development and learning of young boys?

- Why is it important for programs to provide a range of materials including open-ended, closed-ended, and those in-between?

- Why do classroom materials and equipment for young boys need to offer a range of challenges and be continually changed to increase these challenges?

- Why do young boys struggle with instructional approaches that require them to sit still for long periods of time?

- Why is it not a good idea to compare the work of young children? Why should each child's effort and work be acknowledged and appreciated?

- Why is the use of concrete manipulatives and materials often very helpful when a young child is learning complex, abstract concepts in a variety of content areas?

- How does using meta-cognitive processes help young children learn?

- Why does the author suggest that once a child is suspected of having a delay or disability—by a teacher, parent, or expert—this often becomes a self-fulfilling expectation or prophecy? What does this mean? Can it be a problem?

CHAPTER 8

Play in the Outdoors

I take my five-year-old grandson to the park on a regular basis. When we come to the park's stream, he picks up sticks, throws them into the water, and watches them float in the current. When we come to the area of huge tree stumps and dead trunks lying on the ground, he loves to climb on the stumps and tries to walk across the dead trunks. This environment triggers his interests and activities. Interestingly, on later visits, he starts collecting sticks a long time before we actually get to the stream and talks about playing on the trees before we reach them.

Boys love the outdoors for many reasons. They have lots of space to explore and experiment. They can run, jump, and climb. They can be messy and push the limits. They can make lots of noise—which they love to do. They also take risks! And they can become totally involved in whatever they are doing. The outdoors is an ideal goodness-of-fit for young boys, matching well with their interests, behaviors, learning styles, and natural predispositions. Early childhood and elementary programs should find numerous ways to use the outdoors to let young children—especially young boys—"mess around" with the environment, learn from nature, and explore and experiment.

This chapter begins by discussing play, exploring Piaget's cognitive play stages and Parten's social play stages, and considers various aspects of an ideal playground.[1] The chapter also explores the vast amount of choices of outdoor environments young children can enjoy, both with the early childhood program and with their families beyond the playground: outdoor museums, greenbelts, wetlands, trails, and parks.

Characteristics of Play

All children play. From birth, children explore their social and physical world through the use of their senses. This active engagement provides many important opportunities for the development and learning of all children.[2] Play is an excellent goodness-of-fit for young boys because it is under their control

Chapter 8: Play in the Outdoors   **OH BOY!**

Notes from the Field

Snow Days

It had been snowing all weekend, but was beginning to come to a stop. A few flurries continued and it was still quite cold. My kindergarteners were very used to the snow and going outside to enjoy it. We decided to go to the toboggan run and check out the new snow. All of the children were well clothed with hats, scarves, boots, and mittens.

After stopping to break some huge icicles hanging off of a rock formation, we continued on to the toboggan run and enjoyed the new snow, although it made the run pretty slow. Once they had exhausted tobogganing, the children were not ready to go back home. Luckily, I had some matches in my pocket so we decided to see if we could make a fire in the snow.

We selected a protected area at the top of the toboggan run. After clearing off a patch of ground, the children had to figure out how to find dry twigs after a snow storm. Some of the children were ingenious and removed the damp bark off of the twigs they found; others found twigs still on the trees, but on the leeward side of the storm, and thus protected from it. All of the children realized sticks on the ground would just be too wet. With the help of scraps of paper we found in pockets (candy wrappers, etc.), we were able to get a good fire going, and to warm cold hands and feet.

and involves integrated, whole-child learning. For boys who struggle socially and/or academically, play provides many opportunities to be successful and to learn developmentally appropriate social skills. Play is especially attractive to boys because it involves real, tangible interaction with the environment—both social and physical—in a hands-on, interactive, and concrete way.

Here are the five characteristics of play, as explained in the book, *Play and Early Childhood Development*.[3]

- **Positive affect.** Maybe the most obvious aspect of play is that children not only choose to play, but want to all of the time! This tells us that at some level, they find play enjoyable. Even if risk and fear are components of a play activity, they continue to do it.

- **Non-literality.** A central task for a young child is to understand the real world and to come to grips with living and learning in the real world. Unlike adults, children have limited experience and need to learn everything about the world in a short period of time. This can be very demanding and frustrating. Play is an escape from this reality. In play, almost all but the basic rules of social interaction and physical reality can be discarded. Cody can be Superman, the craft table can be a surgeon's operating table, the timid child can become a hero, and the block is a fast car. Not only does play enable children to escape reality, but it also helps them deal with it. They can play out a tragedy they just witnessed; and they can do something they were told they should not do. In play, children can experiment with words, actions, ideas, and social relationships—they can take untold risks with few consequences.

- **Intrinsic motivation.** Children play because it's internally satisfying, and when it is no longer satisfying, they stop. However, one of the important things about play is that once it is no longer self-motivating (when it becomes boring or repetitive), children can change it, making it more challenging and interesting, and thus more intrinsically motivating.

- **Process-oriented.** Have you ever seen a group of children build a fort? Once it's finished, what do they do? Invariably they destroy it and build another one. Why? Because in play children enjoy the process—it's the process that's fun, not the end product (and of course, much of play has no end product).

- **Free choice.** It seems that children have a deep belief that play must be self-chosen. In fact, the research of King discovered that kindergartners considered the same activities to be play if they were self-chosen, and work if they were assigned by the teacher.[4] Many of us have watched a preschooler happily wash dishes in the kitchen sink, only to protest when asked to wash the dishes!

Play Stage Theories

There are two play stage theories—Piaget's cognitive play and Parten's social play—that are helpful in our understanding of young children's play. Both are developmental—meaning children begin at the easiest and simplest stage and progress through each stage sequentially until they reach the highest, or most complex stage.

These two play theories can also operate together. For example, a child may be engaged in constructive play and cooperative play at the same time (building a fort), or symbolic play and solitary play at the same time (driving his car to work on a road built of unit blocks).

Piaget's Cognitive Play Stages

Piaget's cognitive theory was discussed in Chapter 4. Here, we examine how play reflects a child's concept of the world. In Piaget's theory of play, there are four levels of *cognitive play stages*: *functional, constructive, symbolic,* and *games with rules.*[5]

- **Functional play.** Children use objects in a way that reflects their physical characteristics: sticks float in water, blocks can be stacked (and knocked down), balls roll and bounce. Functional play also reflects how the physical body functions: rolls, slides, swings, runs, jumps, rides a tricycle. Play at this stage is driven by the physical characteristics of objects and materials, and of the child.

- **Constructive play.** Here, objects and materials—such as blocks, art supplies, wood and nails, Legos, Tinker toys, and sand and water—are used to create new and different things; to construct. However, constructive play cannot occur before the child has explored the physical properties of the objects and materials. Children can also use their bodies to construct something new such as a dance or a pyramid.

- **Symbolic play.** At this stage, children use materials and objects symbolically to represent something else: a block becomes a phone, a doll is a baby, and a stick is a sword. Further, the child can also represent something else: a doctor, hero, racecar driver, teacher, and parent.

- **Games with rules.** This is a collective activity where pre-established rules are agreed on, and then used to control the activity such as Duck-Duck-Goose; Mother May I; and Red Light, Green Light. Many children under the age of eight struggle to engage in games with rules, requiring an adult to continually reinforce the rules.

Children must developmentally progress through each stage; and no one stage has more value to a child's development and learning than another stage.[6]

Parten's Social Play Stages

Many young boys struggle with behavioral issues in the classroom; they are socially and emotionally immature. Emotional regulation requires three developmental achievements: brain maturity, knowing what is expected, and being able to demonstrate the required behavior.[7] Many young boys struggle with all three of these areas. While brain maturation is generally a matter of age and gender, the other two components can be developed through social play.

In the *social play stages—solitary, parallel, associative,* and *cooperative*—children progress from playing by themselves, which they begin to do as infants, to

being able to play cooperatively with other children.[8] To be able to play with peers, young children have to be able to control their own needs for the good of the play event; they also need to want to do so. Because play is pleasurable for young children, and young children are naturally social, they are motivated to progress through the social play stages. However, children need to progress through each stage at their own speed; progress through the stages cannot be forced.

- **Solitary play.** The toddler who is gleefully banging away on pots and pans in the kitchen with a wooden spoon is engaged in solitary play. The five-year-old blowing bubbles while taking a bath is also involved in solitary play.

- **Parallel play.** Have you ever noticed that at certain times the swing set on the playground is empty and at other times it is completely full, yet when there are children on the swings they pretty much ignore each other? This is parallel play: children playing alone usually involved in the same kind of play, yet in the physical presence of other children. Children playing in the sandbox often engage in parallel play as well.

- **Associative play.** Here children are becoming more social—they are interested in other children playing next to them: what they are playing with, what they are making, how they are playing. They might even use ideas from the other children—using a cup to create a sand building and/or taking a toy from a child because it is nicer than theirs. While they are interacting with their peers at this stage, they are still focusing on their own play activity.

- **Cooperative play.** This is the highest form of social play: it is play where the child's self-interests are subsumed for the good of the play activity. Play is the ultimate thing! Children who are able to negotiate roles in a dramatic play episode—deciding who will be the doctor, baby, or parent—exhibit true cooperative play; a child who insists he must play the doctor each time has not yet reached this stage.

While cooperative play is the highest level of Parten's social play stages, this does not mean children cannot go back to playing at the other levels, or cannot benefit from the other three levels. Many adults spend countless hours playing Solitaire, a solitary play activity.

The Playground Environment

Most early childhood programs and elementary schools have some kind of playground. Early childhood playgrounds are regulated by each state's licensing authority; and school playgrounds by each district's own standards—or the private school's governing board—usually focusing on health, safety, and durability. In both cases, the U.S. Consumer Product Safety Commission's (CPSC) *Public Playground Safety Handbook* and the *Guide to ADA Accessibility*

Guidelines for Play Areas are the documents that detail safety and ADA access requirements.[9]

These playgrounds are the first level of outdoor activity for most children in organized settings. And they are often woefully inadequate. Two major problems of many early childhood and school playgrounds are as follows.

- They are artificial—most playground equipment is made of brightly painted metal and plastic. Many playgrounds today have rubber surfaces or ground up rubber tires under the equipment, and fake grass. While this may satisfy ADA and CPSC requirements, these settings do not offer the play value of real grass, mud, sand, and water.

- Almost all of the equipment on these playgrounds is only for functional play: climbing, swinging, sliding, and riding tricycles or bikes. And based on Piaget's cognitive play stages, this is the simplest, most basic form of play. This means children soon get bored and desperately desire opportunities for more complex and challenging activities—both in cognitive and social play.

General Guidelines for Playgrounds

It is important to remember that the purpose of a playground should be to support the overall development and learning of children. As such, much of the playground's value comes from providing a variety of opportunities that are not provided within the classroom, as opposed to simply duplicating inside activities or teaching goals and objectives that are designed for the indoor classroom.

Playgrounds designed for children's programs must respond to an array of issues: climate, visual appeal, materials, vandalism, maintenance, budgets, liability, program/school rules and regulations, and parent preferences. It is not possible here to provide advice for all of these program-specific issues; however, one way to create a playground that meets children's needs is to examine Richard Dattner's *Criteria for Design*.

- **Array of experiences.** Does the playground provide a vast array of experiences for the child?
- **Control of experiences.** Are there opportunities for children to control their experiences—build, collect, spill, transport, construct, and dig?

- **Graduated challenge.** Does the playground provide a range of old and new experiences, practice play, and new challenges?

- **Choice.** Can children control the environment and select their level of risk?

- **Exercise of fantasy.** Is dramatic play encouraged through general structures—houses, forts, tunnels, bridges, and stages?

- **Separation from adults.** Are children allowed to make mistakes, stumble, fall, delight in freedom, and create their own social rules and their own rules of order?

- **Durability.** Will the playground withstand the typical play of normal children? Will it withstand the local weather conditions?

- **Interest.** Does the playground provide for two kinds of interests: initial interest (such as being attractive because of colors and potential use), and prolonged interest (that which holds the child's interest day after day)?

- **Adaptability.** Does the equipment have more than just one use so it can be adapted and defined by children in a variety of ways?

- **Develop motor skills.** Does the playground encourage large and small muscle development, and hand-eye coordination?

- **Strengthen social relationships.** Does the playground encourage all the levels of Parten's social play scale?

- **Encourage intellectual development.** Does the playground encourage language development; class inclusion; labeling; learning about birds, animals, and plants; and acquisition of a vast amount of basic scientific knowledge?[10]

Design and Build Guidelines

Below are a number of specific suggestions to consider when designing and building a playground to provide optimum opportunities for the development and learning of young boys. Not all programs will be able to carry out all of these suggestions, but they provide a standard or prototype.

Include Hard, Soft, and In-Between Playground Surfaces

Three specific suggestions for playground surfaces are: hard (concrete or asphalt), soft (sand), and in-between (grass). A playground needs all three.

- **Asphalt or Concrete.** These surfaces provide a solid foundation for:
  - tricycles, bikes, wagons, and other wheeled toys;
  - ball games that require a hard, flat surface;
  - opportunities for all sorts of fantastic outdoor art activities with large chalks and house-paint brushes;
  - opportunities for games such as Hopscotch;
  - opportunities to bring the classroom outside—art easels, hollow blocks, dramatic play props, sand and water tables, and the woodworking bench (this enables children to use more space, make more noise, and be able to make a bigger mess—all positive attributes!); and
  - a place for children to play outside when it's too wet to play in the sand or on the grass.

- **Sand.** Recently, I built a playground in my family's backyard. It included a slide, platform, tire-net, and two-story playhouse. The fall zone for the slide is sand. When young children come over to play on the playground, they spend 30-40 minutes climbing and sliding, and then settle into the sandbox for the rest of their stay! I told my wife I could have just built the sandbox. Sand is probably the most versatile material after water, and when sand and water are combined, the options are endless. As pointed out in Chapter 7, sand and water together is the ultimate form of an open-ended play material. Water can be added through the use of a garden hose; when designing a playground, it is good to put a faucet close to the garden and sand areas.

- **Grass.** Unfortunately, more and more playgrounds lack natural grass. Grass is needed because it's a natural surface that children enjoy. It provides a great surface for group games, picnics, folk dancing, family social activities, and reading stories under a shade tree. A large, uncluttered area of grass is ideal; grass hills to run up and roll down are also fun. Grass is also a part of nature—full of bugs, worms, insects, weeds, flowers, and clover; and therefore, must be watered, cut, and fertilized. Grass, of course, is also a favorite surface for going barefoot.

Plant a Garden

All playgrounds should include a vegetable garden.[11] Children are naturally interested in growth, the world around them, and exploring objects close to them on the ground.[12] Not only is a garden a fantastic way to learn about the science of growth, decay, fertilization, pests, nutrition, and caring for plants, it is also a great way to involve men in early childhood programs.

Many of the basic concepts that underline STEM education can be learned through gardening (but it must be developmentally appropriate). For children who struggle academically and behaviorally, the garden is a wonderful place where they can get dirty and mess around in the earth, see the results of their efforts, and feel proud of their contributions. The garden also creates a natural daily and weekly schedule (as opposed to rigid, adult-imposed, artificial schedules) where watering, weeding, harvesting, and other tasks must take place.

Provide Materials and Loose Parts to Encourage Constructive Play

According to Ihn, constructive play is the favorite outdoor activity of preschool age children; and many boys—including those with somewhat delayed verbal skills and social abilities—thrive on constructive play.[13] Yet most playgrounds have few materials and equipment that encourage constructive play.

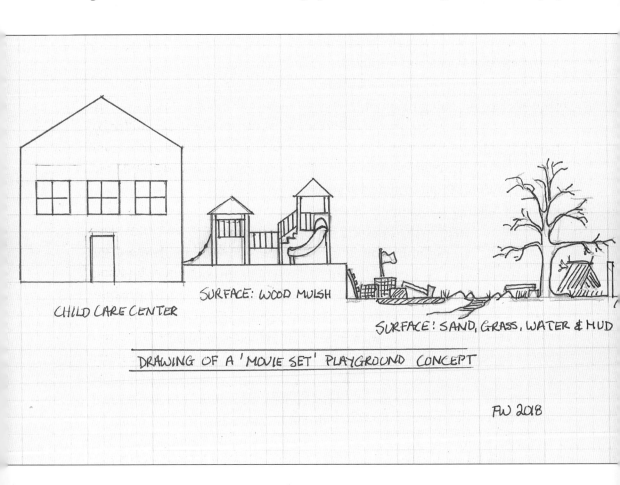

Sand and water are fantastic for this, as are loose parts like sticks, stones, milk crates, boxes, car tires, clean pieces of splinter-free wood, tools to move sand and dirt, and a variety of blocks. Many playgrounds do not offer these materials because they can make the playground look messy, teachers don't want to have to collect them at the end of each day, and they need to be carefully checked and maintained on a regular basis.

One option to these dilemmas is to design what I call a "movie set playground." From the perspective of the program or school, the playground appears to be a typical plastic and painted steel playground with slides, ladders, monkey bars, and platforms. Behind this formal structure is an area of ground sunken two feet below the ground level, filled with sand, water, mud, and a rich assortment of building materials and loose parts. None of this sunken area can be seen from the program or nearby neighborhood.[14]

Include Shade Areas

More and more regulatory agencies are requiring shade on playgrounds due to skin damage from exposure to the sun. Obviously, shade issues differ by geography; they are also very complex. While shade provides protection from the sun's rays in summertime, shade can also create cold and icy patches in the winter, including the shade from local buildings.

Ideally, sun movement and shade patterns should be determined not only before the playground is designed, but also before the location of the playground is chosen. Some years ago, I designed a playground for a new building in western Texas (which is extremely hot). The playground was located on the west side of the building (the hottest and windiest side) since the east side, the logical place for the playground, was the parking lot. It most cases, it seems, the location of the playground is the last consideration of architects and designers.

Provide Indoor/Outdoor Transition Space

One of the great things about buildings in Latin America is that the distinction between the inside and outside is almost indiscernible. Even the airport in Brasilia, Brazil smoothly transitions from inside to outside, with plants, open sky, and pleasant breezes. The schools and early childhood buildings there also have this wonderful feel to them, with all of the classrooms open to a central courtyard. Clearly in these countries, the warm climate makes this possible.

However, the designers of the Children's Houses (infant and child care programs) in communities of the Bruderhof—a communal religious society that

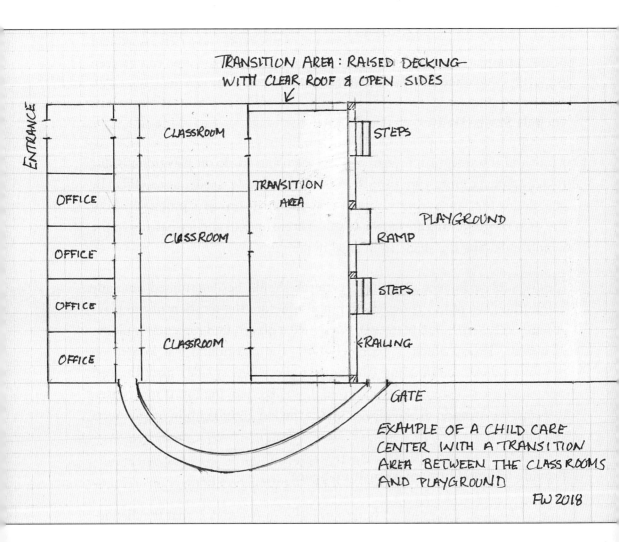

Example of a child care center with a transition area between the classrooms and playground
FW 2018

manufactures Community Playthings (early childhood equipment and toys)—have used their experience from living in Paraguay to adapt this concept for cold climates. They accomplish this by building a transition deck between classrooms and the playground—an area with a raised wooden floor that is covered with a clear corrugated roof to let in the sun and has open side walls. Access to the classrooms is by door, but access to the playground is open. Thus, the transition area is protected from rain, snow, and wind, but is otherwise outdoors. Here, children can use wheeled toys, blocks, art, woodworking materials, and the sand and water table, without getting cold and wet, yet the setting provides more freedom than the indoors. It's the best of both worlds!

Maintenance

Most early childhood programs and schools strive to create playgrounds that are low maintenance—low cost and minimum need for human effort—which is one reason many lack grass, sand, native trees, and shrubs. However, if we are going to view the outdoors as a significant learning environment, then we have to invest both time and financial resources in its care and maintenance. Consider the time and energy devoted to keeping the classroom clean, attractive, in good condition, and equipped with the latest materials and equipment. Few question this commitment. The same devotion needs to extend to the playground if we truly appreciate its value.

Outdoor Environments Beyond the Playground

Beyond the early childhood program and school, children benefit from more opportunities to develop and learn in a variety of challenging, interesting, and natural settings. In Bronfenbrenner's *ecological systems theory*, the early childhood program/school, family, and community are important ecological components that contribute to the development and learning of the child.[15] However, to best support children, these systems must work together and support each other.

When programs use the rich outdoor resources of their communities they create positive outcomes that tell families of the educational value of using the outdoors, and informs them of the many community resources available for their use (the reverse is also true, when families inform their children's programs of community resources they use and enjoy). In today's world of childhood obesity and the limited physical activities of young children, *any* family time spent outside benefits the child.

There are many ways adults interact with children when visiting community resources. The first responsibility is supervision—for both health and safety.[16] However, program staff must be careful to adjust rules so that children can truly benefit from the outdoors. Children's structured activities should be balanced with opportunities to run, climb, shout, throw sticks into the water, and build dams. Field trips are a wonderful avenue for teachers and parent volunteers to share with children the topics they are passionate about: tress, local birds, wild flowers, rocks and rock formations, local animals, and the history of the area. In so doing, teachers need to keep in mind each child's zone of proximal development and carefully scaffold the children's experiences (see Chapter 7). The following are a few examples of outdoor field trip sites.

Outdoor Museums

Most large cities have a variety of museums, including *outdoor museums*. These are often a collection of old buildings—a one-room school house, general store, farm buildings, old dwellings, and sometimes a chapel—arranged like an old town, with local crops grown in gardens and small fields, and a variety of farm animals. They may also offer historical activities in which children can participate such as making jam and apple butter. There are usually no cars allowed in these museums, and volunteers show the children around and answer questions. It's also fun to visit the museum several times a year, making them an ideal site when implementing the Project Approach.

Notes from the Field

Outdoor Museums: A Living History Experience

While raising our young family, my wife and I discovered outdoor museums. When my children were small—all under age five—we enjoyed the outdoor museum called Missouri Town, just outside of Kansas City. We would spend Sunday afternoons enjoying the 1850s town.

There were farmhouses and small residences, a mansion, a one-room school house, outbuildings, a small chapel, and a blacksmith's shop. There were also several gardens with typical plants growing in them: corn, squash, grapes, pumpkins, and potatoes. One of the yards behind a farmhouse featured a collection of old farm equipment. The children loved to get up on the pieces of farm equipment, hold the steering wheel, and pretend they were ploughing the field and harvesting the crops.

At the end of the town was a pleasant, easy hike through a typical Missouri wood. My family especially enjoyed this trail in spring, when all of the wild flowers were in bloom and birds were nesting in the trees, as well as in fall, with colorful leaves and berries to pick and collect.

The museum also offered occasional cooking and arts and crafts activities for the children. The cooking involved preserving fruit from the garden and making different kinds of jams and juices. One art activity my children especially enjoyed was making wallpaper—with water, food coloring, vinegar, and cooking oil.

When our children were older—between four and 10—we enjoyed the Littleton Outdoor Museum in Littleton, Colorado. This outdoor museum also had a collection of typical old buildings. In addition to these buildings, the museum featured an icehouse (the farm was next to a lake) that included a large boat used for transporting the ice and a collection of tools for cutting the ice and then loading it onto the boat. The one-room schoolhouse was, as one could imagine, a favorite place for our children to visit.

This museum also housed a collection of familiar farm animals: pigs, cows, sheep, oxen, draft horses, and chickens (including bantams). On different visits we could see the animals working on the farm as well as some new babies. Volunteers worked in the garden and cared for the animals (in traditional clothes).

We greatly enjoyed these outdoor museums as a family. The children had lots of space to run and climb; they could observe the animals, walk through buildings, and learn about the crops and vegetables. Neither of these museums was ever crowded.

Wetlands, Greenways, and Trails

Children love nature and are interested in all sorts of natural phenomena and occurrences.[17] Many cities have greenways, wetlands, and trails where children can explore birds, waterfowl, animals, butterflies, and local vegetation that often cannot be found in traditional city parks. Of particular interest during the year are the fall and spring migration of wild birds and all of the natural activity in ponds and pools that occurs in the spring.

Many city parks and recreation departments provide guided tours and educational fieldtrips for their wetlands and greenways. These departments often have well developed websites that provide needed information about everything they offer. Early childhood programs and schools should develop a relationship with local departments and discover the rich variety of natural resources available in their area.

However, while traditional programs are beneficial for young children who visit these areas, do not forget the tremendous value of outdoor play. This is the opportunity for children to play in water and mud, build a fort together as a group, explore, make a snow cave in the newly fallen snow, and pretend to be explorers. As we have pointed out, most young boys love to explore, take risks, challenge their bodies, and discover cause-and-effect connections and relationships.

Traditional Parks and Playgrounds

Traditional city parks usually include playgrounds for children of various ages, expansive grass areas and mature trees, picnic tables, and other additions unique to the specific area: a petting zoo, little train, or wading stream.

The parks are more structured than wetlands, greenways, and trails, and often offer the same type of opportunities provided at the school or early childhood program (the equipment might even be identical). To take advantage of this, teachers should bring lots of loose parts and props for games with rules and constructive play, and enjoy opportunities not available in the school playground such as playing in the streams and ponds, building forts under the tree, collecting leaves, and discovering new flowers and other plants. Many programs do not have the expansive grass that is typically found in these parks. When I taught at a small elementary school in Taos, New Mexico, we would walk from the school to the city park several times a week to enjoy a variety of group games in the park.

Chapter Review

This chapter explored the use of the outdoors with young children, especially young boys. It described the characteristics of play and then covered Piaget's cognitive play stages and Parten's social play stages. Next, it discussed designing playgrounds, beginning with Dattner's criteria for design and then describing elements to consider in making good playgrounds for young children: surfaces, creating a garden, encouraging constructive play, providing shade and transition spaces, and the importance of maintenance. The chapter then described the value of going beyond the program or school playground to use outdoor spaces in the community: outdoor museums, greenways, trails, and traditional city parks. It emphasized the rich learning that occurs in using these spaces in nature: birds and animals, ecology, the seasons—including bird migration, growth, and decomposition.

Chapter 8: Play in the Outdoors **OH BOY!**

Questions to Ask Yourself

- Why is play so important for the development and learning of young children, and why should young boys engage in lots of play?

- How does play promote the development of all domains, while also stimulating important brain development?

- What skills and concepts can young children learn through engaging in constructive play?

- Why don't many playgrounds for young children—both in parks and in early childhood programs—support the development of complex social and cognitive play?

- How do young children benefit from exploring outdoor environments beyond the program and traditional park playgrounds?

CHAPTER 9

Men in the Lives of Young Children

Young Boys Need Men

Men provide a goodness-of-fit for young boys. Men were boys once, so they understand some of the behavioral, social, and academic challenges young boys experience in early childhood programs and elementary schools. They also naturally engage in activities that young boys enjoy and are therefore, attracted to such as rough-and-tumble play, use of the outdoors, playing with blocks in the block area, woodworking, building forts, and playing competitive games and various sports activities. Not only do men interact with young boys while engaging in these activities, but their very involvement and enthusiasm conveys to boys that these activities are legitimate and worthy of their time and attention.[1]

Studies show that in the classroom setting many female teachers prefer to engage in art, literacy, and dramatic play activities, while men seem to be more comfortable with floor activities, movement, rough-and-tumble play, construction challenges, and messy and noisier activities and environments.[2] We also know that men and women interact differently with infants and young children. Men tend to be more physical, stimulating, and playful, while women tend to be more nurturing, soothing, and conversational. And we know that when infants and young children want to be comforted, they seek out a female caregiver, and when they want to be stimulated and entertained, they seek out male caregivers.[3] Because young girls are often more advanced in language development than young boys, female teachers are often attracted to working with girls as opposed to boys.[4]

At an age when young children are trying to figure out their society's gender roles and behaviors, men provide boys with healthy role models. As children develop and mature, they need to explore societal constructs of gender; boys especially need positive role models who can interact appropriately with them in a variety of typical male-oriented activities, while also providing role models for healthy masculinity.[5]

However, more and more children do not have healthy male role models in their daily lives. This could be for a variety of reasons including an increase of female-headed households, domestic violence, the high unemployment of many minority men, and incarceration. And men who are physically involved in the home life of young children desperately need support and information about their important role. Thus, boys need men throughout their early childhood and elementary school experiences.

But, there is a lack of men in the classroom: fathers, uncles, boyfriends, grandfathers, teachers, caregivers, administrators, specialists, and volunteers. According to the U.S. Bureau of Labor Statistics, 2.7% of preschool teachers and 19.1% of elementary and middle school teachers are men.[6] While these are American statistics, UNESCO reports similar gender differences in every developed country.[7] Additionally, most men like to be around other men, so when there are few men in programs, it becomes much more difficult to attract male involvement of family members.

There are two fundamental ways to increase the number of men in the lives of young boys when attending early childhood and elementary school programs: increase the involvement of male family members, and increase the number of men who teach and serve young boys in our programs. This chapter will explore both of these areas, beginning with a discussion of some of the reasons it is difficult to involve men in programs that serve young children including fathers and other male relatives, and male teachers and other professionals. It will then provide suggestions to increase the involvement of male family members and how to recruit and retain more male teachers and caregivers.

Barriers to Involving Men in the Lives of Young Children

While more and more males are becoming actively involved in the care and education of their own children, and efforts are being made to increase father/

male relative involvement and the number of male teachers and caregivers, barriers still exist. Here are some of these barriers.

- Resistance from some families who believe that men should not care for or teach young children. This view also extends to male volunteers in the program and is especially true of some new immigrant families whose cultures even forbid young girls from being around men who are not related to them.

- Resistance from many early childhood directors and elementary school principals who are uncomfortable with men in their programs. Also, for a variety of reasons, some women in the field have strong animas towards men.[8]

- Pressure applied to fathers and other male relatives who want to volunteer by male friends and relatives who believe this is not a masculine thing to do, and that only the women in the family should work closely with their child's program.[9]

- Often activities, family events, and volunteer opportunities are mostly things women enjoy doing and are scheduled at inconvenient times for fathers, which of course, is also inconvenient for mothers who work outside of the home.

- Some fathers are absent from the home and many fathers simply see no need to be involved with their children's programs; they feel that it is the job of the mother; and they believe that mothers are more effective in working with the program and school, which is predominantly female.

- Some men feel insecure and incompetent when talking to child care and school staff about their children, and when volunteering in the program.[10]

- A prevailing societal view that women are naturally more capable and able to care for young children than men. Many also believe that young boys and girls do not need caregivers of different genders; they think that for children this age, gender does not matter.

- Pressure applied to men in the field from other men who do not view caring and nurturing young children as a legitimate male occupation, resulting in a lack of support and camaraderie for the few men who do enter the field.

- A view by many that the early childhood and elementary education fields do not pay enough for "heads of the family." Ironically, in today's world, more and more women are the "head of the family," and thus this concern should apply to them as well.

- A deeply held belief by some female teachers that men do not belong in the field, and that this is one of only a few professions where women dominate and control and should continue to dominate and control.[11]

Increasing the Involvement of Male Family Members

Beginning with the work of Froebel, the early childhood field recognized the importance of partnering with parents—usually mothers. Head Start continued to pioneer the concept of parent involvement in the care and education of young children. Today, all early childhood programs work to provide a variety of ways to involve parents through family activities, parent education and support, and the use of parent volunteers throughout the program.

K-12 schools, on the other hand, were slow to embrace parent involvement. Initially, K-12 programs viewed themselves as the experts, and parents as either unneeded or even as an obstacle to their children's progress and education.[12] This attitude was clearly illustrated in the way public school special education programs worked with families of children with special needs up through the 1980s.[13]

When schools did begin to include families in activities, parents were still viewed as peripheral, and "free labor," rather than as critical elements in their children's development and education. Parent involvement was considered a way for school experts to increase their influence by telling parents how to raise their children and how to support the school's important work.[14] With pressure from national organizations such as the Parent Teacher Association, modeling of true program-family partnerships by Head Start, and research that linked the critical value of parent involvement to the success of students, schools are finally committed to involve parents in forming real partnerships in the development and education of their children.

However, two major challenges remain for schools and early childhood programs: 1) minority parents are still often reluctant or unable to become deeply engaged in their children's school activities; and 2) the majority of parents who become involved are overwhelmingly female.

All Staff Need to Understand the Reasons Fathers and Other Men Should Be Involved

Before a program or school attempts to increase the role of fathers and other male relatives in their program, all staff, including specialists and administrators, need to understand why this is important.[15] Ideas to review with staff include the following:

- research shows that when fathers (or other men in the child's life) are involved in programs for young children, the children are more successful emotionally, socially, and cognitively;

- early childhood programs and schools have a responsibility both to support men in their roles as caregivers and to teach them how to support their children in early care and education; and

- two contemporary challenges including the increase in the number of men sharing child care at home, and the increase of the number of mothers who work full-time outside the home, require early childhood programs and schools to find ways to work directly with fathers and other men involved with children in the home.[16]

Before a program can begin to directly address these issues, an honest examination of the program's climate for males is needed. The best way to start this process is for the program to hire a *male advocate* whose role is to set up a positive male-oriented program or initiative. However, this person can only be effective if he is totally supported by the program's administration, which must be committed to the need for male involvement in the program or school. In large programs, a separate staff position can be created; in smaller programs, someone already on staff who is committed to increasing male involvement can be chosen for this role.

The main responsibility of the male advocate is to increase the number of men directly involved with children in the program. This begins with challenging any negative attitudes that exist in the program or school about men being actively involved. Because programs for young children have historically not included men, a variety of negative attitudes and behaviors have crept into the overall culture of many programs. Some of the more pervasive ones are:

- a belief that men do not work well with young children; they do not know what they are doing;

- a belief that men are often too rough;

- when men do get involved with young children, they want to be in charge, but they depend on women to do all of the hard work that is involved in education and child care;

- the feeling that when men fight for the custody of their children they are doing so as a way to get back at the child's mother and don't really care about the children;

- a view that fathers tend to be emotionally absent from their children; and

- the belief that women have learned important parenting skills while growing up that most men have not learned, which is detrimental to young children who are cared for by men.[17]

Additionally, many women in early childhood programs and elementary schools, like all women and men in society, have been raised with a variety of stereotypical gender behaviors and attitudes since they were very young.

And both mothers and female staff members may have negative attitudes toward men due to their own life experiences.[18] These attitudes are hard to change. However, staff members need to fully understand that a critical part of their professional role as teachers and caregivers is to find ways to involve men. These changes must begin with a program-wide self-examination process, which should be led by the male advocate or other leader. For example, if the male advocate observes a parent conference without a father, he must determine whether any effort was made to bring in the father or father figure (maybe offer to change the time or location for the conference or make sure child care services are provided during the conference). The male advocate needs to challenge negative attitudes and behaviors as well.

Determine How Staff Communicate with Men in the Program

Just as men are comfortable interacting with other men, so too are women comfortable talking to other women. This is only natural as women have common issues to discuss, similar communication styles, and a comfort zone with other women. Further, women in early childhood and elementary programs are used to addressing issues of concern with mothers of children and not fathers (or other male members of the family). They have years of practice working with mothers to communicate, solve problems, and address concerns. Often, these women are also friends with some of the mothers outside of the program or school. Programs should determine whether staff members initiate communication with fathers, whether this involves discussions about parenting, the child, and their child's experience in the program, and whether fathers initiate communication with staff. Programs should also look at whether the nature of this communication is respectful, supportive, and helpful.[19]

Many men are new to the business of working with their child's school or early childhood program. They are uncertain, insecure, and feel inadequate. They also have a communication style different from women. Program staff need to recognize this and support and encourage male involvement.

Implement a Male Friendly Program

Once a full evaluation of the program has been completed, the program can begin to create a male-friendly approach to early care and education. The initial registration of the child into the program or school can be the best time to determine the significant males who are involved in the care and education of the child. Because of the diversity of family structures in the U.S. today, a child may have a biological father, stepfather, foster father, teen father, grandfather, or a non-related man who serves as a father figure. It's imperative for the program to know which men are involved in the child's life. Further, this is a great time to begin building the very important relationship between the child's father or significant male caregiver and the program. A checklist can be used to determine the kinds of support provided by the significant male—leisure, physical care, emotional support, financial support, exploration of the community, and discipline.

The father or the father figure should be invited to the intake along with the mother. When this occurs, it is critical for the person doing the intake to direct some questions to the father and not just ask the mother for all of the information. The father can be asked about employment, involvement with the child at home, hobbies and interests, and ways he can contribute to the program. This information can be used to build a relationship with the father or father figure including requests for volunteering and involvement in projects he has indicated he enjoys.

There are also several environmental factors that can be implemented to make men feel more welcome in the program or school. Are there pictures on the wall of things men typically enjoy doing—working on cars and trucks, construction, carpentry, mountain climbing, and sports? Images of men must be evident throughout the program and school: pictures of fathers and other men on office walls; sports, automobile, construction, and woodworking magazines in the entrance area; books of men in a variety of activities and family events; and pictures of men in curricular materials, government reports, marketing materials, and teacher training manuals.

And, of course, men like to be around men. Do they see other men in the program? Do they see fathers being included, male faculty being respected, and examples of men nurturing young children in the program? Do they see activities and projects that men typically enjoy such as building or repairing a playground, working in a vegetable garden, barbequing, building furniture for the classrooms, and/or helping instruct children on the woodworking bench? To increase male involvement, the program must make a concerted effort to ensure that they are welcoming to men. The environment needs to clearly convey that "men are welcome here." Some additional male-friendly components that need to be a part of the program or school include:

- adult-size chairs need to be available in all program areas, including on the playground;

- the program should have a bathroom that is clearly welcome to be used by both men and women and that includes a diaper changing area;

- a male physical presence needs to be present throughout the program including the waiting area, offices, and common areas—books, magazines, pictures, artifacts, and the overall décor; and

- there should be areas where fathers and their children can be together while waiting to visit with staff.[20]

Provide Program Activities Targeted Just to Men

Most men enjoy doing activities with other men that utilize their skills and interests, and that bring together men interested in helping care for and educate their young children. There are two kinds of male activities that work well in early childhood programs. The first is projects that contribute directly to the welfare of the program or school. These might be building or remodeling a playground; planting and caring for a vegetable garden; and building equipment for classrooms such as shelving, a loft, or a puppet stage.[21] Men—and some women—enjoy activities that allow them to use their carpentry, gardening, construction, and other skills.

Because these activities do not involve interacting with children in the program they can be scheduled at times that are convenient to the men involved. Men can also volunteer to help children use the results of these projects such as working on the gardening project and learning how to use the woodworking bench. They can instruct teachers in how to engage with children in these activities if necessary, especially if they are unavailable during the school day.[22]

The second area of activities for male involvement are fatherhood support groups that teach parenting skills. These groups offer opportunities for men to learn about programs available for their children in the school district, local parks and recreation departments, or religious education networks, and to learn about other topics that support child development and learning. They also work for men to teach skills to each other and to network with each other, especially regarding the development and education of their children. Here are some possible topics for support groups:

- discipline;

- the critical role of men in the lives of children;

- how young children develop and learn;

- helping children with homework;

- managing children's access to TV, computers, and all forms of technology;

- dealing with conflicts in the home, especially around issues relating to children;

- use of the community for low-cost activities and community resources that can be enjoyed with their children such as libraries, food banks, and children's museums; and specific agencies that can provide services to their children (health clinics, dentists, psychologists);

- transition activities, either "to the big school" from a separate early childhood program, or from kindergarten to first grade in a large program;

- special education and gifted programs: what they are, how their child might benefit, and critical parent roles and responsibilities;

- conflict resolution techniques—with other adults and children; and

- different *parenting styles—authoritarian, permissive, uninvolved/neglectful,* and *authoritative.* One challenge for many men, especially those who grew up in military or traditional families, is their parenting style. Many fathers—and some mothers—believe the man's role in the home is to be the disciplinarian or authoritarian. As a result, they often use inappropriate—and sometimes abusive—discipline. Various parenting styles need to be described so that fathers can adopt an approach to meet the overall developmental needs of their children.

Figure Ten

Parenting Styles

There are four different parenting styles:

Authoritarian
These are parents who believe that their authority is unquestioned; they set the rules, which are non-negotiable; punishment is often strict, sometimes physical. Expectations of their children are high—sometimes too high. Many fathers are authoritarian—especially those in the military and those who did not have a positive male role model when they were growing up.

Permissive
Permissive parents are warm and have a relaxed approach to discipline. They have low expectations and when rules are broken there are few consequences. These parents often engage in the democratic approach to rule making. Some fathers—especially those who are rarely directly involved with their children—are permissive. Sometimes they give in to their children because of a feeling of guilt; or they reward them to compete with the child's mother.

Uninvolved/Neglectful
These are parents who are not involved with their children and who do not really want to be. They are disinterested and emotionally absent. Many fathers are accused of being uninvolved, but this is often a result of being excluded from the child's life—for a variety of reasons.

Authoritative
This style is a balance of control and consistency, implemented with warmth and encouragement. Parents have high demands of their children, but these expectations match each individual child's developmental age and ability. They provide reasons for rules and limits, but are also open to reasonable negotiations. Authoritative fathers are responsive to their son's unique styles and they do not compare him academically with siblings. They also see the need for one-on-one time between a son and the important male role model in the home.[23]

Fatherhood support groups need to be led by competent trainers, preferably a man of the same or similar economic and racial background as the participants. Leaders for these workshops can be recruited from local men's groups, colleges and universities, and state and local education and mental health training institutes. There are networks of proficient people available to lead these activities.

Survey Men on How They Want to Be Involved

In determining activities, projects, and support group topics it's a good idea to survey the men involved in the care of their children about how they would like to participate in the program. This activity serves two functions:

- it lets men know the program or school cares about their opinions and involvement with their children; and

- it helps the program identify the ideas and interests that are uniquely important to men in the program.[24]

It is important for early childhood programs and schools to offer workshops and training programs on topics that men want and not those the program thinks they need. Certainly, staff can help scaffold choices by suggesting ideas to fathers as a result of discussions, questions, and/or concerns, but no one wants to be told: "You are a bad parent and so you need to learn these things to become a good parent." A variety of surveys should be conducted throughout the program year—questionnaires, idea boxes, and personal solicitations of ideas can be used to gather information. Many programs now use technology for parent communication so a link on the website to solicit ideas might work. Based on the results of these surveys, the following is a list of some possible ways that the program can involve men:

- weekend family activities such as swimming, nature walks, and visits to cultural events;

- special events for the whole family such as awards, parties, and picnics;

- open-house—having the entire family come to the program to learn about how it functions and what it provides;
- classroom, playground, and field trip volunteering opportunities;
- program committees—for governance, fundraising, field trips, and special activities; and
- parenting topics for men only.

Many men are reluctant to engage in activities in which they lack experience. For this reason, it is important to gradually introduce men into classroom volunteering, decision-making committees, and activities where few men are present. A plan to involve men in the early childhood program should start with activities they are comfortable doing and in settings that are familiar.

Assess Male Involvement Activities

Program staffs need to determine which activities successfully involve fathers, and those that do not; further, they need to consider whether there are obvious reasons some activities are more successful than others. Often fathers and other men attend only a few activities during the year, and when they do, some fathers are very involved with their children, while others stand around and just talk with other men.[25] Factors that influence the success of male involvement include the following.

- **Time.** Is the activity at a time when the male family member is available?
- **Place.** Is the activity in a setting where men are comfortable (e.g., the playground or park) as opposed to the classroom, if they have not become comfortable in the classroom?
- **Activity.** Is the activity something men enjoy and are good at such as gardening, repairing the playground, or making something out of wood for the classroom?

- **Company.** Is the activity with other men or mostly women? Is it with strangers or people the men know?

- **Topics.** Is the meeting or activity something men are interested in or have they been told they must attend? Was the topic chosen because it was identified through a survey?

- **Meaningful.** Is it clear how this activity or class will help participants with their children or provide direct support for the children's program or school?[26]

Practice Effective Communication with Men

Effective communication between parents and the program or school is at the center of any good parent involvement program. Research on the communication used in parent involvement shows that:

- early childhood and elementary school staffs often communicate directly with mothers, while ignoring fathers; and

- fathers tend to avoid communicating with staff.[27]

Many fathers have not experienced the same cultural training on parenting that women have received; thus, a major purpose of program communication is to convey parenting knowledge and provide support to fathers and other male caregivers.[28] For communication to be effective, both fathers and other involved men need to be actively engaged with staff members. Staffs should take the initiative to communicate with the men involved in caring for and raising their children; once the initial barrier is overcome, men are often open to and even want more communication. One of the best times to initiate communication with a father or male caregiver is when children are dropped off and picked up.

Early childhood programs and schools need to provide training and support and implement employee evaluation procedures that are designed to improve the ability of staff to work effectively with the fathers or other male caregivers of young children. Some of this training should teach educators how to solve conflicts and problems at the lowest level, rather than always moving them up the authority chain. Staff should also be taught how to handle the common concerns and problems that parents—including fathers—address with them.

Support Men in Classroom Volunteering

By volunteering, fathers learn healthy ways to interact with their own children and are introduced to activities they can do with their children outside of the classroom. Male volunteers also gain information about the experiences their children have in the program. It is important to support men in working with their children in the program or school. Most men will initially gravitate to experiences they are comfortable with such as helping children on the woodworking bench, playing in the block area, supervising on the playground, and working in the garden. Program and school staffs can support them as they learn to feel comfortable in new situations such as reading to children, setting up the paint area, and actively engaging in dramatic play. Programs should avoid the temptation of asking men to "do the heavy lifting"—moving furniture, fixing equipment, and taking out the trash.[29] Men who volunteer in the classroom want to work with children, not engage in non-child related activities. Fathers and other men involved should be directly asked to volunteer in the classroom, playground, and on field trips. Further, staffs who may feel uncomfortable with men volunteering in their programs need coaching and help from the program or school administration.

Epstein's Framework: A Family Involvement Model

As a result of the increased understanding of the importance of involving families in the development and education of students, several parent involvement models have been created. Here, we examine one of these models as a way to explore a structured approach to increasing parent involvement; in this case, to increase the direct involvement of male family members.

Joyce Epstein is the Director of the Center on School, Family, and Commu-

Notes from the Field

Visiting a Fire Station

In chatting with the father of one of my kindergarten students, I discovered that he was a member of the local volunteer firefighters. We arranged for the class to visit the fire station, and for him to provide a tour. The father accompanied us on the moderate walk from the school to the fire station. He then demonstrated to the children how to hold the fire hose and let them try on the heavy coats and hats. They even got to "shoot" the water from the hose (with careful help from the father). He helped each one up onto the fire truck so they could get a real feel for the excitement.

On return to the classroom, I was able to procure some old firefighter hats, coats, and hoses. They were added to the dramatic play area. Books about firefighters and big fire engines were added to the literacy center. This visit triggered lots of dramatic play about firefighters, art work having to do with fire engines and firefighters, and even the creation of toy fire trucks on the woodworking bench.

Engaging a parent volunteer—in this case a father—greatly expanded the learning opportunities for all of the children, but especially for the boys.

nity Partnerships at Johns Hopkins University. Her book, *School, Family and Community Partnerships*, lists six components of home-school partnerships.[30] While this framework is designed for K-12 programs, it can work equally well for early childhood programs. Here are the six components.

- **Parenting.** The program needs to provide advice and assistance in all things parenting to support the child's overall growth and development. Also, the program must find ways to enable teachers and other important staff to learn as much as possible about the diverse families and children they serve. For men, this provides them with information and support regarding how to work closely with their children, including appropriate ways to discipline them.

- **Communicating.** The program needs to keep families up-to-date regarding program issues and individual student progress, while also responding to concerns and issues from the families. Thus, the communication must be two-way, and must be in the home language of the significant adults in the family. Men must be deliberately involved; specific communication regarding male-focused activities, volunteering, and projects must be included.

- **Volunteering.** Programs need to improve outreach to families and train staff on ways to include families—especially men—in the care and education of their child. This is particularly true for populations who tend to be underserved and who are resistant to being involved.

- **Learning at home.** Programs need to provide suggestions and support for a variety of ways—including directly involving men—that parents can provide different learning activities at home, including reading to their children, controlling TV and technology access, and using available community resources, including those that lend themselves to male activities.

- **Decision-making.** Parents, including fathers, need to be actively involved in the governance of their child's early childhood program or school, and not just in various fundraising projects (although some men have expertise in this area and love to be involved). The specific opportunities for governance depend on the program, but a sense of control over their child's care and education is very important for all parents, but especially those who often feel they are not involved in this important endeavor.

- **Collaborating with the community.** A program or school is embedded within a community; therefore, a central role of the program or school is to help families access community resources. This means informing families and assisting them in accessing and using the resources such as parks, wetlands, health and mental health centers, recreational sports programs, community gardens, children's museums, and other community agencies. Early childhood and educational programs also need to provide direct services to the community such as visiting senior centers, planting trees and flowers, cleaning up a neighborhood, and using the facility for neighborhood concerts, art shows, and community gatherings.[31]

Increasing Male Staff in Early Childhood Programs

The preceding section looked at ways to increase the number of fathers and male extended family members in early childhood programs and schools. What follows is an examination of ways to increase men in the early childhood and elementary fields as paid staff focusing on these areas: increase salaries and benefits; create master teachers; and challenge societal attitudes.

Increase Salaries and Benefits

Clearly, one reason there are few men in the early childhood field is poor pay and other benefits—vacation time, health care, in-service training, and retirement.[32] This is also obviously a critical issue for women in the field—especially those who are heads of their households. For this reason, a discussion about increasing pay and benefits must focus on the entire profession—not just men.

While Head Start and state-funded preschool programs are tax supported, as are child care programs funded through federal block grants, the majority of early childhood programs—including some of those in public schools (for which parents must pay tuition)—are not. Further, even in these publicly-funded programs, staffs rarely receive adequate pay and benefits. This is a rather interesting phenomenon because while all K-12 public education, community colleges, and public four-year institutions for higher learning receive significant tax support, in the U.S., most infant and early childhood programs do not. In other countries such as Finland, Australia, and France, public funds are used to support quality early infant and education programs; in some countries, these programs are an integral part of the overall public school system—with teachers receiving the same pay, benefits, and training as K-12 teachers.[33]

We cannot expect parents to pay more than they are already paying, thus significant tax support is needed. There are only two options for this support: a significant federal contribution like the funding for Head Start, or the incorporation of child care and early childhood programs within the local public schools (with pay and benefits on the same scale as those of the teachers in the district) like the *Ecole Maternelle* programs in France.[34]

Either way, adequate pay and benefits are a must. A recent federal document, *High Quality Learning Settings Depend on a High Quality Workforce: Low Compensation Undermines Quality* makes a very persuasive argument supporting this point.[35]

Create Master Teachers

In many early childhood programs, the only way for a teacher to progress financially within the program is to become an administrator or specialist, or to teach older children. However, this does not work well for those who prefer to stay in the classroom with infants or young children. It also means that we lose many good teachers including teachers with experience working with boys and male teachers.[36]

In France, the preschool program is a part of the overall K-12 school system and it is called the *Ecole Maternelle*. Teachers in these Ecole Maternelles receive the same level of college training to become a teacher and are paid on the same scale as K-12 teachers. Throughout the French school system there are Master Teachers, who after being a regular teacher for a given period can take additional coursework and assessments to become a Master Teacher.

Master Teachers work as coaches and trainers for other teachers in the program. For these teachers—both men and women—the Master Teacher position allows for higher salaries, authority, and status, while maintaining the role of a teacher in the school.[37] And this includes teachers in the Ecole Maternelle. Male Master Teachers would become excellent role models for future male teachers in early education and elementary schools.

Challenge Societal Attitudes

Changing society's views of men as nurturing people capable of caring for and teaching young children is a very difficult task. Books about teachers of young children primarily show women in these tasks; marketing materials for early childhood programs, elementary schools, early childhood college programs, and before/after school programs that serve young children only profile female teachers and providers. Even scholarly and government reports on the health, care, and education of young children rarely show men as parents, caregivers, and teachers. New research continues to show a bias towards women nurturing and caring for young children, although there is a beginning shift by younger people toward more appreciation of the ability and need of men to help care for young children.[38]

Changing society's view will take time, effort, deliberation, and persistence. Maybe the best approach is simply to increase the number of men in the field—fathers, other male relatives, caregivers, teachers, administrators, and community volunteers. By doing so, we provide public visibility of men in the field and move towards the normalization of men in early childhood and elementary school programs. Here are some specific ideas to change societal views of including men in the field.

- **Make it a social justice issue.** There are two social justice issues that we need to stress regarding men in early childhood and elementary education: 1) in an open, free society, men have a right to choose to become teachers and caregivers of young children—and to be able to make this a career; and 2) young children, including boys, have a right to have male role models in their early childhood programs and schools. Both these issues must be advocated for in the popular and traditional media, teacher conferences, college classrooms, and professional organizations.

- **Mobilize parent support.** We need to find ways to convince parents not only of the value of having men in their children's programs, but also to be advocates for such a view. In this way, parents can become our allies. Parent Teacher Associations, Head Start Policy Councils, parent committees in early childhood programs, school assemblies, school-wide advocacy groups, and school boards can be utilized in this campaign.

- **Create male support groups.** As we have mentioned, men in college programs and within early childhood and elementary school programs often experience a total lack of support from other men. We need to create support groups where men can socialize, express feelings of frustration, and gain needed support for challenging the societal status quo. Male college student groups, male teacher groups within Head Start programs and schools, and local support groups in professional early childhood and education associations must be mobilized to support men in our field.

- **Positively profile men in the field.** Men in the field should be profiled in newspaper articles and social media posts; awards, scholarships, and conference presentations should highlight these efforts.

- **Include influential men on the program or school's boards, committees, and fundraising activities.** Include male politicians, firefighters, police, local athletes, and other men on high-profile boards and committees so that the public can see men involved in these programs. These men can advocate for early childhood programs and elementary schools.

- **Provide mentors.** Colleges and universities should create mentorship programs for young men enrolled in early childhood and elementary education teacher preparation programs. Preferably, the mentor will be from one of these two departments or a related area such as psychology or sociology. The mentor should support his male students, help them navigate the complexities of college such as access to scholarships, and introduce them to local, national, and international organizations that support male teachers of young children. Once in the field, large organizations such as school districts, regional Head Start associations, and religious school networks should provide mentors for their male teachers—supporting and helping them address the barriers we discussed earlier in this chapter.

- **Use publications and conferences.** *Men Teach* is an online site that disseminates articles from around the world about efforts to increase men in education.[39] This is a great source of information and support for men in the early childhood field—either as practicing teachers or those enrolled in college preparing to become teachers. National and international early childhood conferences such as NAEYC, Head Start, and the World Forum Foundation could dedicate more time, space, and presentations to highlight the desperate need for more male teachers throughout the world and to develop specific strategies to address the lack of men in the field.

Chapter Review

This chapter focused on ways to involve men in early childhood programs and schools. It began by exploring some of the barriers that limit men caring for and educating young children including low pay and a deep belief by many that women are simply better equipped for this important task. The chapter then described in detail ideas for creating a male-friendly program—both for fathers and other male relatives, and for male teachers, caregivers, and other staff. It examined ways to increase male involvement in programs and described actions that early childhood programs and schools need to take before initiating a male-involvement initiative including training staff, examining the program's overall climate, and evaluating staff-male communication. The chapter stressed that men tend to like to be around other men, necessitating programs targeted just for men and creating activities where men can be around other men. It then examined Epstein's framework for parent-program partnerships as a model for parent participation. Finally, the chapter discussed ways to increase the number of male teachers and caregivers in the field including increasing salaries and benefits, creating a master teacher category, and challenging social attitudes about men caring for young children.

Chapter 9: Men in the Lives of Young Children — **OH BOY!**

Questions to Ask Yourself

- Why is it so important to have men in the lives of young children—especially boys—in the early childhood program and school?

- What are some reasons it is difficult to get men—fathers, grandparents, boyfriends—involved with programs that serve young children?

- What are specific ways programs can involve men?

- If you are the parent of a young child, would you be comfortable with him/her being taught by a man? Why or why not? Would you help your program or school attract more male teachers?

- Do you know any men who are infant, early childhood or elementary school teachers, or specialists working with young children—or men in college preparing for these roles? What are their experiences?

Notes

Introduction: Why We Need to Focus on Young Boys

1. Francis Wardle, "Are We Short Changing Boys?," *Exchange*, May/June 1991, 48-51.

2. Francis Wardle, *A Shropshire Lad: The Early Life of a Boy in the Wheathill Bruderhof* (Denver: unpublished, 2014).

Chapter 1: The Challenge of Boys

1. Richard Gargiulo and Emily Bouck, *Special Education in Contemporary Society*, 6th ed. (Thousand Oaks: SAGE Publications, 2018); National Center for Education Statistics (NCES), *Digest of Educational Statistics, 2009* (Washington D.C.: U.S. Department of Education, 2011); David Sadker and Karen Zittleman, *Teachers, Schools, and Society: A Brief Introduction to Education*, 2d ed. (New York: McGraw Hill, 2013); U.S. Department of Education Office of Civil Rights, *Civil Rights Data Collection, Data Snapshot: Early Childhood Education, Brief #2*, http://ocrdata.ed.gov (accessed May 25, 2016).

2. U.S. Department of Education Office of Civil Rights, *Civil Rights Data Collection, Data Snapshot: Early Childhood Education, Brief #2*, http://ocrdata.ed.gov (accessed May 25, 2016).

3. Ibid.

4. U.S. Bureau of Labor Statistics, *Highlights of Women's Earnings in 2013, BLM Report 1051* (Washington, D.C.: U.S. Printing Office, December 2014).

5. See Notes from the Field: Observations from a Head Start Program: Where do Boys Play?

6. Barbara Holmes, Jamel Gibson, and Dietrich Morrison-Danner, "Reducing Aggressive Male Behavior in Elementary School: Promising Practices," *Contemporary Issues in Education Research* 7, no. 4 (2014): 253-258; J.M. Frabutt, W. Clark, and G. Speach, *Social and Emotional Wellness in Private Schools* (paper presented at the Advancing School Mental Health Conference, Albuquerque, NM, 2010).

7. UNESCO Bangkok, *The Impact of Women Teachers on Girls' Education: Advisory Brief*, http://bangkok.unesco.org (2006).

8. Francis Wardle, "Are We Short Changing Boys?," *Exchange*, May/June 1991, 48-51.

9. Kathleen Stassen Berger, *The Developing Person Through Childhood and Adolescence*, 9th ed. (New York: Worth Publishers, 2017).

10. Ibid.

11. Beth Harry and Janette Klingner, *Why are So Many Minority Students in Special Education?* (New York: Teachers College Press, 2006); U.S. Department of Education Office of Civil Rights, *Civil Rights Data Collection, Data Snapshot: Early Childhood Education, Brief #2*, http://ocrdata.ed.gov (accessed May 25, 2016).

12. U.S. Department of Education Office of Civil Rights, *Civil Rights Data Collection, Data Snapshot: Early Childhood Education, Brief #2*, http://ocrdata.ed.gov (accessed May 25, 2016).

13. Richard Gargiulo and Emily Bouck, *Special Education in Contemporary Society*, 6th ed. (Thousand Oaks: SAGE Publications, 2018); Ann Schimke, "Suspended Countless Times as a Child, this Professor is Tackling Racial Disparities in Preschool Discipline," *Chalkbeat*, March 22, 2016, https://chalkbeat.org/posts/co/2016/03/22/suspended-countless-times-as-a-child-this-professor-is-tackling-racial-disparities-in-preschool-discipline/#.V8BQazWUK8B (accessed May 5, 2016); U.S. Department of Education Office of Civil Rights, *Civil Rights Data Collection, Data Snapshot: Early Childhood Education, Brief #2*, http://ocrdata.ed.gov (accessed May 25, 2016).

14. Nancy Hill and Stacie Craft, "Parent-School Involvement and School Performance: Mediated Pathways among Socioeconomically Comparable African American and Euro-American Families," *Journal of Educational Psychology* 95, no. 1 (March 2003): 74-83; Richard Gargiulo and Emily Bouck, *Special Education in Contemporary Society*, 6th ed. (Thousand Oaks: SAGE Publications, 2018).

15. Richard Gargiulo and Emily Bouck, *Special Education in Contemporary Society*, 6th ed. (Thousand Oaks: SAGE Publications, 2018).

16. Francis Wardle, *Collaboration with Families and Communities* (San Diego: Bridgepoint Education, 2013).

17. National Resource Center on ADHD, "Data & Statistics," *CHADD: The National Resource on ADHD* http://www.chadd.org/understanding-adhd/about-adhd/data-and-statistics.aspx (accessed 2016); Janet Lerner and Beverley Johns, *Learning Disabilities and Related Mild Disabilities*, 12th ed. (Belmont: Wadsworth Publishing, 2011).

18. U.S. Department of Education Office of Civil Rights, *Civil Rights Data Collection, Data Snapshot: Early Childhood Education, Brief #2*, http://ocrdata.ed.gov (accessed May 25, 2016).

19. Richard Gargiulo and Emily Bouck, *Special Education in Contemporary Society*, 6th ed. (Thousand Oaks: SAGE Publications, 2018).

20. Kathleen Stassen Berger, *The Developing Person Through Childhood and Adolescence*, 9th ed. (New York: Worth Publishers, 2017).

21. Richard Gargiulo and Emily Bouck, *Special Education in Contemporary Society*, 6th ed. (Thousand Oaks: SAGE Publications, 2018); U.S. Department of Education Office of Civil Rights, *Civil Rights Data Collection, Data Snapshot: Early Childhood Education, Brief #2*, http://ocrdata.ed.gov (accessed May 25, 2016).

22. Richard Gargiulo and Emily Bouck, *Special Education in Contemporary Society*, 6th ed. (Thousand Oaks: SAGE Publications, 2018).

23. U.S. Department of Education Office of Civil Rights, *Civil Rights Data Collection, Data Snapshot: Early Childhood Education, Brief #2*, http://ocrdata.ed.gov (accessed May 25, 2016).

24. Alfie Kohn, *Punished by Rewards: The Trouble with Gold Stars, Incentive Plans, A's, Praise, and Other Bribes* (New York: Houghton Mifflin Harcourt, 1993).

25. Albert Bandura, "Toward a Psychology of Human Agency," *Perspectives on Psychological Science* 1, no. 2 (2006): 164-180; Erik Erikson, *Childhood and Society*, 2d ed. (New York: Norton, 1963); Jeanne Ellis Ormrod, *Human Learning*, 7th ed. (Upper Saddle River: Pearson, 2011).

26. Kathleen Stassen Berger, *The Developing Person Through Childhood and Adolescence*, 9th ed. (New York: Worth Publishers, 2017).

27. Richard Gargiulo and Emily Bouck, *Special Education in Contemporary Society*, 6th ed. (Thousand Oaks: SAGE Publications, 2018).

28. Ibid.

29. Linda Bambara, Rachel Janney, and Martha Snell, *Behavior Support*, 3rd ed. (Baltimore: Brookes Publishing, 2015); Brenda Scheuermann and Judy Hall, *Positive Behavioral Supports for the Classroom*, 3rd ed. (Upper Saddle River: Pearson, 2016).

30. Jeanne Ellis Ormrod, *Human Learning*, 7th ed. (Upper Saddle River: Pearson, 2011).

31. Ibid.

32. National Center for Education Statistics (NCES), *Digest of Educational Statistics, 2009* (Washington D.C.: U.S. Department of Education, 2011); David Sadker and Karen Zittleman, *Teachers, Schools, and Society: A Brief Introduction to Education*, 2d ed. (New York: McGraw Hill, 2013).

33. Sonia Nieto and Patty Bode, *Affirming Diversity: The Sociopolitical Context of Multicultural Education* (Upper Saddle River: Pearson, 2012).

34. Ibid.

35. Albert Bandura, "Toward a Psychology of Human Agency," *Perspectives on Psychological Science* 1, no. 2 (2006): 164-180; Albert Bandura "Self-Efficacy Mechanism in Human Agency," *American Psychologist* 37, no. 2 (1982): 122-147; Jeanne Ellis Ormrod, *Human Learning*, 7th ed. (Upper Saddle River: Pearson, 2011).

36. Francis Wardle, "Are We Short Changing Boys?," *Exchange*, May/June 1991, 48-51.

37. A high-level national conference called to address ways to improve American education because the Russians placed a person in space via Sputnik before the U.S. did.

38. Sue Bredekamp and Carol Copple, eds., *Developmentally Appropriate Practice in Early Childhood Programs* (Washington, D.C.: NAEYC, 1987).

39. Friedrich Froebel, *The Education of Man* (New York: A. Lovell & Company, 1885).

40. Ibid.

41. John Dewey, *Experience and Education* (New York: Touchstone, 1938).

42. Polly Greenberg, "Lucy Sprague Mitchell: A Major Missing Link Between Early Childhood Education in the 1980s and Progressive Education in the 1890s-1930s," *Young Children* 42, no. 5 (July 1987): 70-84; Carolyn Edwards, Lella Gandini, and George Forman, eds., *The Hundred Languages of Children: The Reggio Emilia Approach to Early Childhood Education* (Greenwich: Ablex, 1993); Francis Wardle, *Introduction to Early Childhood Education: A Multidimensional Approach to Child-Centered Care and Learning* (Boston: Allyn & Bacon, 2003).

43. Jerome Bruner, *The Process of Education* (Cambridge: Harvard University Press, 1960).

44. Ibid.

45. Sue Bredekamp and Carol Copple, eds., *Developmentally Appropriate Practice in Early Childhood Programs* (Washington, D.C.: NAEYC, 1987).

46. Ibid.

47. L.A. Shepard and M.L. Smith, "Escalating Academic Demand in Kindergarten: Some Nonsolutions," *Elementary School Journal* 89, no. 2 (1988): 135-146.

Chapter 2: Causes: How Did We Get Here?

1. Young Pai, Susan Adler, and Linda Shadiow, *Cultural Foundations of Education*, 4th ed. (Upper Saddle River: Pearson, 2006).

2. Richard Gargiulo and Emily Bouck, *Special Education in Contemporary Society*, 6th ed. (Thousand Oaks: SAGE Publications, 2018).

3. Young Pai, Susan Adler, and Linda Shadiow, *Cultural Foundations of Education*, 4th ed. (Upper Saddle River: Pearson, 2006).

4. John Wiles and Joseph Bondi, *Curriculum Development: A Guide to Practice*, 9th ed. (Upper Saddle River: Pearson, 2015).

5. National Commission on the Excellence in Education, *A Nation at Risk: The Imperative for Educational Reform* (Washington D.C.: U.S. Printing Office, 1983).

6. Olga S. Jarrett, "Recess," in *The Sage Encyclopedia of Contemporary Early Childhood Education*, ed. Donna Couchenour and J. Kent Chrisman (Thousand Oaks: SAGE Publications, 2016), 1146-1149.

7. Ibid.

8. Ibid.

9. G. Jacobs, "School Readiness," in *The Sage Encyclopedia of Contemporary Early Childhood Education*, ed. Donna Couchenour and J. Kent Chrisman (Thousand Oaks: SAGE Publications, 2016), 1283-1286; Gayle Mindes, "Standards-based Curriculum and Assessment," in *The Sage Encyclopedia of Contemporary Early Childhood Education*, ed. Donna Couchenour and J. Kent Chrisman (Thousand Oaks: SAGE Publications, 2016), 1146-1149.

10. See "Goals 2000" Figure One.

11. Kathleen Stassen Berger, *The Developing Person Through Childhood and Adolescence*, 9th ed. (New York: Worth Publishers, 2017); Laura E. Berk, *Child Development*, 9th ed. (Upper Saddle River: Pearson, 2017); Larry Fenson et al., "Variability in Early Communicative Development," *Monographs of the Society for Research in Child Development* 59, no. 5 (1994); Campbell Leaper, Kristin J. Anderson, and Paul Sanders, "Moderators of Gender Effects on Parents' Talk to their Children: A Meta-Analysis," *Developmental Psychology* 34, no. 1 (1998): 3-27; Beatrice Whiting and Carolyn Price Edwards, "A Cross-Cultural Analysis of Sex-Differences in the Behavior of Children Ages 3 through 11," in *Childhood Socialization*, ed. G. Handle (Hawthorne: Aldine de Gruyter, 1988), 281-297.

12. Richard Gargiulo and Emily Bouck, *Special Education in Contemporary Society*, 6th ed. (Thousand Oaks: SAGE Publications, 2018).

13. Francis Wardle, *Approaches to Early Childhood and Elementary Education: Education in a Competitive and Globalizing World Series* (New York: Nova Science Publishers, 2009); Young Pai, Susan Adler, and Linda Shadiow, *Cultural Foundations of Education*, 4th ed. (Upper Saddle River: Pearson, 2006).

14. Ann Miles Gordon and Kathryn Williams Browne, *Beginnings and Beyond*, 10th ed. (Clifton Park: Delmar, 2016).

15. National Commission on the Excellence in Education, *A Nation at Risk: The Imperative for Educational Reform* (Washington D.C.: U.S. Printing Office, 1983).

16. Young Pai, Susan Adler, and Linda Shadiow, *Cultural Foundations of Education*, 4th ed. (Upper Saddle River: Pearson, 2006).

17. Head Start, Early Childhood Learning and Knowledge Center, "Getting Young Children and Their Families Ready for School and Ready for Life," *U.S. Department of Health and Human Services, Administration for Children & Families*, https://eclkc.ohs.acf.hhs.gov/ (accessed 2018).

18. Ibid.

19. Young Pai, Susan Adler, and Linda Shadiow, *Cultural Foundations of Education*, 4th ed. (Upper Saddle River: Pearson, 2006).

20. Young Pai, Susan Adler, and Linda Shadiow, *Cultural Foundations of Education*, 4th ed. (Upper Saddle River: Pearson, 2006); G. Jacobs, "School Readiness," in *The Sage Encyclopedia of Contemporary Early Childhood Education*, ed. Donna Couchenour and J. Kent Chrisman (Thousand Oaks: SAGE Publications, 2016), 1283-1286; Gayle Mindes, "Standards-based Curriculum and Assessment," in *The Sage Encyclopedia of Contemporary Early Childhood Education*, ed. Donna Couchenour and J. Kent Chrisman (Thousand Oaks: SAGE Publications, 2016), 1146-1149.

21. The Lanham Act funded several early childhood programs, such as the Kaiser Shipyards in Portland, Oregon, so that mothers could work in the factories.

22. Ana Page et al., "Advocacy: From Awareness to Action," *Exchange*, May/June 2016, 23-29.

23. Barbara Bowman, "Standards: At the Heart of Educational Equity," *Young Children* 61, no. 5 (2006): 42-48.

24. Sharon L. Kagan et al., "Alignment: A Missing Link in Early Childhood Transitions?," *Young Children* 61, no. 5 (September 2006): 26-32.

25. National Commission on the Excellence in Education, *A Nation at Risk: The Imperative for Educational Reform* (Washington D.C.: U.S. Printing Office, 1983).

26. See "Goals 2000" Figure One; Richard Gargiulo and Emily Bouck, *Special Education in Contemporary Society*, 6th ed. (Thousand Oaks: SAGE Publications, 2018).

27. U.S. Department of Education Office of Civil Rights, *Civil Rights Data Collection, Data Snapshot: Early Childhood Education, Brief #2*, http://ocrdata.ed.gov (accessed May 25, 2016).

28. Colorado Department of Education, *Colorado 2000: A Plan for Achieving the National Education Goals in Our Communities* (Denver: Colorado Department of Education, 1991).

29. Jacob Kang-Brown et al., *A Generation Later: What We've Learned about Zero Tolerance in Schools* (New York: Vera Institute of Justice, 2013).

30. American Psychological Association Zero Tolerance Task Force, "Are Zero Tolerance Policies Effective in the Schools?: An Evidentiary Review and Recommendations," *American Psychologist* 63, no. 9 (2008): 852-862.

31. Jacob Kang-Brown et al., *A Generation Later: What We've Learned about Zero Tolerance in Schools* (New York: Vera Institute of Justice, 2013).

32. American Psychological Association Zero Tolerance Task Force, "Are Zero Tolerance Policies Effective in the Schools?: An Evidentiary Review and Recommendations," *American Psychologist* 63, no. 9 (2008): 852-862.

33. Jacob Kang-Brown et al., *A Generation Later: What We've Learned about Zero Tolerance in Schools* (New York: Vera Institute of Justice, 2013).

34. Jacob Kang-Brown et al., *A Generation Later: What We've Learned about Zero Tolerance in Schools* (New York: Vera Institute of Justice, 2013); U.S. Department of Education Office of Civil Rights, *Civil Rights Data Collection, Data Snapshot: Early Childhood Education, Brief #2*, http://ocrdata.ed.gov (accessed May 25, 2016).

35. American Psychological Association Zero Tolerance Task Force, "Are Zero Tolerance Policies Effective in the Schools?: An Evidentiary Review and Recommendations," *American Psychologist* 63, no. 9 (2008): 852-862.

36. Dan Gartrell, *Education for a Civil Society: How Guidance Teaches Young Children Democratic Life Skills* (Washington D.C.: NAEYC, 2012).

37. Ann Schimke, "Suspended Countless Times as a Child, this Professor is Tackling Racial Disparities in Preschool Discipline," *Chalkbeat*, March 22, 2016, https://chalkbeat.org/posts/co/2016/03/22/suspended-countless-times-as-a-child-this-professor-is-tackling-racial-disparities-in-preschool-discipline/#.V8BQa-zWUK8B (accessed May 5, 2016); U.S. Department of Education Office of Civil Rights, *Civil Rights Data Collection, Data Snapshot: Early Childhood Education, Brief #2*, http://ocrdata.ed.gov (accessed May 25, 2016).

38. Richard Gargiulo and Emily Bouck, *Special Education in Contemporary Society*, 6th ed. (Thousand Oaks: SAGE Publications, 2018).

39. Ibid., 5.

40. Ibid.

41. Ibid.

42. U.S. Department of Education, "Provisions Related to Children With Disabilities Enrolled by Their Parents in Private Schools," *U.S. Department of Education*, March 2011, https://www2.ed.gov/admins/lead/speced/privateschools/idea.pdf.

43. Richard Gargiulo and Emily Bouck, *Special Education in Contemporary Society*, 6th ed. (Thousand Oaks: SAGE Publications, 2018).

44. Beth Harry and Janette Klingner, "Discarding the Deficit Model," *Educational Leadership* 64, no. 5 (2007): 16-21.

45. Richard Gargiulo and Emily Bouck, *Special Education in Contemporary Society*, 6th ed. (Thousand Oaks: SAGE Publications, 2018).

46. Ibid.

47. Beth Harry and Janette Klingner, "Discarding the Deficit Model," *Educational Leadership* 64, no. 5 (2007): 16-21.

48. Gayle Mindes, "Standards-based Curriculum and Assessment," in *The Sage Encyclopedia of Contemporary Early Childhood Education*, ed. Donna Couchenour and J. Kent Chrisman (Thousand Oaks: SAGE Publications, 2016), 1146-1149.

49. Richard Gargiulo and Emily Bouck, *Special Education in Contemporary Society*, 6th ed. (Thousand Oaks: SAGE Publications, 2018); Beth Harry and Janette Klingner, "Discarding the Deficit Model," *Educational Leadership* 64, no. 5 (2007): 16-21.

50. Richard Gargiulo and Emily Bouck, *Special Education in Contemporary Society*, 6th ed. (Thousand Oaks: SAGE Publications, 2018).

51. Richard Gargiulo and Emily Bouck, *Special Education in Contemporary Society*, 6th ed. (Thousand Oaks: SAGE Publications, 2018); G. Jacobs, "School Readiness," in *The Sage Encyclopedia of Contemporary Early Childhood Education*, ed. Donna Couchenour and J. Kent Chrisman (Thousand Oaks: SAGE Publications, 2016), 1283-1286; Gayle Mindes, "Standards-based Curriculum and Assessment," in *The Sage Encyclopedia of Contemporary Early Childhood Education*, ed. Donna Couchenour and J. Kent Chrisman (Thousand Oaks: SAGE Publications, 2016), 1146-1149.

52. National Resource Center on ADHD, "Data & Statistics," *CHADD: The National Resource on ADHD* http://www.chadd.org/understanding-adhd/about-adhd/data-and-statistics.aspx (accessed 2016); Janet Lerner and Beverley Johns, *Learning Disabilities and Related Mild Disabilities*, 12th ed. (Belmont: Wadsworth Publishing, 2011).

53. American Psychiatric Association, *Diagnostic and Statistical Manual of Mental Disorders*, 5th ed. (Arlington: American Psychiatric Publishing, 2013).

54. Ibid.

55. Candace Cortiella, *The State of Learning Disabilities* (New York: National Center for Learning Disabilities, 2011); Janet Lerner and Beverley Johns, *Learning Disabilities and Related Mild Disabilities*, 12th ed. (Belmont: Wadsworth Publishing, 2011).

56. Richard Gargiulo and Emily Bouck, *Special Education in Contemporary Society*, 6th ed. (Thousand Oaks: SAGE Publications, 2018), 209.

57. The Guardian, "Boys Trail Girls in Literacy and Numeracy When Starting School," *The Guardian*, https://www.theguardian.com/education/2015/oct/13/boys-trail-girls-literacy-numeracy-when-starting-school, (accessed May 25, 2016).

58. Lauren Lowry, "Fact or Fiction? The Top 10 Assumptions about Early Speech and Language Development," *The Hanen Centre*, 2012, http://www.hanen.org/SiteAssets/Articles---Printer-Friendly/Public-Articles/Fact-or-Fiction-.aspx.

Chapter 3: Young Boys are Unique

1. Sue Bredekamp and Carol Copple, eds., *Developmentally Appropriate Practice in Early Childhood Programs: Serving Children Birth through Age 8*, 3rd ed. (Washington, D.C.: NAEYC, 2009).

2. Ibid., 11.

3. Ibid.

4. Ann Miles Gordon and Kathryn Williams Browne, *Beginnings and Beyond*, 6th ed. (Clifton Park: Delmar, 2004).

5. Ibid.

6. Jeanne Ellis Ormrod, *Human Learning*, 7th ed. (Upper Saddle River: Pearson, 2011).

7. C. Eliason and L. Jenkins, *A Practical Guide to Early Childhood Curriculum*, 9th ed. (Upper Saddle River: Pearson, 2012).

8. Ibid.

9. Sue Bredekamp and Carol Copple, eds., *Developmentally Appropriate Practice in Early Childhood Programs: Serving Children Birth through Age 8*, 3rd ed. (Washington, D.C.: NAEYC, 2009), 12.

10. Richard Gargiulo and Emily Bouck, *Special Education in Contemporary Society*, 6th ed. (Thousand Oaks: SAGE Publications, 2018).

11. Casey Quinlan, "The Beginning of 'Two Cultures': By Preschool, Boys And Girls Are Already Segregated," *ThinkProgress*, February 29, 2016, https://thinkprogress.org/the-beginning-of-two-cultures-by-preschool-boys-and-girls-are-already-segregated-219b6b4e76d0/.

12. Anthony Pellegrini, "Rough and Tumble Play and Social Competence: Contemporaneous and Longitudinal Relations," in *The Future of Play Research*, ed. A. Pellegrini (Albany: University of New York Press, 1995), 107-126.

13. Myra Sadker and David Sadker, *Failing at Fairness: How Our Schools Cheat Girls* (New York: Scribner, 1994).

14. Lisa Zamosky, "How Boys and Girls Learn Differently," *WebMD*, March 25, 2011, https://www.webmd.com/parenting/features/how-boys-and-girls-learn-differently#2; Michael Gurian and Kathy Stevens, *The Minds of Boys* (San Francisco: Jossey-Bass, 2007).

15. Spencer A. Rathus, *Childhood: Voyages in Development*, 6th ed. (Belmont: Cengage Learning, 2017).

16. Kathleen Stassen Berger, *The Developing Person Through Childhood and Adolescence*, 9th ed. (New York: Worth Publishers, 2017).

17. Spencer A. Rathus, *Childhood: Voyages in Development*, 6th ed. (Belmont: Cengage Learning, 2017).

18. Alexander Thomas and Stella Chess, *Temperament and Development* (Oxford, England: Brunner/Mazel, 1977); Alexander Thomas and Stella Chess, "Temperament and Personality," in *Temperament in Childhood*, ed. G.A. Kohnstamm, J.E. Bates, and M.K. Rothbart (Oxford, England: John Wiley and Sons, 1989), 249-261; Sue Bredekamp and Carol Copple, eds., *Developmentally Appropriate Practice in Early Childhood Programs: Serving Children Birth through Age 8*, 3rd ed. (Washington, D.C.: NAEYC, 2009); Laura E. Berk and Adam Winsler, *Scaffolding Children's Learning: Vygotsky and Early Childhood Education* (Washington, D.C.: NAEYC, 1995).

19. Spencer A. Rathus, *Childhood: Voyages in Development*, 6th ed. (Belmont: Cengage Learning, 2017).

20. Richard Gargiulo and Emily Bouck, *Special Education in Contemporary Society*, 6th ed. (Thousand Oaks: SAGE Publications, 2018); Sonia Nieto and Patty Bode, *Affirming Diversity: The Sociopolitical Context of Multicultural Education* (Upper Saddle River: Pearson, 2012).

21. Kenneth Cushner, Averil McClelland, and Philip Safford, *Human Diversity in Education: An Intercultural Approach*, 8th ed. (New York: McGraw-Hill Education, 2015).

22. Ibid.

23. U.S. Bureau of Labor Statistics, *Highlights of Women's Earnings in 2013, BLM Report 1051* (Washington, D.C.: U.S. Printing Office, December 2014).

24. Kathleen Stassen Berger, *The Developing Person Through Childhood and Adolescence*, 9th ed. (New York: Worth Publishers, 2017).

25. Kathleen Stassen Berger, *The Developing Person Through Childhood and Adolescence*, 9th ed. (New York: Worth Publishers, 2017); Francis Wardle, *Collaboration with Families and Communities* (San Diego: Bridgepoint Education, 2013).

26. James Johnson, James Christie, and Francis Wardle, *Play, Development and Early Education* (Boston: Allyn & Bacon, 2005); T.G. Power, *Play and Exploration in Children and Animals* (Mahwah: Erlbaum, 2000); Brian Sutton-Smith, "Playfighting as Folkplay Amongst Preschool Children," *Western Folklore* 47, no. 3 (July 1988): 161-176.

27. Anthony Pellegrini, "Rough and Tumble Play and Social Competence: Contemporaneous and Longitudinal Relations," in *The Future of Play Research*, ed. A. Pellegrini (Albany: University of New York Press, 1995), 107-126.

28. Anthony Pellegrini, "A Longitudinal Study of Popular and Rejected Children's Rough and Tumble Play," *Early Education and Development* 2, no. 3 (1991): 205-213.

29. James Johnson, James Christie, and Francis Wardle, *Play, Development and Early Education* (Boston: Allyn & Bacon, 2005); Anthony Pellegrini, "Rough and Tumble Play and Social Competence: Contemporaneous and Longitudinal Relations," in *The Future of Play Research*, ed. A. Pellegrini (Albany: University of New York Press, 1995), 107-126.

30. Jennifer St. George, Richard Fletcher, and Kerrin Palazzi, "Comparing Fathers' Physical and Toy Play and Links to Child Behaviour: An Exploratory Study," *Infant and Child Development* 26, no. 1 (January/February 2017).

31. Spencer A. Rathus, *Childhood: Voyages in Development*, 6th ed. (Belmont: Cengage Learning, 2017).

32. Erik Erikson, *Childhood and Society*, 2d ed. (New York: Norton, 1963).

33. Ibid.

34. Jeanne Ellis Ormrod, *Human Learning*, 7th ed. (Upper Saddle River: Pearson, 2011).

35. Francis Wardle, *Introduction to Early Childhood Education: A Multidimensional Approach to Child-Centered Care and Learning* (Boston: Allyn & Bacon, 2003).

36. Jeanne Ellis Ormrod, *Human Learning*, 7th ed. (Upper Saddle River: Pearson, 2011).

37. Rebecca Isbell and Sonia Akiko Yoshizawa, *Nurturing Creativity: An Essential Mindset for Young Children's Learning* (Washington, D.C.: NAEYC, 2016).

38. Jean Piaget, *The Origins of Intelligence in Children*, trans. Margaret Cook (New York: International Universities Press, 1952).

39. Francis Wardle, "Play as Curriculum," *Earlychildhood NEWS*, http://www.earlychildhoodnews.com/earlychildhood/article_view.aspx?ArticleId=127 (accessed July 1, 2016).

40. Richard Louv, *Last Child in the Woods: Saving Our Children from Nature-Deficit Disorder* (Chapel Hill: Algonquin Books, 2006).

41. Francis Wardle, "Intergenerational Learning: Gardening with Grandpa," *Exchange*, 2016, 87-90.

42. Albert Bandura, *Social Foundations of Thought and Action: A Social Cognitive Theory* (Englewood Cliffs: Prentice Hall, 1986); Albert Bandura, *Self-Efficacy: The Exercise of Control* (New York: Freeman, 1997).

43. Jeanne Ellis Ormrod, *Human Learning*, 7th ed. (Upper Saddle River: Pearson, 2011).

44. Ibid.

45. Albert Bandura, "Human Agency in Social Cognitive Theory," *American Psychologist* 44, no. 9 (September 1989): 1175-1184.

46. Dale H. Schunk, "Self-efficacy and Achievement Behaviors," *Educational Psychology Review* 1, (1989): 173-208.

47. Ibid.

48. Ibid.

Chapter 4: The Solution: Theoretical Underpinnings

1. Sue Bredekamp and Carol Copple, eds., *Developmentally Appropriate Practice in Early Childhood Programs: Serving Children Birth through Age 8*, 3rd ed. (Washington, D.C.: NAEYC, 2009), 10-16.

2. Rima Shore, *Rethinking the Brain: New Insights into Early Development* (New York: Families and Work Institute, 1997).

3. Rima Shore, *Rethinking the Brain: New Insights into Early Development* (New York: Families and Work Institute, 1997); Eric Jensen, *Teaching with the Brain in Mind*, 2d ed. (Alexandria: ASCD, 2005).

4. Eric Jensen, *Teaching with the Brain in Mind*, 2d ed. (Alexandria: ASCD, 2005).

5. Barbara Clark, *Growing up Gifted: Developing the Potential of Children at School and at Home*, 8th ed. (Upper Saddle River: Pearson, 2013); Tiffeni Goesel, "Rediscovering Kindergarten: The Life and Legacy of Friedrich Froebel," *Community Playthings*, April 21, 2015, http://www.communityplaythings.com/resources/articles/2015/rediscovering-kindergarten.

6. David Elkind, *Giants in the Nursery: A Biographical History of Developmentally Appropriate Practice* (St. Paul: Redleaf Press, 2015).

7. Jean Piaget, *The Origins of Intelligence in Children*, trans. Margaret Cook (New York: International Universities Press, 1952).

8. Ibid.

9. Kathleen Stassen Berger, *The Developing Person Through Childhood and Adolescence*, 9th ed. (New York: Worth Publishers, 2017).

10. Jean Piaget, *The Origins of Intelligence in Children*, trans. Margaret Cook (New York: International Universities Press, 1952).

11. Laura E. Berk and Adam Winsler, *Scaffolding Children's Learning: Vygotsky and Early Childhood Education* (Washington, D.C.: NAEYC, 1995).

12. Ibid.

13. Howard Gardner, Frames of Mind: The Theory of Multiple Intelligences (New York: Basic Books, 1983).

14. Barbara Holmes, Jamel Gibson, and Dietrich Morrison-Danner, "Reducing Aggressive Male Behavior in Elementary School: Promising Practices," *Contemporary Issues in Education Research* 7, no. 4 (2014): 253-258; Cynthia Johnson and Shauna Gooliaff, "Teaching to Strengths: Engaging Young Boys in Learning," *Reclaiming Children and Youth* 21, no. 4 (2013): 28-31.

15. Howard Gardner, *Frames of Mind: The Theory of Multiple Intelligences* (New York: Basic Books, 1983).

16. Eric Jensen, *Teaching with the Brain in Mind*, 2d ed. (Alexandria: ASCD, 2005).

17. Barbara Holmes, Jamel Gibson, and Dietrich Morrison-Danner, "Reducing Aggressive Male Behavior in Elementary School: Promising Practices," *Contemporary Issues in Education Research* 7, no. 4 (2014): 253-258.

18. Francis Wardle, "Folk Dancing for Young Children," *Earlychildhood NEWS*, http://www.earlychildhoodnews.com/earlychildhood/article_view.aspx?ArticleId=301.

19. Barbara Holmes, Jamel Gibson, and Dietrich Morrison-Danner, "Reducing Aggressive Male Behavior in Elementary School: Promising Practices," *Contemporary Issues in Education Research* 7, no. 4 (2014): 253-258.

20. Francis Wardle, "Folk Dancing for Young Children," *Earlychildhood NEWS*, http://www.earlychildhoodnews.com/earlychildhood/article_view.aspx?ArticleId=301; Francis Wardle, *Introduction to Early Childhood Education: A Multidimensional Approach to Child-Centered Care and Learning* (Boston: Allyn & Bacon, 2003).

21. Douglas H. Clements and Julie Sarama, "Experimental Evaluation of the Effects of a Research-Based Preschool Mathematics Curriculum," *American Educational Research Journal* 45, no. 2 (2008): 443-494.

22. Barbara Holmes, Jamel Gibson, and Dietrich Morrison-Danner, "Reducing Aggressive Male Behavior in Elementary School: Promising Practices," *Contemporary Issues in Education Research* 7, no. 4 (2014): 253-258; Francis Wardle, "Lifelike Pedagogy: The Project Approach with a Brazilian Twist," *Young Children* 69, no. 2 (2014): 76-81.

23. Mary Jo Pollman, *Blocks and Beyond: Strengthening Early Math and Science Skills Through Spatial Learning* (Baltimore: Brookes, 2010).

24. Ibid.

25. Francis Wardle, *Introduction to Early Childhood Education: A Multidimensional Approach to Child-Centered Care and Learning* (Boston: Allyn & Bacon, 2003).

26. Howard Gardner, "Teaching for Multiple Intelligences," *Educational Leadership* 55, no. 1 (1997): 9-12; Kristen Nicholson-Nelson, *Developing Students' Multiple Intelligences* (New York: Scholastic Professional Books, 1998).

27. Katherine K. Delaney and Susan B. Neuman, "Literacy," in *The Sage Encyclopedia of Contemporary Early Childhood Education*, ed. Donna Couchenour and J. Kent Chrisman (Thousand Oaks: SAGE Publications, 2016), 813-817.

28. Barbara Holmes, Jamel Gibson, and Dietrich Morrison-Danner, "Reducing Aggressive Male Behavior in Elementary School: Promising Practices," *Contemporary Issues in Education Research* 7, no. 4 (2014): 253-258.

29. Howard Gardner, "Teaching for Multiple Intelligences," *Educational Leadership* 55, no. 1 (1997): 9-12; Kristen Nicholson-Nelson, *Developing Students' Multiple Intelligences* (New York: Scholastic Professional Books, 1998).

30. Barbara Clark, *Growing up Gifted: Developing the Potential of Children at School and at Home*, 8th ed. (Upper Saddle River: Pearson, 2013), 190.

31. Erik Erikson, *Childhood and Society*, 2d ed. (New York: Norton, 1963).

32. S.C. Crockenberg and E.M. Leerkes, "Parental Acceptance, Postpartum Depression, and Maternal Sensitivity: Mediating and Moderating Processes," *Journal of Family Psychology* 17, no. 1 (2003): 80-93.

33. David A. Wolfe, "Risk Factors for Child Abuse Perpetration," in *Violence Against Women and Children, Vol. 1: Mapping the Terrain*, ed. Jacquelyn White, Mary Koss, and Alan Kazdin (Washington D.C.: American Psychological Association, 2011), 31-53.

34. John Dewey, *Experience and Education* (New York: Touchstone, 1938).

35. Alfie Kohn, *The Schools Our Children Deserve: Moving Beyond Traditional Classrooms and "Standards"* (Boston: Houghton Mifflin, 1999).

Chapter 5: Policies and Program Practices

1. S. DeZutter and M.K. Kelly, "Social Competence Education in Early Childhood," in *Handbook of Research on the Education of Young Children*, 3rd ed., ed. N. Saracho and B. Spodeck (New York: Routledge, 2013), 206-218; Gayle Mindes, "Standards-based Curriculum and Assessment," in *The Sage Encyclopedia of Contemporary Early Childhood Education*, ed. Donna Couchenour and J. Kent Chrisman (Thousand Oaks: SAGE Publications, 2016), 1146-1149.

2. J. Johnson, "Play, Curriculum, and Pedagogy," in *The Sage Encyclopedia of Contemporary Early Childhood Education*, ed. Donna Couchenour and J. Kent Chrisman (Thousand Oaks: SAGE Publications, 2016), 1007-1010.

3. Ibid.

4. Claudio Sanchez, "What the U.S. Can Learn From Finland, Where School Starts at Age 7," *National Public Radio, Weekend Edition Sunday*, March 8, 2014, https://www.npr.org/2014/03/08/287255411/what-the-u-s-can-learn-from-finland-where-school-starts-at-age-7.

5. Ibid.

6. Ibid.

7. Timothy Walker, "The Joyful, Illiterate Kindergartners of Finland," *The Atlantic*, October 1, 2015, https://www.theatlantic.com/education/archive/2015/10/the-joyful-illiterate-kindergartners-of-finland/408325/.

8. Ibid.

9. Ibid.

10. Ibid.

11. Ibid.

12. Timothy Walker, "The Joyful, Illiterate Kindergartners of Finland," *The Atlantic*, October 1, 2015, https://www.theatlantic.com/education/archive/2015/10/the-joyful-illiterate-kindergartners-of-finland/408325/; Roger Neugebauer, "Early Childhood Programs Wordwide: More Alike than Different (An Interview with David Weikert)," in *Inside Child Care: Trend Report*, ed. Roger Neugebauer (Redmond: Exchange Press, 1999); Claudio Sanchez, "What the U.S. Can Learn From Finland, Where School Starts at Age 7," *National Public Radio, Weekend Edition Sunday*, March 8, 2014, https://www.npr.org/2014/03/08/287255411/what-the-u-s-can-learn-from-finland-where-school-starts-at-age-7.

13. John Dewey, *Experience and Education* (New York: Touchstone, 1938).

14. Joan P. Isenburg, "Arts Integration," in *The Sage Encyclopedia of Contemporary Early Childhood Education*, ed. Donna Couchenour and J. Kent Chrisman (Thousand Oaks: SAGE Publications, 2016), 82-84.

15. John Dewey, *Experience and Education* (New York: Touchstone, 1938).

16. Eric Jensen, *Teaching with the Brain in Mind*, 2d ed. (Alexandria: ASCD, 2005).

17. Spencer A. Rathus, *Childhood: Voyages in Development*, 6th ed. (Belmont: Cengage Learning, 2017).

18. Erik Erikson, *Childhood and Society*, 2d ed. (New York: Norton, 1963).

19. G. Jacobs, "School Readiness," in *The Sage Encyclopedia of Contemporary Early Childhood Education*, ed. Donna Couchenour and J. Kent Chrisman (Thousand Oaks: SAGE Publications, 2016), 1283.

20. Ibid.

21. Massachusetts Department of Education, *Early Childhood Program Standards for Three and Four Year Olds* (Malden: Massachusetts Department of Education, 2005).

22. G. Jacobs, "School Readiness," in *The Sage Encyclopedia of Contemporary Early Childhood Education*, ed. Donna Couchenour and J. Kent Chrisman (Thousand Oaks: SAGE Publications, 2016), 1283.

23. Francis Wardle, *Approaches to Early Childhood and Elementary Education* (New York: Nova Science Publishers, 2009).

24. Sue Bredekamp and Carol Copple, eds., *Developmentally Appropriate Practice in Early Childhood Programs: Serving Children Birth through Age 8*, 3rd ed. (Washington, D.C.: NAEYC, 2009).

25. Richard Gargiulo and Emily Bouck, *Special Education in Contemporary Society*, 6th ed. (Thousand Oaks: SAGE Publications, 2018).

26. Donna Ford, "Culturally Different Students in Special Education: Looking Backward to Move Forward," *Exceptional Children* 78, no. 4 (2012): 391-405; Richard Gargiulo and Emily Bouck, *Special Education in Contemporary Society*, 6th ed. (Thousand Oaks: SAGE Publications, 2018); Beth Harry and Janette Klingner, *Why are So Many Minority Students in Special Education?* (New York: Teachers College Press, 2006); Beth Harry and Janette Klingner, "Discarding the Deficit Model," *Educational Leadership* 64, no. 5 (2007): 16-21.

27. National Center for Education Statistics (NCES), *Digest of Educational Statistics, 2009* (Washington D.C.: U.S. Department of Education, 2011); Beth Harry and Janette Klingner, *Why are So Many Minority Students in Special Education?* (New York: Teachers College Press, 2006); Beth Harry and Janette Klingner, "Discarding the Deficit Model," *Educational Leadership* 64, no. 5 (2007): 16-21.

28. Richard Gargiulo and Emily Bouck, *Special Education in Contemporary Society*, 6th ed. (Thousand Oaks: SAGE Publications, 2018).

29. Ibid.

30. Ibid.

31. Francis Wardle, "How Children Build Images of Themselves," *Exchange*, July 1995, 44-47.

32. Joshua Bleiberg and Darrell M. West, "Special Education: The Forgotten Issue in No Child Left Behind Reform," *Brookings*, June 18, 2013, https://www.brookings.edu/blog/up-front/2013/06/18/special-education-the-forgotten-issue-in-no-child-left-behind-reform/.

33. Jacob Kang-Brown et al., *A Generation Later: What We've Learned about Zero Tolerance in Schools* (New York: Vera Institute of Justice, 2013).

34. Ibid.

35. Ibid.

36. Ibid.

37. Spencer A. Rathus, *Childhood: Voyages in Development*, 6th ed. (Belmont: Cengage Learning, 2017).

38. Dan Gartrell, *Education for a Civil Society: How Guidance Teaches Young Children Democratic Life Skills* (Washington D.C.: NAEYC, 2012).

39. Jacob Kang-Brown et al., *A Generation Later: What We've Learned about Zero Tolerance in Schools* (New York: Vera Institute of Justice, 2013).

Chapter 6: Curricular Approaches

1. Jeremy P. Meyer, "Nearly One in Three Colo. Graduates Needs Remedial Courses in College, Study Finds," *The Denver Post*, May 6, 2016, https://www.denverpost.com/2010/02/08/nearly-one-in-three-colo-graduates-needs-remedial-courses-in-college-study-finds/.

2. Jerome Bruner, *The Process of Education* (Cambridge: Harvard University Press, 1960); Peter Oliva, *Developing the Curriculum*, 5th ed. (Boston: Longman Publishers, 2001).

3. Sue Bredekamp and Carol Copple, eds., *Developmentally Appropriate Practice in Early Childhood Programs: Serving Children Birth through Age 8*, 3rd ed. (Washington, D.C.: NAEYC, 2009), 10-16.

4. Head Start, Early Childhood Learning and Knowledge Center, "Getting Young Children and Their Families Ready for School and Ready for Life," *U.S. Department of Health and Human Services, Administration for Children & Families*, https://eclkc.ohs.acf.hhs.gov/ (accessed 2018).

5. James Johnson, James Christie, and Francis Wardle, *Play, Development and Early Education* (Boston: Allyn & Bacon, 2005); Olga S. Jarrett, "Recess," in *The Sage Encyclopedia of Contemporary Early Childhood Education*, ed. Donna Couchenour and J. Kent Chrisman (Thousand Oaks: SAGE Publications, 2016), 1146-1149.

6. Peter Oliva, *Developing the Curriculum*, 5th ed. (Boston: Longman Publishers, 2001).

7. John Wiles and Joseph Bondi, *Curriculum Development: A Guide to Practice*, 9th ed. (Upper Saddle River: Pearson, 2015).

8. Elizabeth Jones and John Nimmo, *The Emergent Curriculum* (Washington, D.C.: NAEYC, 1994); Elizabeth Jones, "The Emergence of Emergent Curriculum," *YC Young Children* 67, no. 2 (March 2012): 66-68.

9. Elizabeth Jones, "The Emergence of Emergent Curriculum," *YC Young Children* 67, no. 2 (March 2012): 66-68.

10. Elizabeth Jones and John Nimmo, *The Emergent Curriculum* (Washington, D.C.: NAEYC, 1994); Elizabeth Jones, "The Emergence of Emergent Curriculum," *YC Young Children* 67, no. 2 (March 2012): 66-68.

11. Elizabeth Jones and John Nimmo, *The Emergent Curriculum* (Washington, D.C.: NAEYC, 1994), 11.

12. Elizabeth Jones, "The Emergence of Emergent Curriculum," *YC Young Children* 67, no. 2 (March 2012): 66-68.

13. Laura E. Berk and Adam Winsler, *Scaffolding Children's Learning: Vygotsky and Early Childhood Education* (Washington, D.C.: NAEYC, 1995).

14. Judy Harris Helms and Lillian Katz, *Young Investigators: The Project Approach in the Early Years*, 2d ed. (New York: Teachers College Press, 2010).

15. Beau Fly Jones, et al., *Designing Learning and Technology for Educational Reform* (Oak Brook: North Central Regional Educational Laboratory, 1994).

16. Sylvia Chard, "Project Approach," in *The Sage Encyclopedia of Contemporary Early Childhood Education*, ed. Donna Couchenour and J. Kent Chrisman (Los Angeles: SAGE Publications, 2016), 1108-1111.

17. Ibid.

18. Francis Wardle, *A Shropshire Lad: The Early Life of a Boy in the Wheathill Bruderhof* (Denver: unpublished, 2014).

19. Marcelo Rodrigues, *Lifelike Pedagogy*, trans. A.C. Morgan and N. Morgan (São Paulo, Brazil: Escola do Max Editora, 2010).

20. Ibid., 123.

21. Ibid.

22. Francis Wardle, *A Shropshire Lad: The Early Life of a Boy in the Wheathill Bruderhof* (Denver: unpublished, 2014).

23. Erik Erikson, *Childhood and Society*, 2d ed. (New York: Norton, 1963).

24. Ibid.

25. Jean Piaget, *The Origins of Intelligence in Children*, trans. Margaret Cook (New York: International Universities Press, 1952); John Dewey, *Experience and Education* (New York: Touchstone, 1938); Joseph McVicker Hunt, *Intelligence and Experience* (Oxford, England: Ronald, 1961); John H. Flavell, *The Developmental Psychology of Jean Piaget* (Princeton: D. Van Nostrand, 1963); Erik Erikson, *Childhood and Society*, 2d ed. (New York: Norton, 1963); Lawrence Kohlberg, "Stages of Moral Development as a Basis for Moral Education," in *Moral Education: Interdisciplinary Approaches*, ed. C.M Beck, B.S. Crittenden, and E.V. Sullivan (Toronto, Canada: University of Toronto Press, 1971), 23-92.

26. Mary Hohmann and David P. Weikart, *Educating Young Children: Active Learning Practices for Preschool and Child Care Programs*, 2d ed. (Ypsilanti: HighScope Press, 2002), 297.

27. HighScope Educational Research Foundation, "Preschool," *HighScope*, https://highscope.org/preschool (accessed 2018).

28. Mary Hohmann and David P. Weikart, *Educating Young Children: Active Learning Practices for Preschool and Child Care Programs*, 2d ed. (Ypsilanti: HighScope Press, 2002).

29. Central Advisory Council for Education (England), *The Plowden Report: Children and their Primary Schools, Vol. 1 and 2* (London: Her Majesty's Stationery Office, 1967).

30. Joseph Featherstone, "The Primary School Revolution in Britain," *The New Republic*, August 10, September 2, and September 9, 1967; Francis Wardle, *Introduction to Early Childhood Education: A Multidimensional Approach to Child-Centered Care and Learning* (Boston: Allyn & Bacon, 2003).

31. Joseph Featherstone, "The Primary School Revolution in Britain," *The New Republic*, August 10, September 2, and September 9, 1967.

32. Francis Wardle, *Approaches to Early Childhood and Elementary Education: Education in a Competitive and Globalizing World Series* (New York: Nova Science Publishers, 2009).

33. Ibid.

Chapter 7: Aspects of a Classroom

1. Francis Wardle, "Are We Short Changing Boys?," *Exchange*, May/June 1991, 48-51.

2. James Johnson, James Christie, and Francis Wardle, *Play, Development and Early Education* (Boston: Allyn & Bacon, 2005).

3. Ibid.

4. Elizabeth Prescott, "The Physical Environment: A Powerful Regulator of Experience," *Exchange*, November/December 1994, 9-15.

5. Francis Wardle, "Play as Curriculum," *Earlychildhood NEWS*, http://www.earlychildhoodnews.com/earlychildhood/article_view.aspx?ArticleId=127, (accessed July 1, 2016).

6. Mary Hohmann and David P. Weikart, *Educating Young Children: Active Learning Practices for Preschool and Child Care Programs*, 2d ed. (Ypsilanti: HighScope Press, 2002), 297.

7. D.F. Gullo, "Kindergarten Environments," in *The Sage Encyclopedia of Contemporary Early Childhood Education*, ed. Donna Couchenour and J. Kent Chrisman (Los Angeles: SAGE Publications, 2016), 786-789.

8. Ann. S. Epstein, *The Intentional Teacher: Choosing the Best Strategies for Young Children's Learning* (Washington D.C.: NAEYC, 2007).

9. Sandra Duncan, Jody Martin, and Rebecca Kreth, *Rethinking the Classroom Landscape: Creating Environments that Connect Young Children, Families, and Communities* (Lewisville: Gryphon House, 2016).

10. Marilou Hyson, "Approaches to Learning," in *The Sage Encyclopedia of Contemporary Early Childhood Education*, ed. Donna Couchenour and J. Kent Chrisman (Los Angeles: SAGE Publications, 2016), 73-77.

11. Ibid.

12. Jeanne Ellis Ormrod, *Human Learning*, 7th ed. (Upper Saddle River: Pearson, 2011).

13. Ibid.

14. Saul McLeod, "Bruner," *Simply Psychology*, 2008, https://www.simplypsychology.org/bruner.html (accessed July 1, 2016).

15. Walter Isaacson, *Einstein: His Life and Universe* (New York: Simon & Schuster, 2007).

16. J. Q. Chen, "Multiple Intelligences," in *The Sage Encyclopedia of Contemporary Early Childhood Education*, ed. Donna Couchenour and J. Kent Chrisman (Los Angeles: SAGE Publications, 2016), 890-891.

17. Ibid.

18. Laura E. Berk and Adam Winsler, *Scaffolding Children's Learning: Vygotsky and Early Childhood Education* (Washington, D.C.: NAEYC, 1995), 171.

19. Ibid.

20. Barbara Rogoff, *Apprenticeship in Thinking: Cognitive Development in Social Context* (New York: Oxford University Press, 1990).

21. Laura E. Berk and Adam Winsler, *Scaffolding Children's Learning: Vygotsky and Early Childhood Education* (Washington, D.C.: NAEYC, 1995).

22. Ibid.

23. National Council of Teachers of Mathematics, *Principles and Standards for School Mathematics* (Reston: National Council of Teachers of Mathematics, 2000).

24. Danielle B. Davis and Dale C. Farran, "Positive Early Math Experiences for African American Boys: Nurturing the Next Generation of STEM Majors," *Young Children* 73, no. 2 (May 2018).

25. Sue Bredekamp and Carol Copple, eds., *Developmentally Appropriate Practice in Early Childhood Programs: Serving Children Birth through Age 8*, 3rd ed. (Washington, D.C.: NAEYC, 2009).

26. Jeanne Ellis Ormrod, *Human Learning*, 7th ed. (Upper Saddle River: Pearson, 2011).

27. Ibid.

28. Ibid.

29. Walter S. Gilliam, "Pre-Kindergartners Left Behind: Expulsion Rates in State Pre-kindergarten Programs," *Foundation for Child Development*, May 4, 2005, https://www.fcd-us.org/assets/2016/04/ExpulsionCompleteReport.pdf.

30. Jeanne Ellis Ormrod, *Human Learning*, 7th ed. (Upper Saddle River: Pearson, 2011).

31. Sue Bredekamp and Carol Copple, eds., *Developmentally Appropriate Practice in Early Childhood Programs: Serving Children Birth through Age 8*, 3rd ed. (Washington, D.C.: NAEYC, 2009).

32. Dan Gartrell, *Education for a Civil Society: How Guidance Teaches Young Children Democratic Life Skills* (Washington D.C.: NAEYC, 2012).

33. Margaret King, "Guidance with Boys in Early Childhood Classrooms," in *The Power of Guidance: Teaching Social-Emotional Skills in Early Childhood Classrooms*, ed. Dan Gartrell (Washington D.C.: NAEYC, 2004), 106-124.

34. Julee J. Newberger, "New Brain Development Research: A Wonderful Window of Opportunity to Build Public Support for Early Childhood Education!," *Young Children* 52, no. 4 (1997): 4-9.

35. Dan Gartrell, *Education for a Civil Society: How Guidance Teaches Young Children Democratic Life Skills* (Washington D.C.: NAEYC, 2012).

36. Alfie Kohn, *Beyond Discipline: From Compliance to Community*, 2nd ed. (Alexandria: ASCD, 2006).

37. Jeanne Ellis Ormrod, *Human Learning*, 7th ed. (Upper Saddle River: Pearson, 2011).

38. Erik Erikson, *Childhood and Society*, 2d ed. (New York: Norton, 1963).

39. Dan Gartrell, *Education for a Civil Society: How Guidance Teaches Young Children Democratic Life Skills* (Washington D.C.: NAEYC, 2012).

40. Ibid.

41. Ibid.

42. Walter S. Gilliam, "Pre-Kindergartners Left Behind: Expulsion Rates in State Pre-kindergarten Programs," *Foundation for Child Development*, May 4, 2005, https://www.fcd-us.org/assets/2016/04/ExpulsionCompleteReport.pdf.

43. Richard Gargiulo and Emily Bouck, *Special Education in Contemporary Society*, 6th ed. (Thousand Oaks: SAGE Publications, 2018).

44. Ibid.

45. Spencer A. Rathus, *Childhood: Voyages in Development*, 6th ed. (Belmont: Cengage Learning, 2017).

46. Linda Garris Christian, "Understanding Families: Applying Family Systems Theory to Early Childhood Practice," *Young Children* 61, no. 1 (2006): 12-20.

47. Francis Wardle, "Twice Exceptional Students," *Exchange*, 2017, 26-30.

48. Spencer A. Rathus, *Childhood: Voyages in Development*, 6th ed. (Belmont: Cengage Learning, 2017).

49. Jeanne Ellis Ormrod, *Human Learning*, 7th ed. (Upper Saddle River: Pearson, 2011).

Chapter 8: Play in the Outdoors

1. James Johnson, James Christie, and Francis Wardle, *Play, Development and Early Education* (Boston: Allyn & Bacon, 2005).

2. J. Johnson, "Development of Play" in *The Sage Encyclopedia of Contemporary Early Childhood Education*, ed. Donna Couchenour and J. Kent Chrisman (Los Angeles: SAGE Reference, 2016), 1011-1013.

3. James Johnson, James Christie, and Francis Wardle, *Play, Development and Early Education* (Boston: Allyn & Bacon, 2005).

4. Nancy King, "Work and Play in the Classroom," *Social Education* 46, no. 2 (1982): 110-113.

5. James Johnson, James Christie, and Francis Wardle, *Play, Development and Early Education* (Boston: Allyn & Bacon, 2005).

6. Ibid.

7. Claire Cameron, *Hands On, Minds On: How Executive Function, Motor, and Spatial Skills Foster School Readiness* (New York: Teachers College Press, 2018).

8. James Johnson, James Christie, and Francis Wardle, *Play, Development and Early Education* (Boston: Allyn & Bacon, 2005).

9. U.S. Consumer Product Safety Commission, *Public Playground Safety Handbook* (Bethesda: U.S. Consumer Product Safety Commission, 2015); U.S. Access Board, *Americans With Disabilities Act (ADA) Accessibility Guidelines for Buildings and Facilities; Play Areas,* 36 CFR Part 1191, Washington D.C., November 20, 2000.

10. Richard Dattner, *Design for Play* (Cambridge: MIT Press, 1969).

11. Francis Wardle, "Intergenerational Learning: Gardening with Grandpa," *Exchange*, 2016, 87-90.

12. C.B. Hillman, Planting the Seeds: Life Lessons from the Garden," *Exchange*, 2016, 28-31.

13. H. Ihn, "Analysis of Preschool Children's Equipment Choices and Play Behaviors in Outdoor Play," *Early Childhood News* 10, no. 4 (1998): 20-25.

14. Francis Wardle, "Supporting Constructive Play in the Wild: Guidelines for Learning Outside," *Exchange*, July/August 2000, 26-29.

15. Urie Bronfenbrenner, *The Ecology of Human Development: Experiments by Nature and Design* (Cambridge: Harvard University Press, 1979); Urie Bronfenbrenner, "Developmental Ecology through Space and Time: A Future Perspective," in *Examining Lives in Context: Perspectives on the Ecology of Human Development*, ed. P. Moen, G.H. Elder, Jr., and K. Luscher (Washington D.C.: American Psychological Association, 1995), 619-647.

16. Jody Martin, *Preschool Health and Safety Matters* (Silver Spring: Gryphon House, 2011).

17. C.B. Hillman, Planting the Seeds: Life Lessons from the Garden," *Exchange*, 2016, 28-31; Rusty Keeler, "Marvelous Mud: Outdoor Environments," *Exchange*, March/April 2011, 78-79; Richard Louv, *Last Child in the Woods: Saving Our Children from Nature-Deficit Disorder* (Chapel Hill: Algonquin Books, 2006).

Chapter 9: Men in the Lives of Young Children

1. Francis Wardle, "Are We Short Changing Boys?," *Exchange*, May/June 1991, 48-51.

2. Francis Wardle, *A Shropshire Lad: The Early Life of a Boy in the Wheathill Bruderhof* (Denver: unpublished, 2014).

3. Kathleen Stassen Berger, *The Developing Person Through Childhood and Adolescence*, 9th ed. (New York: Worth Publishers, 2017).

4. Ibid.

5. Ibid.

6. Bureau of Labor Statistics, U.S. Department of Labor, *Occupational Outlook Handbook: Childcare Workers*, https://www.bls.gov/ooh/personal-care-and-service/childcare-workers.htm (accessed August 2, 2018); *Occupational Outlook Handbook: Preschool and Childcare Center Directors*, https://www.bls.gov/ooh/management/preschool-and-childcare-center-directors.htm (accessed August 5, 2018); *Occupational Outlook Handbook: Kindergarten and Elementary School Teachers*, https://www.bls.gov/ooh/education-training-and-library/kindergarten-and-elementary-school-teachers.htm (accessed August 20, 2018).

7. Seth Spaulding and Ranjan Chaudhuri, "UNESCO's World Education Report: Its Evolution, Strengths, and Possible Futures," *International Journal of Educational Development* 19, no. 1 (1999): 53-63.

8. Daniel Castner, "It's a Man's Field Too: Men as Caregivers," in *Go Where You Belong: Male Teachers as Cultural Workers in the Lives of Children, Families, and Communities*, ed. Lemuel W. Watson and C. Sheldon Woods (Rotterdam, Netherlands: Sense Publishers, 2011), 55-62.

9. Francis Wardle, "Men in Early Childhood are not Appreciated," in *Go Where You Belong: Male Teachers as Cultural Workers in the Lives of Children, Families, and Communities*, ed. Lemuel W. Watson and C. Sheldon Woods (Rotterdam, Netherlands: Sense Publishers, 2011), 67-71.

10. Jay Fagan and Glen Palm, *Fathers and Early Childhood Programs* (Clifton Park: Delmar Learning, 2004).

11. Robert Michael Capuozzo, "Calling my Maleness into Question," in *Go Where You Belong: Male Teachers as Cultural Workers in the Lives of Children, Families, and Communities*, ed. Lemuel W. Watson and C. Sheldon Woods (Rotterdam, Netherlands: Sense Publishers, 2011), 107-112.

12. Richard Gargiulo and Emily Bouck, *Special Education in Contemporary Society*, 6th ed. (Thousand Oaks: SAGE Publications, 2018); Howard Kirschenbaum, "From Public Relations to Partnerships: A Changing Paradigm in School, Family, and Community Relations," *George Washington University, The Communitarian Network*, https://www2.gwu.edu/~ccps/pop_schl.html.

13. Richard Gargiulo and Emily Bouck, *Special Education in Contemporary Society*, 6th ed. (Thousand Oaks: SAGE Publications, 2018).

14. Richard Gargiulo and Emily Bouck, *Special Education in Contemporary Society*, 6th ed. (Thousand Oaks: SAGE Publications, 2018); Howard Kirschenbaum, "From Public Relations to Partnerships: A Changing Paradigm in School, Family, and Community Relations," *George Washington University, The Communitarian Network*, https://www2.gwu.edu/~ccps/pop_schl.html.

15. Jay Fagan and Glen Palm, *Fathers and Early Childhood Programs* (Clifton Park: Delmar Learning, 2004).

16. Ibid.

17. Jay Fagan and Glen Palm, *Fathers and Early Childhood Programs* (Clifton Park: Delmar Learning, 2004); Lemuel W. Watson, "Introduction: Addressing the Culture of Gender Bias," in *Go Where You Belong: Male Teachers as Cultural Workers in the Lives of Children, Families, and Communities*, ed. Lemuel W. Watson and C. Sheldon Woods (Rotterdam, Netherlands: Sense Publishers, 2011), xv-xviii.

18. Ibid.

19. Jay Fagan and Glen Palm, *Fathers and Early Childhood Programs* (Clifton Park: Delmar Learning, 2004).

20. N. Tift, "Is Your Organization Father Friendly? An Introduction to the Agency Audit," *Workshop, Fourth Annual National Summit on Fatherhood*, Washington D.C., June 2001.

21. Jay Fagan and Glen Palm, *Fathers and Early Childhood Programs* (Clifton Park: Delmar Learning, 2004).

22. Francis Wardle, *Collaboration with Families and Communities* (San Diego: Bridgepoint Education, 2013).

23. Diana Baumrind, "Current Patterns of Parental Authority," *Developmental Psychology* 4, no. 1 (January 1971): 1-103.

24. Eugenia Hepworth Berger, "Don't Shut Fathers Out," *Early Childhood Education Journal* 26, no. 1 (1998): 57-61.

25. Jay Fagan and Glen Palm, *Fathers and Early Childhood Programs* (Clifton Park: Delmar Learning, 2004).

26. Ibid.

27. Brent McBride and Thomas Rane, "Father Male Involvement in Early Childhood Programs: Training Staff to Work with Men," in *Clinical and Educational Interventions with Fathers*, ed. Jay Fagan and Alan Hawkins (New York: Haworth Clinical Practice Press, 2001), 171-190.

28. Jay Fagan and Glen Palm, *Fathers and Early Childhood Programs* (Clifton Park: Delmar Learning, 2004).

29. Lemuel W. Watson and C. Sheldon Woods, eds. *Go Where You Belong: Male Teachers as Cultural Workers in the Lives of Children, Families, and Communities* (Rotterdam, Netherlands: Sense Publishers, 2011).

30. Joyce Epstein, *School, Family, and Community Partnerships: Preparing Educators and Empowering Schools* (Boulder: Westview Press, 2010).

31. Ibid.

32. U.S. Department of Health and Human Services and U.S. Department of Education, *High-Quality Early Learning Settings Depend on a High-Quality Workforce: Low Compensation Undermines Quality*, June 2016, https://www2.ed.gov/about/inits/ed/earlylearning/files/ece-low-compensation-undermines-quality-report-2016.pdf.

33. Francis Wardle, *Approaches to Early Childhood and Elementary Education: Education in a Competitive and Globalizing World Series* (New York: Nova Science Publishers, 2009).

34. U.S. Department of Health and Human Services and U.S. Department of Education, *High-Quality Early Learning Settings Depend on a High-Quality Workforce: Low Compensation Undermines Quality*, June 2016, https://www2.ed.gov/about/inits/ed/earlylearning/files/ece-low-compensation-undermines-quality-report-2016.pdf.

35. Ibid.

36. Daniel Castner, "It's a Man's Field Too: Men as Caregivers," in *Go Where You Belong: Male Teachers as Cultural Workers in the Lives of Children, Families, and Communities*, ed. Lemuel W. Watson and C. Sheldon Woods (Rotterdam, Netherlands: Sense Publishers, 2011), 55-62.

37. Francis Wardle, *Approaches to Early Childhood and Elementary Education: Education in a Competitive and Globalizing World Series* (New York: Nova Science Publishers, 2009).

38. Juliana Menasce Horowitz, et al., "Americans Widely Support Paid Family and Medical Leave, but Differ Over Specific Policies," *Pew Research Center, Social & Demographic Trends*, March 23, 2017, http://www.pewsocialtrends.org/2017/03/23/gender-and-caregiving/.

39. http://www.menteach.org/.

Bibliography

American Psychiatric Association. *Diagnostic and Statistical Manual of Mental Disorders*. 5th ed. Arlington: American Psychiatric Publishing, 2013.

American Psychological Association Zero Tolerance Task Force. "Are Zero Tolerance Policies Effective in the Schools?: An Evidentiary Review and Recommendations." *American Psychologist* 63, no. 9 (2008): 852-862.

Bambara, Linda, Rachel Janney, and Martha Snell. *Behavior Support*. 3rd ed. Baltimore: Brookes Publishing, 2015.

Bandura, Albert. "Human Agency in Social Cognitive Theory." *American Psychologist* 44, no. 9 (September 1989): 1175-1184.

———. "Self-Efficacy Mechanism in Human Agency." *American Psychologist* 37, no. 2 (1982): 122-147.

———. *Self-Efficacy: The Exercise of Control*. New York: Freeman, 1997.

———. *Social Foundations of Thought and Action: A Social Cognitive Theory*. Englewood Cliffs: Prentice Hall, 1986.

———. "Toward a Psychology of Human Agency." *Perspectives on Psychological Science* 1, no. 2 (2006): 164-180.

Baumrind, Diana. "Current Patterns of Parental Authority." *Developmental Psychology* 4, no. 1 (January 1971): 1-103.

Berger, Eugenia Hepworth. "Don't Shut Fathers Out." *Early Childhood Education Journal* 26, no. 1 (1998): 57-61.

Berger, Kathleen Stassen. *The Developing Person Through Childhood and Adolescence*. 9th ed. New York: Worth Publishers, 2017.

Berk, Laura E. *Child Development*. 9th ed. Upper Saddle River: Pearson, 2017.

———, and Adam Winsler. *Scaffolding Children's Learning: Vygotsky and Early Childhood Education*. Washington, D.C.: NAEYC, 1995.

Bleiberg, Joshua, and Darrell M. West. "Special Education: The Forgotten Issue in No Child Left Behind Reform." *Brookings*, June 18, 2013. https://www.brookings.edu/blog/up-front/2013/06/18/special-education-the-forgotten-issue-in-no-child-left-behind-reform/.

Bowman, Barbara. "Standards: At the Heart of Educational Equity." *Young Children* 61, no. 5 (2006): 42-48.

Bredekamp, Sue, and Carol Copple, eds. *Developmentally Appropriate Practice in Early Childhood Programs.* Washington, D.C.: NAEYC, 1987.

Bronfenbrenner, Urie. "Developmental Ecology through Space and Time: A Future Perspective." In *Examining Lives in Context: Perspectives on the Ecology of Human Development*, edited by P. Moen, G.H. Elder, Jr., and K. Luscher, 619-647. Washington D.C.: American Psychological Association, 1995.

_____. *The Ecology of Human Development: Experiments by Nature and Design.* Cambridge: Harvard University Press, 1979.

Bruner, Jerome. *The Process of Education.* Cambridge: Harvard University Press, 1960.

Cameron, Claire. *Hands On, Minds On: How Executive Function, Motor, and Spatial Skills Foster School Readiness.* New York: Teachers College Press, 2018.

Capuozzo, Robert Michael. "Calling my Maleness into Question." In *Go Where You Belong: Male Teachers as Cultural Workers in the Lives of Children, Families, and Communities*, edited by Lemuel W. Watson and C. Sheldon Woods, 107-112. Rotterdam, Netherlands: Sense Publishers, 2011.

Castner, Daniel. "It's a Man's Field Too: Men as Caregivers." In *Go Where You Belong: Male Teachers as Cultural Workers in the Lives of Children, Families, and Communities*, edited by Lemuel W. Watson and C. Sheldon Woods, 55-62. Rotterdam, Netherlands: Sense Publishers, 2011.

Central Advisory Council for Education (England). *The Plowden Report: Children and their Primary Schools, Vol. 1 and 2.* London: Her Majesty's Stationery Office, 1967.

Chard, Sylvia. "Project Approach." In *The Sage Encyclopedia of Contemporary Early Childhood Education*, edited by Donna Couchenour and J. Kent Chrisman, 1108-1111. Los Angeles: SAGE Publications, 2016.

Chen, J. Q. "Multiple Intelligences." In *The Sage Encyclopedia of Contemporary Early Childhood Education*, edited by Donna Couchenour and J. Kent Chrisman, 890-891. Los Angeles: SAGE Publications, 2016.

Christian, Linda. "Understanding Families: Applying Family Systems Theory to Early Childhood Practice." *Young Children* 61, no. 1 (2006): 12-20.

Clark, Barbara. *Growing up Gifted: Developing the Potential of Children at School and at Home*. 8th ed. Upper Saddle River: Pearson, 2013.

Clements, Douglas H., and Julie Sarama. "Experimental Evaluation of the Effects of a Research-Based Preschool Mathematics Curriculum." *American Educational Research Journal* 45, no. 2 (2008): 443-494.

Colorado Department of Education. *Colorado 2000: A Plan for Achieving the National Education Goals in Our Communities*. Denver: Colorado Department of Education, 1991.

Cortiella, Candace. *The State of Learning Disabilities*. New York: National Center for Learning Disabilities, 2011.

Crockenberg, S.C., and E.M. Leerkes. "Parental Acceptance, Postpartum Depression, and Maternal Sensitivity: Mediating and Moderating Processes." *Journal of Family Psychology* 17, no. 1 (2003): 80-93.

Cushner, Kenneth, Averil McClelland, and Philip Safford. *Human Diversity in Education: An Intercultural Approach*. 8th ed. New York: McGraw-Hill Education, 2015.

Dattner, Richard. *Design for Play*. Cambridge: MIT Press, 1969.

Davis, Danielle B., and Dale C. Farran. "Positive Early Math Experiences for African American Boys: Nurturing the Next Generation of STEM Majors." *Young Children* 73, no. 2 (May 2018).

Delaney, Katherine, and Susan B. Neuman. "Literacy." In *The SAGE Encyclopedia of Contemporary Early Childhood Education*, edited by Donna Couchenour and J. Kent Chrisman, 813-817. Thousand Oaks: SAGE Publications, 2016.

Dewey, John. *Experience and Education*. New York: Touchstone, 1938.

DeZutter, S., and M.K. Kelly. "Social Competence Education in Early Childhood." In *Handbook of Research on the Education of Young Children*, 3rd ed., edited by N. Saracho and B. Spodeck, 206-218. New York: Routledge, 2013.

Duncan, Sandra, Jody Martin, and Rebecca Kreth. *Rethinking the Classroom Landscape: Creating Environments that Connect Young Children, Families, and Communities.* Lewisville: Gryphon House, 2016.

Edwards, Carolyn, Lella Gandini, and George Forman, eds. *The Hundred Languages of Children: The Reggio Emilia Approach to Early Childhood Education.* Greenwich: Ablex, 1993.

Eliason, C., and L. Jenkins. *A Practical Guide to Early Childhood Curriculum.* 9th ed. Upper Saddle River: Pearson, 2012.

Elkind, David. *Giants in the Nursery: A Biographical History of Developmentally Appropriate Practice.* St. Paul: Redleaf Press, 2015.

Epstein, Ann. S. *The Intentional Teacher: Choosing the Best Strategies for Young Children's Learning.* Washington D.C.: NAEYC, 2007.

Epstein, Joyce. *School, Family, and Community Partnerships: Preparing Educators and Empowering Schools.* Boulder: Westview Press, 2010.

Erikson, Erik. *Childhood and Society.* 2d ed. New York: Norton, 1963.

Fagan, Jay, and Glen Palm. *Fathers and Early Childhood Programs.* Clifton Park: Delmar Learning, 2004.

Featherstone, Joseph. "The Primary School Revolution in Britain." *The New Republic*, August 10, September 2, and September 9, 1967.

Fenson, Larry, P.S. Dale, J.S. Reznick, E. Bates, D.J. Thal, and S.J. Pethick. "Variability in Early Communicative Development." *Monographs of the Society for Research in Child Development* 59, no. 5 (1994).

Flavell, John H. *The Developmental Psychology of Jean Piaget.* Princeton: D. Van Nostrand, 1963.

Ford, Donna. "Culturally Different Students in Special Education: Looking Backward to Move Forward." *Exceptional Children* 78, no. 4 (2012): 391-405.

Froebel, Friedrich. *The Education of Man.* New York: A. Lovell & Company, 1885.

Gardener, Howard. *Frames of Mind: The Theory of Multiple Intelligences.* New York: Basic Books, 1983.

_____. "Teaching for Multiple Intelligences." *Educational Leadership* 55, no. 1 (1997): 9-12.

Gargiulo, Richard, and Emily Bouck. *Special Education in Contemporary Society*. 6th ed. Thousand Oaks: SAGE Publications, 2018.

Gartrell, Dan. *Education for a Civil Society: How Guidance Teaches Young Children Democratic Life Skills*. Washington D.C.: NAEYC, 2012.

Gilliam, Walter S. "Pre-Kindergartners Left Behind: Expulsion Rates in State Pre-kindergarten Programs." *Foundation for Child Development*, May 4, 2005. https://www.fcd-us.org/assets/2016/04/ExpulsionCompleteReport.pdf.

Goesel, Tiffeni. "Rediscovering Kindergarten: The Life and Legacy of Friedrich Froebel." *Community Playthings*, April 21, 2015. http://www.communityplaythings.com/resources/articles/2015/rediscovering-kindergarten.

Gordon, Ann Miles, and Kathryn Williams Browne. *Beginnings and Beyond*. 10th ed. Clifton Park: Delmar, 2016.

Greenberg, Polly. "Lucy Sprague Mitchell: A Major Missing Link Between Early Childhood Education in the 1980s and Progressive Education in the 1890s-1930s." *Young Children* 42, no. 5 (July 1987): 70-84.

The Guardian. "Boys Trail Girls in Literacy and Numeracy When Starting School." *The Guardian*. https://www.theguardian.com/education/2015/oct/13/boys-trail-girls-literacy-numeracy-when-starting-school (accessed May 25, 2016).

Gullo, D.F. "Kindergarten Environments." In *The Sage Encyclopedia of Contemporary Early Childhood Education*, edited by Donna Couchenour and J. Kent Chrisman, 786-789. Los Angeles: SAGE Publications, 2016.

Gurian, Michael, and Kathy Stevens. *The Minds of Boys*. San Francisco: Jossey-Bass, 2007.

Harry, Beth, and Janette Klingner. "Discarding the Deficit Model." *Educational Leadership* 64, no. 5 (2007): 16-21.

_____. *Why are So Many Minority Students in Special Education?* New York: Teachers College Press, 2006.

Head Start, Early Childhood Learning and Knowledge Center. "Getting Young Children and Their Families Ready for School and Ready for Life." *U.S. Department of Health and Human Services, Administration for Children & Families*. https://eclkc.ohs.acf.hhs.gov/ (accessed 2018).

Helms, Judy Harris, and Lillian Katz. *Young Investigators: The Project Approach in the Early Years*. 2d ed. New York: Teachers College Press, 2010.

HighScope Educational Research Foundation. "Preschool." *HighScope*. https://highscope.org/preschool (accessed 2018).

Hill, Nancy, and Stacie Craft. "Parent-School Involvement and School Performance: Mediated Pathways among Socioeconomically Comparable African American and Euro-American Families." *Journal of Educational Psychology* 95, no. 1 (March 2003): 74-83

Hillman, C.B. "Planting the Seeds: Life Lessons from the Garden." *Exchange*, 2016, 28-31.

Hohmann, Mary, and David P. Weikart. *Educating Young Children: Active Learning Practices for Preschool and Child Care Programs*. 2d ed. Ypsilanti: HighScope Press, 2002, 297.

Holmes, Barbara, Jamel Gibson, and Dietrich Morrison-Danner. "Reducing Aggressive Male Behavior in Elementary School: Promising Practices." *Contemporary Issues in Education Research* 7, no. 4 (2014): 253-258.

Horowitz, Juliana Menasce, Kim Parker, Nikki Graf, and Gretchen Livingston. "Americans Widely Support Paid Family and Medical Leave, but Differ Over Specific Policies." *Pew Research Center, Social & Demographic Trends*, March 23, 2017. http://www.pewsocialtrends.org/2017/03/23/gender-and-caregiving/.

Hunt, Joseph Mcvicker. *Intelligence and Experience*. Oxford, England: Ronald, 1961.

Hyson, Marilou. "Approaches to Learning." In *The Sage Encyclopedia of Contemporary Early Childhood Education*, edited by Donna Couchenour and J. Kent Chrisman, 73-77. Los Angeles: SAGE Publications, 2016.

Ihn, H. "Analysis of Preschool Children's Equipment Choices and Play Behaviors in Outdoor Play." *Early Childhood News* 10, no. 4 (1998): 20-25.

Isaacson, Walter. *Einstein: His Life and Universe*. New York: Simon & Schuster, 2007.

Isbell, Rebecca, and Sonia Akiko Yoshizawa. *Nuturing Creativity: An Essential Mindset for Young Children's Learning*. Washington, D.C.: NAEYC, 2016.

Isenburg, Joan P. "Arts Integration." In *The Sage Encyclopedia of Contemporary Early Childhood Education*, edited by Donna Couchenour and J. Kent Chrisman, 82-84. Thousand Oaks: SAGE Publications, 2016.

Jacobs, G. "School Readiness." In *The Sage Encyclopedia of Contemporary Early Childhood Education*, edited by Donna Couchenour and J. Kent Chrisman, 1283-1286. Thousand Oaks: SAGE Publications, 2016.

Jarrett, Olga S. "Recess." In *The Sage Encyclopedia of Contemporary Early Childhood Education*, edited by Donna Couchenour and J. Kent Chrisman, 1146-1149. Thousand Oaks: SAGE Publications, 2016.

Jensen, Eric. *Teaching with the Brain in Mind*. 2d ed. Alexandria: ASCD, 2005.

Johnson, Cynthia, and Shauna Gooliaff. "Teaching to Strengths: Engaging Young Boys in Learning." *Reclaiming Children and Youth* 21, no. 4 (2013): 28-31.

Johnson, J. "Play, Curriculum, and Pedagogy." In *The Sage Encyclopedia of Contemporary Early Childhood Education*, edited by Donna Couchenour and J. Kent Chrisman, 1007-1010. Thousand Oaks: SAGE Publications.

Johnson, James, James Christie, and Francis Wardle. *Play, Development and Early Education*. Boston: Allyn & Bacon, 2005.

Jones, Beau Fly, Gilbert Valdez, Jeri Nowakowski, and Claudette Rasmussen. *Designing Learning and Technology for Educational Reform*. Oak Brook: North Central Regional Educational Laboratory, 1994.

Jones, Elizabeth. "The Emergence of Emergent Curriculum." *YC Young Children* 67, no. 2 (March 2012): 66-68.

_____, and John Nimmo. *The Emergent Curriculum*. Washington, D.C.: NAEYC, 1994.

Kagan, Sharon L., Jude Carroll, James P. Comer, and Catherine Scott-Little. "Alignment: A Missing Link in Early Childhood Transitions?" *Young Children* 61, no. 5 (September 2006): 26-32.

Kang-Brown, Jacob, Jennifer Trone, Jennifer Fratello, and Tarika Daftary-Kapur. *A Generation Later: What We've Learned about Zero Tolerance in Schools*. New York: Vera Institute of Justice, 2013.

Keeler, Rusty. "Marvelous Mud: Outdoor Environments." *Exchange*, March/April 2011, 78-79.

King, Margaret. "Guidance with Boys in Early Childhood Classrooms." In *The Power of Guidance: Teaching Social-Emotional Skills in Early Childhood Classrooms*, edited by Dan Gartrell, 106-124. Washington D.C.: NAEYC, 2004.

King, Nancy. "Work and Play in the Classroom." *Social Education* 46, no. 2 (1982): 110-113.

Kirschenbaum, Howard. "From Public Relations to Partnerships: A Changing Paradigm in School, Family, and Community Relations." *George Washington University, The Communitarian Network*. https://www2.gwu.edu/~ccps/pop_schl.html.

Kohlberg, Lawrence. "Stages of Moral Development as a Basis for Moral Education." In *Moral Education: Interdisciplinary Approaches*, edited by C.M Beck, B.S. Crittenden, and E.V. Sullivan, 23-92. Toronto, Canada: University of Toronto Press, 1971.

Kohn, Alfie. *Beyond Discipline: From Compliance to Community*. 2d ed. Alexandria: ASCD, 2006.

———. *Punished by Rewards: The Trouble with Gold Stars, Incentive Plans, A's, Praise, and Other Bribes*. New York: Houghton Mifflin Harcourt, 1993.

———. *The Schools Our Children Deserve: Moving Beyond Traditional Classrooms and "Standards."* Boston: Houghton Mifflin, 1999.

Leaper, Campbell, Kristin J. Anderson, and Paul Sanders. "Moderators of Gender Effects on Parents' Talk to their Children: A Meta-Analysis." *Developmental Psychology* 34, no. 1 (1998): 3-27.

Lerner, Janet, and Beverley Johns. *Learning Disabilities and Related Mild Disabilities*. 12th ed. Belmont: Wadsworth Publishing, 2011.

Louv, Richard. *Last Child in the Woods: Saving Our Children from Nature-Deficit Disorder*. Chapel Hill: Algonquin Books, 2006.

Lowry, Lauren. "Fact or Fiction? The Top 10 Assumptions about Early Speech and Language Development." *The Hanen Centre*, 2012. http://www.hanen.org/SiteAssets/Articles---Printer-Friendly/Public-Articles/Fact-or-Fiction-.aspx.

Martin, Jody. *Preschool Health and Safety Matters*. Silver Spring: Gryphon House, 2011.

Massachusetts Department of Education. *Early Childhood Program Standards for Three and Four Year Olds.* Malden: Massachusetts Department of Education, 2005.

McBride, Brent, and Thomas Rane. "Father Male Involvement in Early Childhood Programs: Training Staff to Work with Men." In *Clinical and Educational Interventions with Fathers*, edited by Jay Fagan and Alan Hawkins, 171-190. New York: Haworth Clinical Practice Press, 2001.

McLeod, Saul. "Bruner." *Simply Psychology*, 2008. https://www.simplypsychology.org/bruner.html (assessed July 1, 2016).

Meyer, Jeremy P. "Nearly One in Three Colo. Graduates Needs Remedial Courses in College, Study Finds." *The Denver Post*, May 6, 2016. https://www.denverpost.com/2010/02/08/nearly-one-in-three-colo-graduates-needs-remedial-courses-in-college-study-finds/.

Mindes, Gayle. "Standards-based Curriculum and Assessment." In *The Sage Encyclopedia of Contemporary Early Childhood Education*, edited by Donna Couchenour and J. Kent Chrisman, 1146-1149. Thousand Oaks: SAGE Publications, 2016.

National Center for Education Statistics (NCES). *Digest of Educational Statistics, 2009.* Washington D.C.: U.S. Department of Education, 2011.

National Commission on the Excellence in Education. *A Nation at Risk: The Imperative for Educational Reform.* Washington D.C.: U.S. Printing Office, 1983.

National Council of Teachers of Mathematics. *Principles and Standards for School Mathematics.* Reston: National Council of Teachers of Mathematics, 2000.

National Resource Center on ADHD. "Data & Statistics." *CHADD: The National Resource on ADHD.* http://www.chadd.org/understanding-adhd/about-adhd/data-and-statistics.aspx (accessed 2016).

Neugebauer, Roger. "Early Childhood Programs Wordwide: More Alike than Different (An Interview with David Weikert)." In *Inside Child Care: Trend Report*, edited by Roger Neugebauer. Redmond: Exchange Press, 1999.

Newberger, Julee J. "New Brain Development Research: A Wonderful Window of Opportunity to Build Public Support for Early Childhood Education!" *Young Children* 52, no. 4 (1997): 4-9.

Nicholson-Nelson, Kristen. *Developing Students' Multiple Intelligences.* New York: Scholastic Professional Books, 1998.

Nieto, Sonia, and Patty Bode. *Affirming Diversity: The Sociopolitical Context of Multicultural Education*. Upper Saddle River: Pearson, 2012.

Oliva, Peter. *Developing the Curriculum*. 5th ed. Boston: Longman Publishers, 2001.

Ormrod, Jeanne Ellis. *Human Learning*. 7th ed. Upper Saddle River: Pearson, 2011.

Page, Ana, Monica Brinkerhoff, Mary Beth Salomone Testa, and Samantha Marshall. "Advocacy: From Awareness to Action." *Exchange*, May/June 2016, 23-29.

Pai, Young, Susan Adler, and Linda Shadiow. *Cultural Foundations of Education*. 4th ed. Upper Saddle River: Pearson, 2006.

Pellegrini, Anthony. "A Longitudinal Study of Popular and Rejected Children's Rough and Tumble Play." *Early Education and Development* 2, no. 3 (1991): 205-213.

———. "Rough and Tumble Play and Social Competence: Contemporaneous and Longitudinal Relations." In *The Future of Play Research*, edited by A. Pellegrini, 107-126. Albany: University of New York Press, 1995.

Piaget, Jean. *The Origins of Intelligence in Children*, translated by Margaret Cook. New York: International Universities Press, 1952.

Pollman, Mary Jo. *Blocks and Beyond: Strengthening Early Math and Science Skills Through Spatial Learning*. Baltimore: Brookes, 2010.

Power, T.G. *Play and Exploration in Children and Animals*. Mahwah: Erlbaum, 2000.

Prescott, Elizabeth. "The Physical Environment: A Powerful Regulator of Experience." *Exchange*, November/December 1994, 9-15.

Quinlan, Casey. "The Beginning of 'Two Cultures': By Preschool, Boys And Girls Are Already Segregated." *ThinkProgress*, February 29, 2016. https://thinkprogress.org/the-beginning-of-two-cultures-by-preschool-boys-and-girls-are-already-segregated-219b6b4e76d0/.

Rathus, Spencer A. *Childhood: Voyages in Development*. 6th ed. Belmont: Cengage Learning, 2017.

Rodrigues, Marcelo. *Lifelike Pedagogy*, translated by A.C. Morgan and N. Morgan. Sao Paulo, Brazil: Escola do Max Editora, 2010.

Rogoff, Barbara. *Apprenticeship in Thinking: Cognitive Development in Social Context.* New York: Oxford University Press, 1990.

Sadker, David, and Karen Zittleman. *Teachers, Schools, and Society: A Brief Introduction to Education.* 2d ed. New York: McGraw Hill, 2013.

Sanchez, Claudio. "What the U.S. Can Learn From Finland, Where School Starts at Age 7." *National Public Radio, Weekend Edition Sunday,* March 8, 2014. https://www.npr.org/2014/03/08/287255411/what-the-u-s-can-learn-from-finland-where-school-starts-at-age-7.

Scheuermann, Brenda, and Judy Hall. *Positive Behavioral Supports for the Classroom.* 3rd ed. Upper Saddle River: Pearson, 2016.

Schimke, Ann. "Suspended Countless Times as a Child, this Professor is Tackling Racial Disparities in Preschool Discipline." *Chalkbeat,* March 22, 2016. https://chalkbeat.org/posts/co/2016/03/22/suspended-countless-times-as-a-child-this-professor-is-tackling-racial-disparities-in-preschool-discipline/#.V8BQazWUK8B.

Schunk, Dale H. "Self-efficacy and Achievement Behaviors." *Educational Psychology Review* 1, (1989): 173-208.

Shepard, L.A., and M.L. Smith. "Escalating Academic Demand in Kindergarten: Some Nonsolutions." *Elementary School Journal* 89, no. 2 (1988): 135-146.

Shore, Rima. *Rethinking the Brain: New Insights into Early Development.* New York: Families and Work Institute, 1997.

Spaulding, Seth, and Ranjan Chaudhuri. "UNESCO's World Education Report: Its Evolution, Strengths, and Possible Futures." *International Journal of Educational Development* 19, no. 1 (1999): 53-63.

St. George, Jennifer, Richard Fletcher, and Kerrin Palazzi. "Comparing Fathers' Physical and Toy Play and Links to Child Behaviour: An Exploratory Study." *Infant and Child Development* 26, no. 1 (January/February 2017).

Sutton-Smith, Brian. "Playfighting as Folkplay Amongst Preschool Children." *Western Folklore* 47, no. 3 (July 1988): 161-176.

Thomas, Alexander, and Stella Chess. *Temperament and Development.* Oxford, England: Brunner/Mazel, 1977.

———. "Temperament and Personality." In *Temperament in Childhood*, edited by G.A. Kohnstamm, J.E. Bates, and M.K. Rothbart, 249-261. Oxford, England: John Wiley and Sons, 1989.

UNESCO Bangkok. *The Impact of Women Teachers on Girls' Education: Advisory Brief.* 2006. http://bangkok.unesco.org.

U.S. Access Board. *Americans With Disabilities Act (ADA) Accessibility Guidelines for Buildings and Facilities; Play Areas.* 36 CFR Part 1191. Washington D.C., November 20, 2000.

U.S. Bureau of Labor Statistics, U.S. Department of Labor. *Highlights of Women's Earnings in 2013, BLM Report 1051*. Washington, D.C.: U.S. Printing Office, December 2014.

———. *Occupational Outlook Handbook: Childcare Workers*. https://www.bls.gov/ooh/personal-care-and-service/childcare-workers.htm (accessed August 2, 2018).

———. *Occupational Outlook Handbook: Kindergarten and Elementary School Teachers*. https://www.bls.gov/ooh/education-training-and-library/kindergarten-and-elementary-school-teachers.htm (accessed August 20, 2018).

———. *Occupational Outlook Handbook: Preschool and Childcare Center Directors*. https://www.bls.gov/ooh/management/preschool-and-childcare-center-directors.htm (accessed August 5, 2018).

U.S. Consumer Product Safety Commission. *Public Playground Safety Handbook.* Bethesda: U.S. Consumer Product Safety Commission, 2015.

U.S. Department of Education. "Provisions Related to Children With Disabilities Enrolled by Their Parents in Private Schools." *U.S. Department of Education*, March 2011. https://www2.ed.gov/admins/lead/speced/privateschools/idea.pdf.

U.S. Department of Education Office of Civil Rights. *Civil Rights Data Collection, Data Snapshot: Early Childhood Education, Brief #2*. http://ocrdata.ed.gov (accessed May 25, 2016).

U.S. Department of Health and Human Services and U.S. Department of Education. *High-Quality Early Learning Settings Depend on a High-Quality Workforce: Low Compensation Undermines Quality*. June 2016. https://www2.ed.gov/about/inits/ed/earlylearning/files/ece-low-compensation-undermines-quality-report-2016.pdf.

Walker, Timothy. "The Joyful, Illiterate Kindergartners of Finland." *The Atlantic*. October 1, 2015. https://www.theatlantic.com/education/archive/2015/10/the-joyful-illiterate-kindergartners-of-finland/408325/.

Wardle, Francis. *A Shropshire Lad: The Early Life of a Boy in the Wheathill Bruderhof*. Denver: unpublished, 2014.

_____. *Approaches to Early Childhood and Elementary Education: Education in a Competitive and Globalizing World Series*. New York: Nova Science Publishers, 2009.

_____. "Are We Short Changing Boys?" *Exchange*, May/June 1991, 48-51.

_____. *Collaboration with Families and Communities*. San Diego: Bridgepoint Education, 2013.

_____. "Folk Dancing for Young Children." *Earlychildhood NEWS*. http://www.earlychildhoodnews.com/earlychildhood/article_view.aspx?ArticleId=301.

_____. "How Children Build Images of Themselves." *Exchange*, July 1995, 44-47.

_____. "Intergenerational Learning: Gardening with Grandpa." *Exchange*, 2016, 87-90.

_____. *Introduction to Early Childhood Education: A Multidimensional Approach to Child-Centered Care and Learning*. Boston: Allyn & Bacon, 2003.

_____. "Lifelike Pedagogy: The Project Approach with a Brazilian Twist." *Young Children* 69, no. 2 (2014): 76-81.

_____. "Men in Early Childhood are not Appreciated." In *Go Where You Belong: Male Teachers as Cultural Workers in the Lives of Children, Families, and Communities*, edited by Lemuel W. Watson and C. Sheldon Woods, 67-71. Rotterdam, Netherlands: Sense Publishers, 2011.

_____. "Play as Curriculum." *Earlychildhood NEWS*. http://www.earlychildhoodnews.com/earlychildhood/article_view.aspx?ArticleId=127 (assessed July 1, 2016).

_____. "Supporting Constructive Play in the Wild: Guidelines for Learning Outside." *Exchange*, July/August 2000, 26-29.

_____. "Twice Exceptional Students." *Exchange*, 2017, 26-30.

Watson, Lemuel W. "Introduction: Addressing the Culture of Gender Bias." In *Go Where You Belong: Male Teachers as Cultural Workers in the Lives of Children, Families, and Communities*, edited by Lemuel W. Watson and C. Sheldon Woods, xv-xviii. Rotterdam, Netherlands: Sense Publishers, 2011.

_____, and C. Sheldon Woods, eds. *Go Where You Belong: Male Teachers as Cultural Workers in the Lives of Children, Families, and Communities*. Rotterdam, Netherlands: Sense Publishers, 2011.

Whiting, Beatrice, and Carolyn Price Edwards. "A Cross-Cultural Analysis of Sex-Differences in the Behavior of Children Ages 3 through 11." In *Childhood Socialization*, edited by G. Handle, 281-297. Hawthorne: Aldine de Gruyter, 1988.

Wiles, John, and Joseph Bondi. *Curriculum Development: A Guide to Practice*, 9th ed. Upper Saddle River: Pearson, 2015.

Wolfe, David A. "Risk Factors for Child Abuse Perpetration." In *Violence Against Women and Children, Vol. 1: Mapping the Terrain*, edited by Jacquelyn White, Mary Koss, and Alan Kazdin, 31-53. Washington D.C.: American Psychological Association, 2011.

Zamosky, Lisa. "How Boys and Girls Learn Differently." *WebMD*. March 25, 2011. https://www.webmd.com/parenting/features/how-boys-and-girls-learn-differently#2

Glossary of Key Terms

A Nation at Risk: The Imperative for Educational Reform: A federal report published in 1983 and written by the President Ronald Reagan's National Commission on Excellence in Education that was highly critical of the outcomes of American public education.

Align: In the vernacular of curriculum standards and outcomes, this is the requirement that curriculum match the state's standards and frameworks—and vice-versa; it is used today to make sure early childhood curricula match the formal K-12 curriculum.

Associative Play: A form of play in which a group of children participate in similar or identical activities without formal organization, group direction, group interaction, or a definite goal.

Attention Deficit Hyperactive Disorder (ADHD): A disorder characterized by symptoms of inattention, hyperactivity, and/or impulsivity.

Authoritarian Parenting Style: A style that establishes parents as the unquestioned authority. Set rules and expected behavior are non-negotiable and must be followed. Parents with an authoritarian style often have very high expectations of their children—sometimes too high. Punishment is often strict, sometimes physical.

Authoritative Parenting Style: A style that is a balance of control and consistency, implemented with warmth and encouragement. These parents have high demands of their children, but expectations match each child's developmental age. They provide reasons for rules and limits, but are also open to reasonable negotiations; they view each child as a unique individual and do not compare their children

Autonomy versus Shame/Doubt: The second of Erikson's stages in which a toddler tries to achieve a sense of autonomy and independence.

Bidirectional Behavior: The two-way nature of an interaction, from child to adult and from adult to child; each influence the other.

Bodily-Kinesthetic Learning Style: One of Gardner's learning styles, bodily-kinesthetic learning is the ability to use one's body for self-expression and physical performance through a combination of physical activity, muscle control, sensations, reflexes, coordination, and movement.

Child-Centered Learning: Refers to a wide variety of educational programs, learning experiences, instructional approaches, and academic-support strategies that are intended to address the distinct learning needs, interests, aspirations, and/or cultural backgrounds of individual students and groups of students.

Closed-Ended Materials: Play materials that only have one function or can only be used in one way such as a puzzle.

Cognitive Play Stages: Piaget's theory of play development in which the child progresses from functional play to games with rules.

Concrete Learners: Students who learn most effectively using real objects; most young children are concrete learners.

Concrete Manipulatives: Real objects such as beads, stones, sticks, and blocks that children use to learn complex, abstract concepts such as math computations.

Constructive Play: Use of objects and materials to create new and different things—to construct—such as blocks, art materials, wood and nails, Legos, Tinker toys, sand and water.

Cooperative Play: The most advanced form of social play: it is play where the child's self-interests are subsumed for the good of the play activity of the group.

Cortisol: A hormone often found at elevated levels in children who are constantly under stress. It can cause long-term brain damage and learning disabilities.

Curricular Philosophy: The underlying rationale of any curriculum; the what and how of the curriculum.

Deficit Model: An educational approach that focuses on what children cannot do or what they struggle to do well.

Developmental Delay: A general term used by individual states that refers to children—ages birth to 9—who perform significantly below developmental norms. It is also one of the 13 federal disability categories.

DSM-5: The *Diagnostic and Statistical Manual of Mental Disorders* (5th ed.) published by the American Psychiatric Association, and used for diagnosing a range of disabilities including ADHD, autism, and various mental health disorders.

Ecole Maternelle: Preschool programs in France (and in international French schools).

Ecological Systems Theory: Bronfenbrenner's theory that describes the importance of various components on the healthy growth and development of the child: family, community, community agencies, and school/early childhood programs. These components need to function together for the child's optimum development.

Elementary and Secondary Education Act (ESEA): One of the programs of the War on Poverty; essentially the first time that the federal government provided direct financial support (with specific conditions) to local schools.

Emergent Curriculum: A curricular approach based on Dewey's philosophy that selects content based on student interests, and teachers and students jointly plan activities and experiences.

Emotional Regulation: The ability of a child to inhibit, control, or maintain an emotional response to accomplish a goal.

Enactive Mode of Representation: In Bruner's three modes of representation, enactive representation involves memory through movement; muscle memory.

Epstein's Framework: A framework for defining six different types of parent involvement. This framework assists educators in developing school and family partnership programs.

Federal Disability Categories: The 13 categories in the Individuals with Disabilities Education Act (IDEA) that constitute the eligibility criteria for children to be served by IDEA. A child must meet one or more of these categories to receive services.

Functional Play: The use of bodily movements, with or without objects, such as running and jumping, sliding, gathering and dumping, manipulating and stacking objects, and informal games without rules.

Games with Rules: A collective activity where pre-established rules are agreed on and then used to control the activity such as Duck-Duck-Goose.

Gender-Role Socialization: The way each society and culture develops male and female behaviors and expectations in their children.

Gifted and Talented Children: Children who possess abilities and talents that can be demonstrated, or have the potential for being developed, at exceptional high levels. Children can be gifted and talented in one of several areas.

Goals 2000: Educate America Act: Set forth eight national goals for U.S. public education. These goals later morphed into standards, which became a central component of the No Child Left Behind Act.

Goodness-of-Fit: A match between a child's unique behaviors, characteristics, and dispositions and the social and physical environment in which the child develops and learns.

Hands-On Learning: Experiencing new information in a concrete manner: to hold, touch, move, smell, see, and manipulate real objects.

Head Start's Performance Standards: Program-based quality expectations used by local Head Start programs to make sure they meet national guidelines.

High-Stakes Assessments: Typically standardized tests used for the purposes of accountability. Test scores are used to determine punishments (such as sanctions, penalties, funding reductions, negative publicity), accolades (awards, public celebration, positive publicity), advancement (grade promotion or graduation for students), or compensation (salary increases or bonuses for administrators and teachers).

Iconic Mode of Representation: In Bruner's three modes of representation, iconic learning involves the process of mentally storing information visually in the form of images or mental pictures.

Individualized Education Program (IEP): Is a plan or program developed to ensure that a child (three to 21) who has a disability identified under the Individuals with Disabilities Education Act (IDEA) and is attending an elementary or secondary educational institution receives specialized instruction and related services.

Individualized Family Service Plan (IFSP): A plan for services for a child under age three who qualifies for early intervention under the Individuals with Disabilities Education Act (IDEA). It lays out the services a baby or toddler should receive and the hoped for results.

Industry versus Inferiority: The fourth of Erikson's stages (six to 12): the need for children to be competent in what they do and to feel good about doing it—especially when compared to peers.

Initiative versus Guilt: The third of Erikson's stages (three to six), it stipulates children need to develop initiative: to try new things, solve problems, and be in control.

Interpersonal Learning Style: One of Gardner's learning styles, children with an interpersonal learning style are good at listening, cooperating in group tasks and projects, seeing things from the perspective of others, and organizing and negotiating group activites.

Intersubjectivity: The process whereby two participants who begin a task with different understandings arrive at a shared understanding that creates a common ground for communication and problem-solving.

Intrinsic Motivation: A characteristic of the British Infant and Primary curriculum that refers to behavior that is driven by internal rewards. In other words, the motivation to engage in a behavior arises from within the individual because it is naturally satisfying.

Key Developmental Indictors: The scope and content of the HighScope curriculum; what children can do, how they perceive the world, and the kinds of experiences important to their development and learning.

Kindergarten: The original kindergarten was created by Froebel in Germany. Literally meaning a "children's garden," its philosophy focuses on use of the outdoors, play, the arts, and natural maturation.

Learning by Doing: A concept of Dewey's educational philosophy that claims one of the best ways to learn many skills and tasks is by actually doing them such as speaking the foreign language, fixing the car, calculating change.

Least Restrictive Environment (LRE): A requirement of the Individuals with Disabilities Act (IDEA) that stipulates children with disabilities must be educated with non-disabled peers so long as they can benefit from the placement.

Lifelike Pedagogy: A version of the Project Approach developed in Brazil that expands the Project Approach to an entire curriculum. It enables students to control every aspect of their learning.

Male Advocate: A role in an early childhood program or school whose main goal is to create programs to encourage male involvement.

Meaningful Learning: By relating new information to knowledge already stored in the memory, children find meaning in the new information. According to research, this new information is remembered and retrieved more easily.

Meta-Cognition: The knowledge of one's learning and cognitive processes and the ability to regulate these processes; being aware of how one learns and using this information to enhance learning.

Methodology: The how of instruction; the broad principles, rules, and processes used by teachers to teach the curriculum.

Musical Learning Style: One of Gardner's learning styles, children with a musical learning style have a talent in and disposition toward music: singing, playing an instrument, and can use rhythms and patterns to assist in learning.

Naturalist Learning Style: One of Gardner's learning styles, children with a naturalistic learning style enjoy the outdoors and have a special talent to learn from nature and natural phenomena.

No Child Left Behind Act: The 2001 reauthorization of the Elementary and Secondary Educational Act (ESEA). It required local school districts to focus on teaching academic skills (math and literacy) and use high-stakes assessments as a condition for receiving federal funds.

Non-Literal Play: A characteristic of play in which children engage in non-real activities; fantasy.

Open-Ended Materials: Play materials that can be used in a variety of ways.

Outdoor Museum: A collection of historic buildings from a specific time period reconfigured into a small town; includes gardens, animals, farm equipment, and period activities.

Parallel Play: Children playing alone and usually involved in the same kind of play, yet in the physical presence of other children.

Pedagogy: This broad term includes how teachers and students relate together as well as the instructional approaches implemented in the classroom.

Permanent Site: The community site that students visit on several occasions when implementing the Project Approach. It must be safe for children and show significant change over time (such as the construction of a building).

Permissive Parenting Style: Permissive parents are warm and have a relaxed approach to discipline. They have low expectations and when rules are broken, there are few, if any, consequences. They often engage in the democratic approach to rule-making.

Prefrontal Cortex: The front part of the brain that controls planning, judgment, and emotional regulation. In general, this part of the brain is less developed in young boys than girls.

Premack Principle: The use of an activity or task the child enjoys and is good at doing to reinforce an activity or task the child struggles with.

Preoperational Stage: The second of Piaget's cognitive stages, children (two to seven) are concrete learners who need to manipulate the environment to create and test schemes.

Private Speech: Talking to oneself to regulate one's own behavior and/or guide learning through scaffolding.

Process-Orientated Play: Play is characterized by process as opposed to the need to achieve a specific goal.

Progressive Education: A form of education that was developed out of Dewey's educational philosophy. It includes learning by doing, meaningful learning, using each child's experiences as the basis for the curriculum, and building classroom and school communities. Projects are one result of progressive education.

Project Approach: A curricular approach based on Dewey's philosophy that provides an in-depth study of an idea or theme by a group of children. A site that is visited on multiple occasions provides the content of this approach.

Representation: Another term for memory; how we retain new information in our minds.

Rough-and-Tumble Play: Physically vigorous behavior such as chase and play fighting that is accompanied by positive feelings between the players.

Response to Intervention (RTI): An alternative process used to determine whether a student has a specific learning disability. The process exposes students to increasing levels of instruction; if they fail, they are deemed to have a specific learning disability.

Scaffolding: A concept based on the work of Vygotsky in which experts (adults or peers) provide children with specific support and structure in learning a skill or concepts, slowly reducing the support and structure as the child learns the skill or concept.

Scheme: The central construct in Piaget's theory. A scheme is a theory or model of how the world works created by the child. By repeatedly interacting with the concrete world the child refines his schemes.

Scope: The content of the curriculum—the subject matter, skills, and other objectives or outcomes to be covered—often during a specific timeframe (i.e. first grade math).

Self-Efficacy: A child's belief in what the child can do, learn, and accomplish; children with a high level of self-efficacy are willing to try new things and risk new endeavors; those without it are reluctant to try anything new.

Self-Fulfilling Expectation/Prophecy: An event that occurs because of the behaviors of those who expect it to occur; a situation in which a person's expectations about future events create the conditions through which these expectations become a reality.

Sensory-Motor Stage: The first of Piaget's cognitive stages; in this stage children (birth to two) learn through a combination of sensory input and physical activity such as seeing an object, grasping the object, placing the object in their mouth, and then tasting the object.

Sequence: The order in which the curricular content is presented for learning.

Social Competence: The set of skills necessary to get along with others and behave constructively in groups. This encompasses skills like empathy, emotional regulation, perspective taking, cooperation, friendliness, and social problem-solving skills.

Social Play Stages: Parten's theory of social play development in which the child progresses from solitary to cooperative play.

Solitary Play: A child playing alone—either with or without objects (toys)—without the involvement or participation of other children or adults.

Specific Learning Disability: The most common of the 13 federal disability categories; a discrepancy between a student's ability and the student's academic performance, usually in literacy or math.

Stereotype Threat: The concept whereby individuals from stereotypically low-achieving groups perform more poorly on tests or tasks than they otherwise would simply because they are aware that their group traditionally does poorly.

Symbolic Mode of Representation: In Bruner's three modes of representation, symbolic representation (over age seven) involves the use of symbols, words, and numbers in the learning process.

Symbolic Play: Children use materials and objects symbolically to represent something else. For example, a block becomes a phone, a doll is a baby, and a stick is a sword.

Time Out: A form of discipline that involves removing a misbehaving child from a classroom or playground activity.

Trust versus Mistrust: The first of Erikson's stages in which the infant needs to develop a sense of trust and a belief in the goodness of the world.

Twice-Exceptional Student: A student who is gifted and talented and also has a special need, or a child with a developmental delay or special need who is also gifted and talented.

Uninvolved/Neglectful Parenting Style: Characterized by a lack of responsiveness to a child's needs. Parents who are not involved with their child and who really do not want to be. They are disinterested and emotionally absent.

Variability: The normal range of development for any given age in any domain; the understanding that human development, especially for young children, is not a straight line, but varies greatly due to many internal and external factors.

Visual-Spatial Learning Style: One of Gardner's learning styles, it involves thinking about objects in different spatial orientations, being able to see objects from different points of view, organizing objects in space, understanding and explaining how objects are arranged in space to each other, and using visual images to enhance memory, information processing, and retrieval.

War on Poverty: A series of federal programs including Head Start and the Elementary and Secondary Education Act (ESEA), developed in the 1960s, and targeted to eliminate poverty in the U.S.

Webbing: A non-linear approach to curriculum planning that allows for divergent and creative ideas, plans, and concepts.

Whole-Child Activities: Learning activities that engage all domains of the child: physical, social, emotional, cognitive, and affective; those activities that recognize children engage multiple domains when learning new skills and concepts; integrated learning.

Whole-Child Learners: The concept that young children learn new information and engage in new experiences using all domains at the same time: cognitive, physical, social, emotional, and affective.

Zero-Tolerance Policies: Absolute policies related to certain aggressive behaviors or possession of certain items, in and near a school. Individual teachers and administrators lack any discretion in implementing these rules; punishment is often punitive.

Zone of Proximal Development (ZPD): The distance between what a child can accomplish during independent problem solving and what the child can accomplish with the help of an adult or more mature child; the zone where learning can take place.

OH BOY! Strategies for Teaching Boys in Early Childhood

About the Author

Francis Wardle grew up on a mixed farm in the wild border country between England and Wales. His early years were filled with damming swift streams, herding sheep, hiking on the local hills, and playing in yellow gorse and purple heather. It was an ideal environment for a very curious, active young boy.

Francis came to the U.S. with his family when he was 16 years of age. He then attended Pennsylvania State University (Art Education), the University of Wisconsin (Foundations of Education), and the University of Kansas (PhD in Curriculum and Instruction, with a minor in Human Development).

He began his formal teaching experience at Da Nahazli School, an alternative school in Taos, New Mexico, and then continued to teach at PACERS school in Kansas City, Missouri. Since then he has had over 20 years of experience with Head Start in a variety of capacities including classroom volunteer, educational coordinator, national program reviewer, and director of Adams County (Colorado) Head Start.

For four years he was the educational director for Children's World Learning Centers.

Since 1997, as a member of Partners of the Americas, Dr. Wardle has visited Brazil on many occasions, building playgrounds, and studying education, culture, and race.

Currently, Dr. Wardle teaches classes for the School of Advanced Studies, the University of Phoenix, and early childhood classes for Red Rocks Community College in Lakewood, Colorado. He has published numerous articles on a variety of early childhood topics in *Exchange* magazine, Young Children, Children Today, Children and Families, and Childhood Education, and he has published eight books on young children, multicultural education, and multiracial families.

He is married with four children and four grandchildren, and lives in Denver, Colorado.

Acknowledgments

First, I must thank my wife for support and encouragement, and for putting up with all my sojourns into a myriad of fantastic writing projects! My four children, Maia, Eirlys, Kealan, and RaEsa taught me about diversity, individual differences, and that each of us is destined for greatness. I would also like to thank Emily Rose, Tina Reeble, Scott Bilstad, and Nancy Rosenow from Exchange Press who took on this project midstream, and provided wonderful direction and leadership. Finally, I must thank each one of my students in the Early Childhood Department at Red Rocks Community College who keep me on my toes, insisting I stay real and down to earth!